MANAGEMENT IN THE MIRROR

MANAGEMENT IN THE MIRROR

Stress and Emotional Dysfunction in Lives at the Top

Bernadette H. Schell

QUORUM BOOKS
Westport, Connecticut • London

Library of Congress Cataloging-in-Publication Data

Schell, Bernadette H. (Bernadette Hlubik), 1952–
    Management in the mirror : stress and emotional dysfunction in
lives at the top / Bernadette H. Schell.
        p.   cm.
    Includes bibliographical references and index.
    ISBN 1–56720–197–0 (alk. paper)
    1. Executives—Psychology.   2. Leadership—Psychological aspects.
3. Success in business.   4. Self-realization.   5. Executives—
Interviews.   I. Title.
    HD38.2.S33   1999
    658.4'001'9—dc21   98–44553

British Library Cataloguing in Publication Data is available.

Library of Congress Catalog Card Number: 98–44553
ISBN: 1–56720–197–0

First published in 1999

Quorum Books, 88 Post Road West, Westport, CT 06881
An imprint of Greenwood Publishing Group, Inc.
www.quorumbooks.com

Printed in the United States of America

The paper used in this book complies with the
Permanent Paper Standard issued by the National
Information Standards Organization (Z39.48–1984).

10 9 8 7 6 5 4 3 2 1

Copyright Acknowledgments

The author and publisher are grateful for permission to reproduce portions of the following copyrighted material:

American Psychiatric Association. (1994). *Diagnostic and statistical manual of mental disorders. Fourth edition. DMS-IV*. Washington, DC: American Psychiatric Association. Reprinted with permission from the Diagnostic and Statistical Manual of Mental Disorders, Fourth Edition. Copyright 1994 American Psychiatric Association.

Baltrusch, H.J.F., Stangel, W., & Waltz, M.E. (1988). Cancer from the biobehavioral perspective: The Type C pattern. *Activas Nervosa Superior*, 30, 18–20. Reprinted with permission.

Cohen, A. (1997). Tapes show JFK weighing war risk. *The Globe and Mail*, October 20, pp. A1, A3. Reprinted with permission from The Globe and Mail.

Chusmir, L.H., & Azevedo, A. (1992). Motivation needs of sampled Fortune-500 CEOs: Relations to organization outcomes. *Perceptual and Motor Skills*, 75, 595–612. © Perceptual and Motor Skills 1992. Reprinted with permission.

Dart, B. (1998). Power leads men to risky business, psychologists say. *The Globe and Mail*, January 31, p. A18. Reprinted with permission from B. Dart of the Cox News Service.

Delacroix, J., & Saudagaran, S.M. (1991). Munificent compensation as disincentives: The case of American CEOs. *Human Relations*, 44, 665–678. Reproduced with permission of Plenum Publishing Corporation.

Gill, A. (1998). Lives lived: Donald Colin (Ben) Webster. *The Globe and Mail,* January 21, p. A18. Reprinted with permission from The Globe and Mail.

Hambrick, D.C., & Fukutomi, G.D.S. (1991). The season of a CEO's tenure. *Academy of Management Review*, 16, pp. 719–742. Reproduced with permission.

Hare, R.D., Hart, S.D., & Harper, T.J. (1991). Psychopathy and the SDM-IV criteria for antisocial personality disorder. *Journal of Abnormal Psychology*, 100, 391–398. Copyright © 1991 by the American Psychological Association. Reprinted with permission.

Harris, M. (1997). Letters: Is your career killing you? *Canadian Business*, 70, 15. Reprinted with permission of the author.

Hart, S.L., & Quinn, R.E. (1993). Roles executives play: CEOs, behavioral complexity, and firm performance. *Human Relations*, 46, 543–574. Reproduced with permission of Plenum Publishing Corporation and the authors.

Heinzl, H., Church, E., Partridge, J., Lush, P., & McFarland, J. (1998). Those wild and crazy annual meetings. *The Globe and Mail*, May 1, p. B23. Reprinted with permission from The Globe and Mail.

Ingram, M. (1998). J.P. Bryan: Hero and/or villain? *The Globe and Mail*, February 10, p. B2. Reprinted with permission from The Globe and Mail.

Jang, B. (1998). Gulf CEO engineers debt strategy. *The Globe and Mail*, March 20, p. B23. Reprinted with permission from The Globe and Mail.

Jang, B. (1998). Bryan leaves Gulf Canada. *The Globe and Mail*, February 10, pp. B1, B10. Reprinted with permission from The Globe and Mail.

Keenan, G., & McFarland, J. (1997). The boy's club. *The Globe and Mail*, September 27, pp. B1, B5. Reprinted with permission from the Globe and Mail.

Kets de Vries, M. F. R. (1993). *Leaders, fools, and imposters*. San Francisco: Jossey-Bass, pp. 29–33. Reprinted with permission.

To my family, and to Darren Larose

A special "thank-you" to the following people: Arthur Johnson of *Canadian Business*, Tamsen Tillson, Eric Valentine, Stewart Tait, Dr. Jean Endicott, my corporate leader friends in the Cayman Islands, Gisele Bonin, and all of the Canadian corporate leaders who participated in our study.

Contents

PART I

On Becoming a Successful Corporate Leader

CHAPTER 1

The Drive to Succeed:
What We Know about Corporate
Leaders, Geniuses, and Other
Creative Leaders

Years of experience have taught me that leaders and followers come
in many shapes and sizes. The more leaders I encounter, the more
difficult I find it to describe a typically effective leadership style.
—M. F. R. Kets de Vries (1993)

A CASE IN POINT (GILL 1998)

Venture capitalist and mystic explorer. Born on April 8, 1930, in
Montreal; died of cancer in Toronto on Dec. 13, 1997, aged 67.
—A. Gill (1998)

Ben Webster wasn't born with a silver spoon in his mouth. It was
gold. Descended from one of the country's wealthiest dynasties, he
had it all and a little bit more: charisma, intelligence, a strong work
ethic and a reservoir of raw energy. Fuelled by an intense curiosity,
appetite for adventure and fascination with all things paranormal,
he lost his fortune more than once but recovered it every time,
becoming one of the most successful high-tech venture capitalists
and eccentric members of the modern Canadian establishment.

Best known for co-founding Velcro Industries in the 1950s, Mr.
Webster kicked himself for selling his shares so early. But the
money helped finance Helix Investments in 1968, and he made a
fortune gambling on the new high-tech economy. His string of corporate successes included Mitel, Enfield, Open Text, Hummingbird
Communications, Corel and Geac Computer. Herbal remedies, a

Broadway play and a diving company that searched for sunken treasure also benefited from Mr. Webster's instincts and the advice of his personal psychics.

An avid mathematician and reader of history, religion, philosophy and science, Mr. Webster concluded that the standard definitions of the universe didn't add up. Like many, he tried LSD in the sixties and it raised his consciousness to the possibility of other realms. Unlike most, he devoted a good part of his life to bridging the gap between reason and psychic phenomena, even funding mind-matter experiments at Princeton University. He decorated his office with a painting of the Great Pyramid (the Helix logo), crystals and a Stonehenge room. Once, flying over the Caribbean, he thought he saw the lost city of Atlantis.

His great-grandfather would not have approved. Senator Lorne Webster built an industrial empire, 250 companies strong, gathered under the mantle of Canadian Import. His will urged his five children to be active followers of Jesus and he specified that any Webster who disgraced his name be automatically excluded.

Ben's father, Colin, carried on the tradition. His mother, Jean, was a Frosst, the family that founded Canada's first pharmaceutical company. Together, they raised a strict Methodist-Presbyterian family in Montreal's Westmount.

At Lower Canada College, Ben led his class, a provincial champion in track and boxing who always went to bed early. After obtaining an engineering degree at Princeton in 1951, he studied for two years in Geneva and worked as an engineer for five years before starting his entrepreneurial career.

Moving to Toronto in the early sixties, Ben met his first wife, Beverley Beattie, and began his spiritual explorations. She later became a Buddhist. They had four children: Benjamin, Colin, Samuel and Alexandra. When they divorced, amicably, in 1974, Ben had already met Madaline McArtle. They married the next year and had a child, Victoria.

Their homes included a castle in Scotland, an estate in Bermuda, his beloved retreat in Muskoka and a Toronto mansion where they held seances, received the Dalai Lama and entertained friends with parapsychics such as the spoon-bender Uri Geller. The family traveled extensively, riding elephants through India and hurtling face-first down the St. Moritz Cresta Run.

In December of 1995, he was diagnosed with lymphoma. This wasn't supposed to happen to a tennis-playing triathlete who meditated daily and followed a strict diet supplemented by vitamins. Frantic, he enlisted more than 60 experts and quickly dismissed most orthodox specialists; after intensive research, he already knew more than they did. In California he found Chinese healers and non-traditional chemotherapy. He came back a changed man.

The illness persisted, but he had found love with a new woman, Margaret Wendt; he spent his last 19 months with her and they planned to wed. According to his son Benjamin, "The icicle lodged in his heart began to melt," as he learned to express his emotions freely and devoted more time to his family. Others saw the transformation differently. "This wasn't my husband," said Madaline, of the man who turned on her and alienated many old friends.

Last September, in Germany, Mr. Webster flatlined eight times and had an out-of-body experience. Bathed in a warm light, he communed with the dead. "I'm wagering," he told Ms. Wendt as he slipped in and out of consciousness. He had seen death, he told friends later, and it was peaceful.

INTRODUCTION

Management in the Mirror is dedicated to all of the Ben Websters around the world who have contributed greatly to society yet who seem to be on a perpetual search for greater success, happiness, and self-actualization.

When we look at Ben Webster, with the little bit that we know of him, he seems to be an individual who had all the elements that make "successful" leaders. Yet, when we read these few short pages about Ben Webster, we get the sense that there was some unfulfilled need deep inside him. Until his death, he searched desperately to fill this void through drugs, parapsychology, and unorthodox religions. Ben was about to begin his third marriage with a woman who allegedly was able to melt the "icicle lodged in his heart" when cancer arrived on his doorstep, and the rest is history.

How many other searching Ben Websters are there in the corporate world? That is a question that over a year ago, Darren Larose, my graduate student, and I asked ourselves. We searched the psychosocial and organizational literature trying to get a clearer understanding of how "successful" corporate leaders and other worldly eminents place themselves on the stress-personality-mood yardstick and on the compensation yardstick, but we came back with just a few answers. The secrets for "success" and "eminence" that we did uncover in our search are the focus of Part I. Thus, Part I details what we know about the particulars surrounding the path to "success":

• the work and personal stressors of the rich and famous;

• strategies used for getting to the top;

- personality traits and behavioral profiles of those who have made it to the top;
- normal moods and mood disorders accompanying those who have made the climb to the top; and
- how status, income, perks, and accoutrements motivate eminents to reach for the top.

Having had our "success" appetites whetted by our literature search, we attempted to validate some hypotheses on Canadian corporate leaders using a 14-page questionnaire. I share our findings on this corporate leader sample in Part II of this book.

Then we return at the book's end to what the case of Ben Webster is all about: accepting that "success" has personal costs and benefits. Webster, it seems, has taught us two more things: (1) that an individual—no matter how famous or wealthy—has to find his or her own happiness from inside and (2) that maybe with a bit more "critically intelligent" knowledge about ourselves, there is a way to find happiness and "success" sooner rather than later. Thus, I share with you in Part II of this book some learnings from present-day corporate leaders and the experts on better "success" coping.

In Chapter 1, we begin to look at the drive to succeed and other beliefs about how "successful" corporate leaders, geniuses, and other creative eminents make their way to the top. In particular, three "success" myths are discussed:

- that the truly successful have some "extraordinary intelligence" that sets them apart from their less successful counterparts;
- that the truly successful have some "special set" of motives that prompts them to walk along the path to success; and
- that the truly successful have some wild and crazy, if not "mad," urges that propel them to the top.

MYTH #1: THE TRULY SUCCESSFUL HAVE EXTRAORDINARY INTELLIGENCE

While Webster may have seemed a bit odd dabbling in parapsychology to find his ingredients for success and happiness, for over 80 years psychosocial experts have similarly analyzed outputs of the eminent dead to try to discover their ingredients for success. Experts (Simonton 1984; Winter & Steward 1977) have posited that in order to move leagues beyond their less successful counterparts, the eminent—whether they be in the corporate world, in the arts, in the sciences, or in politics—must have some extraordinary intelligence. As Dr. Samuel Johnson put it in *Lives of the English Poets*, "The true genius is a mind of large general powers, accidentally determined to some particular direction." But is this really the case?

Starting in the early 1920s, IQ expert Lewis Terman traced a sample of 1,000 children scoring exceptionally high on standardized IQ tests into adulthood to see if they achieved "distinction" in later life. He published his findings in the 1925 classic *Genetic Studies of Genius: Volume 1. Mental and Physical Traits of a Thousand Gifted Children.*

A year later, in 1926, Catherine Cox published her psychohistoric classic, *The Early Mental Traits of Three Hundred Geniuses*, which was essentially a sequel to Terman's work but in reverse. Beginning with a sample of 301 eminent historical personalities, Cox traced their biographies back into childhood, searching for evidence of intellectual and personological precociousness. In fact, for this tracing-back research technique Cox is credited with helping to set the groundwork for psychohistory, the discipline most strongly associated with the determination of what drives or motivates eminent personalities from the past (Simonton 1976b).

Cox's psychohistoric search included a collation of biographical data on the early mental traits and behaviors of 301 geniuses born since 1450. Three independent raters used her collated information to calculate these geniuses' IQ scores, whereby IQ was defined according to the traditional concept of a ratio of mental age to chronological age, and where a score of 100 represents the average IQ. Thus, these raters judged what mental age was normally required for a given precocious act to occur, divided their estimates by the genius' chronological age at the time of the precocious act, and multiplied by 100 to yield a standardized IQ score (Simonton 1984; Cox 1926).

Simonton (1984) gives us an example of IQ back-estimation to help us understand this technique:

As an example of this way of measuring IQ, take John Stuart Mill. Mill began to learn Greek at 3, read Plato at 7, studied geometry and algebra at 8 and calculus at 11. He wrote a history of Rome when he was 6 and could discuss the relative merits of Wellington and Marlborough at age 5. To determine his IQ, one must know the average age at which a person of "normal" intelligence could accomplish these same tasks. Thus the study of calculus usually commences, if at all, around age 18. Dividing the mental age required for calculus (18) by Mill's chronological age (11) and multiplying by 100 yields an IQ score of 164. Taking Mill's entire early biography into account, Cox and her collaborators arrived at an IQ estimate of 190. (p. 44)

Using this estimation procedure, the range of IQ scores calculated by Cox's team for the 301 geniuses was from 115 to 210, with an average genius IQ estimate of 165—far above the norm of 100 for the general population. To place Cox's finding in perspective, only a minuscule portion of the general population has IQ scores in this very high-end range. Given her findings, Cox concluded that IQ is, indeed, related to achieved eminence in adulthood. She cited the following particulars as evidence in support of her argument: Geothe had an estimated IQ of 210, Pascal an estimated IQ of 195, Hume and Michelangelo estimated IQs of 180, and Mozart an estimated IQ of 165 (Simonton 1984; Cox 1926).

Soon after the release of Cox's findings, other scholars began to question her research design. In 1931, for example, White challenged Cox's definition and measurement of intelligence, alleging that her methods were too restrictive. White's empirical study showed, in contrast, that the eminent in all walks of life tend to display exceptional versatility rather than high IQs per se. *That is, successful types in most fields seem to exhibit mental and behavioral competence in a wide array of endeavors* (White 1931).

Six years later, in 1937, Bell similarly argued that studies such as Cox's, which assess intellectual ability on IQ tests alone, need to be viewed with caution, for IQ tests like the Binet have a history of validity deficiencies and cultural biases that need to be recognized. Bell argued, as a case in point, that Henri Poincaré's performance on the early Binet tests was so miserable that if he had been judged as a child on his IQ score instead of as a famous mathematician in adulthood, he would have been rated as an imbecile (Bell 1937).

The debate surrounding the issue of IQ and eminence continued for another 30 years. By early 1960, some psychologists began to argue that updated research on creativity in community populations suggests that the functional relationship between intelligence and creativity is a bit more complicated than originally thought. For example, in 1964, Mc-Nemar maintained that while there appears to be a positive relationship between intelligence and creativity, it tends to vanish in the upper reaches of intelligence. That is, beyond an IQ of around 120, further gains in IQ do not seem to increase the likelihood of creative achievement (McNemar 1964). Cronbach also posited that an IQ of 120 is not all that selective a cutoff point for creative eminence potential, for this score seems to mark the average IQ score of university graduates. Putting this score in perspective, about 10 percent of the general population has an IQ of 120 or higher (Cronbach 1960).

Spurred on by the IQ success controversy and by the improvement in multivariate statistical techniques, in 1976, Simonton reported his rean-alyzed results of Cox's data (Simonton 1976a), in which he separated the IQ scores of the "creative geniuses" from those of "the leader geniuses." Though the average IQ was nearly 170 for the 192 creators in Cox's artist, scientist, philosopher, and musician sample, Simonton concluded, after using appropriate statistical techniques, that *there was no significant statistical association found between intelligence and eminence for these creators.*

Simonton further posited that part of the problem with Cox's creator study sample was that it was just too homogeneous (1976a, 1984). "What can be done with a privileged group of eleven composers who range in eminence from Beethoven, Bach, and Mozart down to no lower than Gluck and Palestrina?" he asked (1984, p. 46). "Almost seven hundred composers are responsible for the works performed in the classical repertoire. The IQs of this top 2 percent range from genius level to supergenius level. If we are to discern a positive relation between eminence and intelligence," Simonton responded, "we must study a much more heterogeneous sample."

Turning now to Simonton's reanalysis of Cox's IQ data on 109 "eminent leaders," Simonton similarly concluded that among the successful leaders in Cox's sample, achieved eminence was uncorrelated with IQ. *He went on to say that, if anything, Cox's IQ estimates seem to bolster the conclusion that excessive intelligence may actually be a handicap in a leader.* As a case in point, the average IQ of the 109 leaders in Cox's sample—including politicians, soldiers, revolutionaries, and religious leaders—was four to six points below that of the 192 creators in her sample (1976a, 1984). Simonton said that the latter finding can be explained, in part, by the realization that creative geniuses like Bach and Beethoven can sometimes afford to be misunderstood by their contemporaries, whereas corporate or political leaders must achieve greatness in their own lifetimes or else fall into permanent oblivion (1984, p. 46). Therefore, for leaders to become eminent, concluded Simonton, other factors besides IQ likely prevail. He outlined the importance of being comprehensible and of being able to form coalitions in various leadership sectors:

The area of leadership may determine just how important it is to be comprehensible. The least intelligent of Cox's 109 leaders are the 27 soldiers—mostly generals and admirals—with a mean IQ of 140, compared with the overall average of 164 for the 301 geniuses. Military leaders are often placed in the position of having to persuade and cajole their soldiers. Napoleon was particularly effective in such morale-boosting tasks, as in his famous 1798 address before the Battle of the Pyramids. Such compatibility with the masses is far less crucial in other domains of leadership.

The IQs of the politicians and revolutionaries in the Cox sample average around 165, a full 25 points above those of the military figures. Prime ministers, legislators, and revolutionaries may have to pay more attention to the intricacies of power brokerage and coalition formation than to the summoning of support from the masses. Interestingly, the 8 most famous U.S. presidents have a mean IQ of only 152, 13 points lower than that for politicians in general. The American chief executive is far more dependent than many other politicians upon direct communication with the public for his political success. (pp. 46–47)

Simonton made another interesting comment about succession, leadership, and intelligence—or lack of it:

It is feasible to have a stupid person assume the highest positions of leadership. In hereditary monarchies, for example, a royal heir can claim by birthright a throne that would be denied if mental capacity were required for succession. Cox deliberately left out of her sample all eminent persons who she believed had not achieved eminence by their own merits. This selection criterion means the omission of some of the most eminent leaders of history—leaders like Louis XIV of France, Elizabeth I of England, and Peter the Great of Russia. (pp. 47–48)

Among monarchs, emphasized Simonton, even the obscure and the incapable go down in the historical records along with their most famous and competent colleagues. For research purposes, therefore, the inclusion of the unworthy or the less worthy in a study sample is an asset: it provides a comparison group for estimating intelligence, fame, leadership, and other pertinent personality attributes. It extends the range of these variables and thus permits a more valid test of their interrelationships.

In summary, Simonton's research was a major landmark that stifled experts' excitement around the myth that a strong relationship exists between IQ and creative or leadership eminence. By 1980, the attention of researchers turned, instead, to other personality variables to help explain the relationship between individual differences in predicting "success" across fields.

MYTH #2: THE TRULY SUCCESSFUL HAVE SOME "SPECIAL SET" OF MOTIVES

In an attempt to extend Cox's findings, in 1980, Walberg, Rasher, and Parkerson reported that 90 percent of the eminent personalities that they studied presented with extremely high intelligence *and* questioning curiosity.

To better understand this notion called "questioning curiosity," researchers began to focus on the role of unconscious factors as success determinants. By 1980, the 1938 work of Murray on motivational needs and the 1950s and 1960s work of McClelland rolled directly in front as experts continued on their quest for the ingredients of eminence.

The Basics of Motivation Theory

Motivational theory, as developed by Murray (1938) and later refined by McClelland and his colleagues (McClelland 1961; Atkinson 1958; McClelland et al. 1953), posits that motivated behavior is largely a function of the strength of various, often unconscious needs of adults at any point in time. These needs are many and include the need for achievement (n-Ach), the need for affiliation (n-Aff), the need for power or dominance (n-Pow or n-Dom), the need for autonomy (n-Aut), and the need for activity inhibition (n-ActI).

Before defining each of these needs, it is useful to review what is meant by the term *motive*. *Motive* is a word often heard in murder mysteries, such that the detective searches for "a motive" for a killing. Used in this sense, a motive is a reason for committing the crime. Thus, the search for a motive is the search for a reason, a process of "thinking and feeling" that causes an adult to act in specific ways.

In the psychohistorical and organizational literature, five commonly measured motivational needs are defined (Simonton 1984; House, Spangler, & Woycke 1991; Steers 1975; Kolb, Rubin, & McIntyre 1979):

(1) *Power/Dominance (n-Pow, n-Dom)*: Adults high on the n-Pow or the n-Dom exhibit a concern with strong, vigorous action that affects other people—action that has an emotional impact on others, on one's own reputation, or on one's own status. Power motivation is occurring, for example, when an adult is affected or is emotionally concerned about getting or maintaining control over another person, such as wanting to win a point in a debate or wanting to avoid weakness or humiliation. Power motivation is occurring, as another example, when an adult is actually doing something to get or to keep control, such as arguing, giving a command, or punishing.

(2) *Affiliation (n-Aff)*: Adults high on the n-Aff exhibit a concern for establishing, maintaining, or restoring close, personal, emotional relationships with others—including those of a boss-subordinate, a husband-wife, or a friend-friend dyad. Affiliation motivation is occurring, for example, when a husband buys his wife flowers for her birthday.

(3) *Achievement (n-Ach)*: Adults high on the n-Ach exhibit a concern for long-term involvement, competition against some standard of excellence, or some unique accomplishment. Above all, the n-Ach characterizes adults motivated or driven by a need for personal accomplishment through their own efforts. Achievement motivation is present, for example, when an adult has a need to make his or her "mark in the world" by getting the top sales record for the year.

(4) *Autonomy (n-Aut)*: Adults high on the n-Aut exhibit a concern for accomplishing tasks without the assistance (or, in some cases, interference) from others. Autonomy motivation is present, for example, when the scientist in the Research and Development (R&D) lab prefers to solve a long-standing problem herself, rather than getting the whole R&D team involved.

(5) *Activity Inhibition (n-ActI)*: Adults high on the n-ActI exhibit a concern for using their available power to achieve institutional or social goals rather than purely personal goals. Activity inhibition is present, for example, when soldiers and leaders fight for their country in a political war, disregarding the personal costs. McClelland says that the his-

torical use of the word "not" in proscriptive statements in the Judeo-Christian tradition, such as "Thou shalt not," reflects the n-ActI. Through the n-ActI, constraint is placed on the often coexisting coercive, exploitative, and self-interested use of the n-Pow.

Adults' motivational needs are measured by experts in a number of ways, including the Thematic Apperception Test (TAT) (McClelland 1961), in which clients write or tell stories to ambiguous pictures shown them by a trained clinician, who then interprets what the stories indicate in terms of prevailing motivational needs; the Personality Research Form (PRF), an inventory developed by Jackson (1967); and the 20-item Manifest Needs Questionnaire (MNQ), developed by Steers and Braunstein in 1976 for organizational members, in particular.

As with Cox's research on IQ, controversy has surrounded the assessment of needs in adults. Because all three of the just-cited tools had been developed in the United States, some critics, including Hofstede (1980) and Trompenaars (1993), have argued that they are culturally biased and are not representative of other cultures valuing different needs. Perhaps it is best to recognize the useful words of O'Reilly and Roberts (Adler 1997, p. 160), who in 1973 cautioned researchers not to assume that the rankings gotten from any of the tools will hold universally but to expect that they may vary from culture to culture. However, cautioned this research pair, varying rankings in cultures do not imply serious cultural bias in the instruments used for getting these rankings. Given that an adult's "internal frame of reference" (i.e., his or her thinking and feeling patterns) will determine the order of importance of his or her needs, and because an adult's frame of reference is determined by his or her culture, it can be said that one's motivational needs are, indeed, partially bound by culture.

The Motivational Profiles of Successful Corporate and Political Leaders

Is there an empirically validated motivational formula for success for corporate leaders and political leaders? Apparently so. Based on a stream of research conducted by experts in the 1960s (Piotrowski & Armstrong 1979), in the 1970s (Steers 1975; Varga 1975; McClelland & Burnham 1976; Winter 1973), in the 1980s (McClelland & Boyatzis 1982), and in the 1990s (House, Spangler, & Woycke 1991), the successful leader in organizations and in political office apparently is more likely to have a higher n-Pow and a higher n-ActI, a weaker but still "unusual" n-Ach motive, and a quite subdued n-Aff and n-Aut. Studies testing the cross-cultural robustness of this profile (Simonton 1976b) have also been confirmatory. McClelland cautioned, however, that there is some variability along this motivational profile theme in corporate and political leaders, for as Kets de Vries once said, "leaders and followers come in many shapes and sizes."

Furthermore, McClelland found that the motivational profile of a corporation's chief executive officer (CEO) says a lot about how the company will fare in the international marketplace. To determine why in the post–World War II era the Japanese automobile manufacturers' sales rose at the expense of the once-dominant American companies, McClelland and one of his students analyzed CEOs' letters written to stockholders for the Nissan, Honda, Toyota, Chrysler, and General Motors corporations. They found for the period between 1952 and 1980 that the imagery in the Japanese CEOs' letters was consistently higher in the n-Ach than was that in the American CEOs' letters. McClelland suggested, therefore, that to make a car with worldwide appeal, car corporation boards should consider putting high n-Ach types at the top of their organizations. On a more general basis, he added, if companies wish to gain a bigger market share, stockholders might want to insist that their CEOs be prolific in n-Ach imagery or become trained in becoming more prolific.

After completing a similar analysis of CEOs' letters to stockholders in the 50 largest industrial firms in the United States in 1992, Chusmir and Azevedo reported a similar trend. They found that when CEOs high in the n-Ach were at the helm, relative growth in sales was reported; when CEOs high in the n-Pow were at the helm, relative growth in profits was reported. Moreover, they said, industrial leaders tend to profile low on the n-Aff. These researchers expounded on their findings:

Another way of looking at the difference between CEOs high in n Ach and those high in n Pow is in terms of the immediacy of their actions. As McClelland (1961) argued, it may be more correct to think in terms of n Ach managers as those who are concerned with rapid growth and n Pow managers as those concerned with slow growth.

If high n Ach managers act more rapidly and with less interpersonal sensitivity than high n Pow managers, they might be better at making the hard decisions needed to rescue organizations that are in trouble financially or competitively.

If high n Pow managers act more slowly and with more interpersonal sensitivity than high n Ach managers, they might be better at running publicly owned organizations where slow, steady profit growth is required to please stockholders and to maintain or increase stock prices. . . .

It is not surprising that need for affiliation scores of the 50 Fortune-500 CEOs were severely skewed. CEOs in this study had a mean n Aff score of close to zero (0.27). Motivation theory is clear that n Aff is not normally a desirable motive need for top-level managers since the effort to please others and to maintain warm, affiliative relationships may get in the way of needed hard decision making. If the "best" managers should be low in n aff, as McClelland and Burnham (1976) argue, it is logical that the CEOs of the top US industrial firms would be very low in that motive need. That was the case in this study. (pp. 609–610)

The Motivational Profiles of Successful Creative Geniuses

Given that experts have been able to uncover a motivational formula for success for corporate and political leaders, is there a similar motivational formula for success for creators? Appparently so. Research data completed over the past few decades indicate that the motive that sets creative geniuses in the arts, in the sciences, and in the social sciences apart from their less eminent peers is not a high n-Pow, as was found for the corporate and political leaders, but a high n-Ach—and hours upon hours of hard work (Simonton 1976b). In 1963, psychologist Frank Barron summed it well when he said, "The biography of the inventive genius commonly records a lifetime of original thinking, though only a few ideas survive and are remembered to fame. Voluminous productivity is the rule and not the exception among the individuals who have made some noteworthy contribution" (p. 139).

Creative eminents' n-Ach outputs speak volumes: Sigmund Freud wrote 330 articles and books; Thomas Edison applied for and got 1,093 U.S. patents; Balzac finished 85 novels by working over 15 hours a day for 20 years; and Picasso completed 20,000 works over the course of his career (Simonton 1976b, p. 139). More recently, H. J. Eysenck, who died in 1997 at age 81, was the author of nearly 60 books and 1,600 scientific papers (Kesterton 1997). Though he was one of the most widely cited psychologists in the world, H. J. Eysenck (like many eminents) loved to stir up controversy. For this reason, he was once dubbed "the psychologist they most love to hate." Though Eysenck openly disclosed that he thought Freud was a charlatan and maybe even crazy, other psychologists around the globe have similarly wondered whether, at times, creative Eysenck wasn't a bit "tad off" himself.

MYTH #3: THE TRULY SUCCESSFUL HAVE SOME "MAD" URGES THAT PROPEL THEM TO THE TOP

Compared to their less successful counterparts in corporations, in politics, and in the arts and sciences, are the truly successful in some way "mad"? The poet John Dryden expressed a widespread belief about successful leaders and creative geniuses when he wrote, "Great wits are sure to madness near allied, And thin partitions do their bounds divide." But what does the empirical evidence say about the presence of "madness" in present-day "successful" types—regardless of their chosen career fields?

Certainly, the list of dead eminents allegedly having unstable, if not "mad," personalities is long and diverse and includes such greats (Simonton 1984) as Newton, Nietzsche, Schumann, Peladeau, and Van Gogh. The truth is, it seems, that "success" does seem to have some personal costs attached to it—but it is presently not at all clear to experts whether unstable or "mad" personality traits create outstanding outcomes, or whether outstanding outcomes, in some way, are responsible for unstable or "mad" personality traits presenting, or bits of both.

For example, the 1978 study team of Goertzel, Goertzel, and Goertzel, investigating 300 eminent leaders and creators, found that 9 percent of their study sample suffered from serious mental illness, 3 percent of their sample attempted suicide, and 2 percent of their sample were successful with their suicide attempts. Moroever, of those who committed suicide or tried to do so, almost all of them were seriously mood-disordered. As another example, in a 1972 study completed by Martindale on eminent poets, almost 50 percent of their study sample presented with mental ill-health symptoms, and about 15 percent were psychotic. Despite the closeting that has gone on around corporate leaders' "madness," in particular, media reports have increasingly suggested that top corporate leaders may actually be suffering from more antisocial traits and mood disorders than is typically suspected by the societal masses (McFarland 1996; Tillson 1996).

So, what is the bottom line on this issue? Are the eminent in business, in politics, in the sciences, and in the arts more "mad" than their less eminent counterparts? To date, emphasizes Simonton, endorsement of the "madness" hypothesis in the eminent remains a big question mark. Part of the problem is that the eminents in business, in politics, and in science tend to be inaccessible for testing, and part of the problem is that readily available test instruments for measuring mood disorders per se just do not exist. Mood disorder diagnoses are generally made by a highly trained mental health expert using a face-to-face interview format. The reality is that many eminents fear showing up for mood disorder assessments because they do not want their findings publicly disclosed. So, like Ben Webster, they tend to suffer in silence, searching for their own answers to happiness.

Though statistics like those cited by the Goertzel team and by Martindale seem, on face, to endorse the "mad genius" stereotype, Simonton (1984, pp. 55–56) warns that such implications cannot be taken as hardcore proof. The issue of finding a suitable comparison group is critical, he warns. Most of the mental ill-health estimates reported for eminent creators have been based on studies that have compared "creative geniuses" with "noncreative subjects," not on studies that have compared "creative geniuses" with "normal individuals" found in the population—which is a more logical comparison.

However, emphasizes Simonton, Barron's 1963 study is more the exception than the rule. Barron compared population "normals" with artistic creators and found that artistic creators are not necessarily "mad," but they do seem more prone to emotional instability and to mood dis-

orders than scientific creators or "normals" in the community population.

Conceivably, Simonton goes on to say, mood disorders in "successful"
types may be more of a consequence than a cause of achieved eminence,
regardless of the career arena to which the eminent self-selects. As Ein-
stein noted, many eminents have encountered fierce opposition to their
ideas—an opposition that may, at times, temporarily undermine their
sanity. Simonton adds that Ignaz Semmelweis died in a mental facility
after a nervous breakdown, precipitated by the controversy around his
discovery that the mortality rates from puerperal fever could be sharply
reduced if obstetricians would only wash their hands before delivering
babies.

It is possible, Simonton concludes, that some professional groups, including corporate leaders, politicians, and lawyers, are as prone as the
creative geniuses in the arts to mood disorders. But the challenge to the
academic community in the 1990s is to properly complete the research
studies that will either confirm or disconfirm such realities. So far, this
just hasn't been done on any large-scale basis.

THE BOTTOM LINE

This chapter opened with a case on Ben Webster, described by friends
as a venture capitalist and a mystic explorer. But for what was Ben exploring? That became the intriguing question that started us on our
search to better understand the ingredients of eminence.

Chapter 1 sought some answers to three myths that have emerged over
the decades regarding the truly successful in society, namely, that compared to their less successful counterparts, the truly successful are genius
intellectually, have unique motivational profiles, and have some special
"madness" tendencies. Our review of the literature in Chapter 1 suggested that, at present, there is strong empirical evidence in support of
only one of these myths.

Though there is some variation along the IQ theme, eminents in the
arts, in business, and in politics tend to be slightly above-normal in intelligence, but not genius level. In fact, noted many recent experts, beyond a certain level of IQ, excessive intelligence may even be a detriment
to success in business and in politics. Thus, the myth suggesting that the
truly successful are intellectual geniuses is just not supported empirically.

From a motivational point of view, however, "successful" types do
seem to profile more consistently, though there is some difference in
profiling between eminent leaders and creators. Corporate leaders and
political leaders, for example, tend to profile with a higher need for

power and a higher need for activity inhibition, a weaker but still "unusual" need for achievement, and a quite subdued need for affiliation and autonomy. Creative eminents, on the other hand, tend to profile with a high need for achievement. Thus, the myth positing that the truly successful have unique motivational profiles has been supported empirically.

When it comes to mental ill health and "madness," the findings have been suggestive that mood disorders, in particular, may be above-average in prevalence in the eminents, as compared to community populations, but more empirical investigation of this matter is needed. Also, suitable instruments for assessing the mood disorders and less homogeneous study samples are required to properly validate or invalidate the myth that the eminents in business, in politics, and elsewhere are somehow "mad."

Parts I and II of *Management in the Mirror* attempt to more fully answer two intriguing questions from Chapter 1: what other ingredients are "part and parcel" of eminence? Given these ingredients, how do present-day corporate leaders see themselves?

REFERENCES

Adler, N. (1997). *International dimensions of organizational behavior*. Cincinnati: South-Western College Publishing, pp. 158–166.

Atkinson, J. W. (1958). *Motives in fantasy, action, and society*. New York: Van Nostrand.

Barron, F. X. (1963). The needs for order and for disorder as motives in creative activity. In C. W. Taylor and F. X. Barron (Eds.), *Scientific creativity*. New York: Wiley.

Bell, E. T. (1937). *Men of mathematics*. New York: Simon & Schuster.

Chusmir, L. H., & Azevedo, A. (1992). Motivation needs of sampled Fortune-500 CEOs: Relations to organization outcomes. *Perceptual and Motor Skills, 75,* 595–612.

Cox, C. (1926). *The early mental traits of three hundred geniuses*. Stanford, CA: Stanford University Press.

Cronbach, L. J. (1960). *Essentials of psychological testing*. 2d ed. New York: Harper & Row.

Gill, A. (1998). Lives lived: Donald Colin (Ben) Webster. *The Globe and Mail*, January 21, p. A18.

Goertzel, M. G., Goertzel, V., & Goertzel, T. G. (1978). *Three hundred eminent personalities*. San Francisco: Jossey-Bass.

Hofstede, G. (1980). Motivation, leadership and organization: Do American theories apply abroad? *Organizational Dynamics, 9,* 42–63.

House, R. J., Spangler, W. D., & Woycke, J. (1991). Personality and charisma in the U.S. presidency: A psychological theory of leader effectiveness. *Administrative Science Quarterly, 36,* 364–396.

Jackson, D. N. (1967). *Personality Research Form Manual*. Goshen, NY: Research Psychologists Press.

Kesterton, M. (1997). Hans Eysenck. *The Globe and Mail*, September 15, p. A20.

Kets de Vries, M. F. R. (1993). *Leaders, fools, and imposters*. San Francisco: Jossey-Bass.

Kolb, D. A., Rubin, I. M., & McIntyre, J. M. (1979). *Organizational psychology*. Englewood Cliffs, NJ: Prentice-Hall, pp. 72–77.

Martindale, C. (1972). Father absence, psychopathology, and poetic eminence. *Psychological Reports*, 31, 843–847.

McClelland, D. C. (1961). *The achieving society*. New York: Van Nostrand.

McClelland, D. C. (1984). *Human motivation*. Glenview, IL: Scott, Foresman.

McClelland, D. C., Atkinson, J. W., Clark, R. A., & Lowell, E. L. (1953). *The achievement motive*. New York: Appleton-Century-Crofts.

McClelland, D. C., & Boyatzis, R. E. (1982). Leadership motive pattern and long-term success in management. *Journal of Applied Psychology*, 67, 737–743.

McClelland, D. C., & Burnham, D. H. (1976). Power is the great motivator. *Harvard Business Review*, 54, 100–110, 159–166.

McFarland, J. (1996). Managing: Is your boss a psychopath? *The Globe and Mail*, January 9, p. B11.

McNemar, O. (1964). Lost: Our intelligence? Why? *American Psychologist*, 19, 871–882.

Murray, H. A. (1938). *Explorations in personality*. New York: Oxford University Press.

Piotrowski, C., & Armstrong, T. R. (1989). The CEO: An analysis of the CNN telecast "Pinnacle." *Psychological Reports*, 65, 435–438.

Simonton, D. K. (1976a). Biographical determinants of achieved eminence: A multivariate approach to the Cox data. *Journal of Personality and Social Psychology*, 33, 218–226.

Simonton, D. K. (1976b). *Greatness: Who makes history and why*. New York: Guilford Press.

Simonton, D. K. (1984). *Genius, creativity, and leadership*. Cambridge, MA: Harvard University Press, pp. 42–62.

Steers, R. M. (1975). Task-goal attributes, n achievement, and supervisory performance. *Organizational Behavior and Human Performance*, 13, 392–403.

Steers, R. M., & Braunstein, D. N. (1976). A behaviorally-based measure of manifest needs in worksettings. *Journal of Vocational Behavior*, 9, 251–266.

Terman, L. (1925). *Genetic studies of genius. Volume 1: Mental and physical traits of a thousand gifted children*. Stanford, CA: Stanford University Press.

Tillson, T. (1996). The CEO's disease. *Canadian Business*, 69, 26–28, 33–34.

Trompenaars, F. (1993). *Riding the waves of culture*. London: Economist Books.

Varga, K. (1975). n Achievement, n power, and effectiveness of research development. *Human Relations*, 28, 571–590.

Walberg, H. J., Rasher, S. P., & Parkerson, J. (1980). Childhood and eminence. *Journal of Creative Behavior*, 13, 225–231.

White, R. K. (1931). The versatility of genius. *Journal of Social Psychology*, 2, 460–489.

Winter, D. G. (1973). *The power motive*. New York: Free Press.

Winter, D. G., & Steward, A. J. (1977). Content analysis as a method of studying political leaders. In M. G. Hermann (Ed.), *A psychological examination of political leaders*. New York: Free Press, pp. 27–61.

CHAPTER 2

The Path to Success:
Work and Personal Stressors
of the Rich and Famous

The most self-conscious people in the world are its leaders. They may also be the most anxious and insecure. As men of action, leaders face risks and uncertainty, and often display remarkable courage in shouldering grave responsibility. But beneath their fortitude, there often lies an agonizing sense of doubt and a need to justify themselves.

—A. Zaleznik (1966)

A CASE IN POINT

In looking at the leadership behavior of former U.S. president Richard Nixon, some political and organizational psychologists have defined him as a paradoxical leader, while others have defined him as a disease-prone, pathologically stressed leader. Why? Five major life episodes in Nixon's psychobiography illustrate his "paradoxical" and "disease-prone" thinking and behaving. These are outlined as follows (Winter & Carlson 1988, p. 77):

(1) At age 10, Nixon announced to his mother, "I would like to be a lawyer—an honest lawyer, who can't be bought by crooks." Yet in 1974, 51 years after Nixon's saying this, he resigned the presidency of the United States in the face of clear evidence that he was guilty of several criminal actions in, perhaps, the biggest political scandal in American history—all of this after earlier asserting on national television, "I am not a crook!"

(2) Upon graduation from college, Nixon described himself as "very liberal, almost populist." But 10 years or so later, he launched his polit-

ical career by attacking a liberal opponent and "hunting down" communists. Twenty-five years after that, he capped his presidency by visiting "Red" China and toasting its communist leader, Chairman Mao Zedong, in Beijing's Great Hall of the People.

(3) Nixon lost elections for the presidency in 1960 and the governorship of California in 1962, after which he told reporters, "You won't have Nixon to kick around anymore, because, gentlemen, this is my last press conference." Yet, by 1968, he was elected president, the first candidate since Grover Cleveland to win a U.S. presidential election after losing one.

(4) In May 1970, Nixon widened the Vietnam War by ordering an invasion of Cambodia. In response, thousands of university students gathered in Washington, D.C., to protest. On the night of May 8–9, 1970, after a press conference in which Nixon strongly defended his actions, he made 51 telephone calls over seven hours and then drove to the Lincoln Memorial at 4:35 A.M. to visit with the protesting students. After telling the students, "I want you to know that I understand just how you feel," he went on to discuss not the war—but travel, architecture, American Indians, and college football.

(5) After February 1971, Nixon audiotaped all of his meetings and telephone conversations. Later, even when it became clear that these tapes would provide the evidence to force his presidential resignation, he did not destroy them. Why?

In these five life episodes, Nixon's leadership actions seem to defy understanding in terms of the dictates of reason or even the pattern of his previous verbalizations about himself. Simply put, Nixon does not seem to "walk" his own "talk." The question is, Why? Might there be some deeper and more complex theoretical link between Nixon's motivational profile, his childhood life stressors, his presidential role stressors, and his apparent "paradoxical" or "disease-prone" leadership behaviors while in office?

Procedure for Discovery

In 1988, researchers David Winter and Leslie Carlson were similarly moved by this question, to which they attempted to find an answer. Since they could not bring Nixon into their offices to do an in-depth inventory analysis of his "thinking and behaving" patterns, they had to devise an alternative procedure. In their first step, Winter and Carlson examined Nixon's profile using TAT-type analysis and his 1969 and 1973 inaugural addresses.

In their second step, Winter and Carlson showed that Nixon's motive profile fitted well with other facts known about his personal and his leadership "thinking and behaving" by gathering evidence from the published record. The latter included books about and by Richard Nixon (including his 1962 and his 1978–1979 autobiographies) and memoirs of six former close aides who continued to have positive, or at least neutral, feelings about him. These aides included (1) John Ehrlichman, Nixon's campaign adviser, White House counsel, and later chief of the Domestic Council; (2) H. R. Haldeman, Nixon's campaign adviser and White House chief of staff from 1969 to 1973; (3) Henry A. Kissinger, presidential assistant for national security and later secretary of state from 1969 to 1974; (4) Herbert G. Klein, campaign adviser and White House director of communications from 1969 to 1973; (5) Ray Price, campaign adviser and White House speechwriter from 1969 to 1974; and (6) William Safire, campaign adviser and White House speechwriter from 1969 to 1973. In all, 65 specific behaviors, thoughts, or background characteristics of Nixon were studied with regard to his n-Ach, n-Aff, and n-Pow traits; these were then compared against 28 traits of persons with a high n-Ach, 14 traits of persons with a high n-Aff, and 21 traits of persons with a high n-Pow.

Hypothesis

Without getting into too many details, these researchers hypothesized that Nixon's "paradoxical" or "disease-prone" behavior during his presidency could likely be explained by a distressing childhood (in Nixon's mind, at least), an atypical leadership profile for the presidency, and a personality-job misfit that was exacerbated by a "high-noise" environment during his term in office.

Theoretical Approach

To elaborate on the latter point, Winter and Carlson (1988) noted that in leadership positions, the "self-healing" side of the n-Ach involves a concern for excellence and unique accomplishment and is often associated with moderate risk taking and entrepreneurial activity. But the n-Ach can have its costs. Leaders who are high on the n-Ach often report suffering from restlessness and burnout in adulthood, breaking rules or using illegal means to become "successful," and having an ongoing need to "outwardly" please their parents, who in childhood had set high performance standards for them.

Moreover, while the n-Aff is often associated with being able to maintain close relations with others in adulthood, it, too, has its costs. When they become very stressed, leaders high on the n-Aff tend to present with a "prickly" and "erratic" defensive orientation toward others. Leaders who are found to have an unusually high n-Aff often report in adulthood to be still suffering from some separation from their parents in childhood. Also, they often report having an intense fear of not receiving praise from their parents, essentially an emotional codependency carryover from childhood.

Finally, a high n-Pow is often associated with a concern for impact and prestige, thus leading to community social power and leadership positions in adulthood. However, an undeveloped or a misplaced n-Pow does have its costs. Stressed leaders high on the n-Pow often report manifesting disease-prone actions, both on and off the job. These include impulsively aggressing toward others, consuming excessive quantities of alcohol, and taking extreme personal and decision-making risks. Parental permissiveness about sex and aggression and an intense sense of status loss seem to be important antecedents of such disease-prone states regarding the n-Pow.

Findings

After completing their analyses, Winter and Carlson concluded, first, that compared to other successful presidential and corporate leaders who typically have motivational profiles high in the n-Pow, somewhat elevated in the n-Ach, and low in the n-Aff, Nixon's motivational profile was uniquely high in the n-Ach, very high in the n-Aff, and only average in the n-Pow. Second, they found that Nixon's sensitivities about rejection in adulthood—brought on, in part, by his childhood insecurities—helped to further explain his pathological distress and, consequently, his paradoxical and sometimes "prickly" leadership behaviors.

These researchers explained their conclusions using excerpts from Nixon's autobiographies and other historic memoirs (pp. 83–91, with some amendments in formatting):

High Achievement Motivation

On the "Self-Healing" Side:

1. Nixon had high aspirations, calculated the odds, and took moderate risks. Here the evidence comes from several memoirs: "He possesses or is possessed by overwhelming ambition; a desire for accomplishment in a historic sense" (Klein). "I've never known him to take a major step without thoroughly outlining its consequences" (Ehrlichman). "He'd check every item of the [formal dinner] menu and each facet of the evening program, adjusting this or that detail until he got it right" (Haldeman).

2. Nixon was persistent. Safire describes Nixon's persistence in poker metaphors: "The next layer [of Nixon's personality] is the poker player with a long record of winning, the politician with a long record of losing, then winning, then losing again, but not quitting until he absolutely had to quit." In his autobiography, Nixon himself recalled the comment of a law school classmate: He "heard me out, sat back, looked me in the eye, and told me something I shall

never forget: 'You don't have to worry. You have what it takes to learn the law—an iron butt.' "

3. Nixon was innovative and successful, especially on complex problems. In his 1969 book, *Nixon Agonistes: The Crisis of the Self-Made Man*, G. Wills describes these behaviors in an account of Nixon's wartime poker-playing: "He was not playing games; with him it was a business. Lock your true Horatio Alger in a brothel, with no chance of leaving it, and he will improve management, streamline method, and raise income; his moral drive must find some outlet. Nick, as always, did his homework. He found poker's local theoreticians, men willing to play and discuss, replay and debate, out of sheer analytic zeal. . . . [One officer reported that] 'we played two-handed poker without money for four or five days, until he had learned the various plays. Soon his playing became tops.' "

4. Nixon displayed entrepreneurial activity. During his early years as a lawyer before World War II, Nixon helped to set up the Citra-Frost Company, an early effort to produce and market frozen orange juice [as stated by S. E. Ambrose in the 1987 book, *Nixon: The Education of a Politician 1913–1962*]. (Unfortunately, the company failed after a year and a half.)

On the "Disease-Prone" Side:

1. Nixon would cheat and use illegal means to reach a desired goal. The facts of Nixon's role in Watergate are of course public knowledge. In his memoirs, Haldeman explained the whole episode in terms that suggest this aspect of achievement motivation: "Why did Nixon go as far as he did? . . . [There was] a belief in, and too great a willingness to accept, the concept that the end justifies the means."

2. Nixon would give and take feedback, and at times his performance would be severely modified because of it. Haldeman illustrated this Nixon behavior in matters ranging from a White House dinner to Nixon's China policy: "The next day Nixon critiqued the dinner as if it had been a major military battle. Every detail was commented upon. . . . By 1967 he had decided that Communist China was a fact of life. Nixon said, 'Any American policy toward Asia must come urgently to grips with the reality of China.' " Safire suggested that this behavior was at the root of Nixon's "tricky Dick" image: "A favorite criticism of Nixon is that he was infuriatingly inconsistent: opportunism, flip-flop, expediency are the words used to describe [him]. . . . [One of] his common denominators: When circumstances change, change your policy."

3. On his early childhood, it is clear that Nixon's parents set high standards. Nixon's own words give the most vivid description of his parents' high standards: "Probably because of Uncle Griffith's urgings, my parents decided to give my musical abilities a real test. Never a day went by when [my father] did not tell me and my four brothers how fortunate we were to be able to go to school. I was determined not to let him down. My biggest thrill in those years was to see the light in his eyes when I brought home a good report card." Furthermore, Nixon's mother was warmer than his father. Again, Nixon's own words illustrate this point: "She radiated warmth and love for her family. It was his temper that impressed me most as a small child."

Very High Affiliation Motivation

On the "Self-Healing" Side:

1. Nixon had a preference for dyads rather than larger groups; and this is where he shone. Several aides recall Nixon's discomfort in large crowds and pleasure at single relationships: "After meeting Nixon individually or in a small group, people usually would say that they had a new and warm feeling for him. 'Isn't it too bad he doesn't come across that warmly in an auditorium or on television,' " they would say (Klein). "[Rebozo] has cheerfully tolerated endless Nixon monologues with patience and equanimity. . . . Nixon has always found it effortless to be with Rebozo" (Ehrlichman).

On the "Disease-Prone" Side:

1. Nixon would be sociable under safe conditions, but "prickly" and defensive under threat. Price describes this aspect of Nixon's behavior most vividly: "One part of Richard Nixon is exceptionally considerate, exceptionally caring, sentimental, generous of spirit, kind. . . . [A second] part is angry, vindictive, ill-tempered, mean-spirited. Those of us who have worked with Nixon over the years often refer to his 'light side' and his 'dark side.' . . . I thought he often misread the nature of press antagonism toward him, and often needlessly exacerbated it by his own overreaction."

2. Moreover, in situations of agreeableness and similarity, Nixon would be pleasant but in situations of discord or dissimilarity, he would become "prickly" or avoidant. Klein documented the positive aspect of this pattern: "The opposite side of Nixon is his loyalty and support for those close to him during a crisis. . . . This crisis loyalty led the President to cling to Haldeman and Ehrlichman as long as possible. . . . He paid too little personal attention to these matters [fiscal integrity] and accepted the advice of lawyers and aides who were overly anxious to please."

   Ehrlichman recalled the negative aspect: "Nothing, Nixon asserted, would ever be gained by showing friendliness toward the [*Washington*] *Post* [a newspaper critic of Nixon]. Kissinger's comments illustrated the cycle in everyday interaction, suggesting yet another motivational basis for the variability or "tricky" aspect of Nixon's political behavior: "When he did see a new personality, he avoided any risk of tension by seeming to agree with everything his interlocuter said. . . . Each member of his entourage was acquainted with a slightly different Nixon subtly adjusted to the President's judgment of the aide or to his assessment of his interlocutor's background."

3. Nixon's sensitivity to rejection by others may have been triggered by early separation from his parents, as suggested in Nixon's autobiography. While Nixon's parents were alive and married throughout his childhood, he nevertheless experienced several lengthy separations from them. At age 11 he was sent away for 6 months to an aunt's house to take music lessons. Shortly after that, he was sent away to stay with another aunt at the time that his younger brother Arthur died. During his teens, his mother took his older brother Harold (ill from tuberculosis) to Arizona for 3 years. With his father and older brothers, Richard visited during school vacations.

Average Power Motivation

On the "Self-Healing" Side:

1. Through early adulthood organizational activity and leadership, Nixon hinted in his autobiography of a power motivation. Prior to his entry to politics, Nixon was an active leader in organizations. He was elected president of his college student body, helped to organize an "alternative" fraternity, and was elected president of several local clubs.

On the "Disease-Prone" Side:

1. Though leaders high in n-pow tend to be active, forceful, and influential in small groups, for Nixon the evidence is largely negative. According to Haldeman, "Nixon was not at his best at this vital art [of persuasion]." Kissinger adds that "The give-and-take of negotiations made him nervous.... [H]e found it painful to insist on his point of view directly," and also that "Nixon hated to give direct orders—especially to those who might disagree with him."

2. Though leaders high in n-pow tend to create a climate of clarity and high morale for subordinates, once again for Nixon, the evidence is largely negative. Klein commented simply that "His weakness was ... in the area of the use of power and the misuse of it." According to Kissinger: "It was all vintage Nixon: a definite instruction, followed by maddening ambiguity and procrastination, which masked the search for an indirect means of solution, capped by a sudden decision.... He shunned persuading or inspiring his subordinates.... He had been too unsure of himself to inspire. [After meeting with Gerald Ford] I suddenly realized that for the first time in years after a Presidential meeting I was free of tension. It was impossible to talk to Nixon without wondering afterward what other game he might be engaged in at the moment."

3. Though leaders high in n-pow tend to be generally good anger managers in order to gain a following, Nixon was known for his hostile and aggressive yelling and actions around his subordinates. Haldeman stated simply that "Nixon also had a terrible temper." Kissinger filled in some details: "The coarse side of his nature was a kind of fantasy in which he acted out his daydreams of how ruthless politicians behaved under stress.... [Many people wondered] when Nixon would launch one of his characteristically vicious counter-attacks."

4. Leaders with power insecurities tend to be alcohol abusers. While this is an elusive topic regarding Nixon, a first-hand statement is available from Ehrlichman: "On election day [in 1962] Nixon had begun greeting defeat with lubrication but without grace." Others, including Morris, said that Nixon drank exceptionally at night and there were many nights when you couldn't reach him at Camp David.

Conclusions

In concluding their study, Winter and Carlson said that by understanding the intricacies of both Nixon's motivational profile and his

"thinking and behaving" patterns when stressed, Nixon's five life episode paradoxes become understandable. They elucidated (p. 97):

(1) The "honest lawyer" and Watergate. Nixon's announcement to his
mother that he would like to be an "honest lawyer" is the kind of long-
range future career goal typical of achievement-motivated young people,
while at the same time it also expresses a strong affiliation-related desire
for his mother's approval. His later involvement in the crimes of Watergate can be seen as a different manifestation of the achievement motive,
using illegal means to reach a goal—reelection—that is both a valued
achievement and a sign of other people's positive evaluation and loyalty.

(2) Nixon's changing political beliefs (from college liberal, to postwar
"Redhunter," to being a guest of Mao Zedong) earned him the nickname
of "Tricky Dick." Such changes of belief and tactics manifest very clearly
the tendency for achievement-motivated people to modify their actions
on the basis of the results of previous actions. Doubtless this flexibility
makes them successful in business, but in politics it can breed corrosive
suspicions.

(3) Nixon's persistence and ultimate success in the 1968 election also
seem to reflect the persistence and use of feedback that is so characteristic
of high n-Ach. Yet Nixon's campaigning was not merely blind persistence but was closely related to his perceived probability of success—as
would be expected of someone high in the n-Ach. Even before President
Kennedy's assassination, Nixon had decided to stay out of the 1964 contest because (in his own words), "Kennedy was almost certainly going
to be re-elected." By 1968, however, as Nixon himself said, "the chances
for a Republican to be elected President . . . looked better all the time.
My chances of being that Republican had also improved."

(4) The bombing of Cambodia was undeniably an aggressive action,
widening an existing war if not actually beginning a new one. While one
might posit that such an action indicates a high n-Pow, the erratic and
ambivalent features of Nixon's behavior at this time suggest that he was
not comfortable with the exercise of "raw" power and force, and that
he, in fact, felt some ambivalence and discomfort. In at least one memo,
Nixon went so far as to endorse the Cambodia invasion on *affiliative*
grounds: because "we are going to find out who our friends are." Perhaps this ambivalence about power and overriding concern with
affiliation is most clearly expressed in his sudden decision to talk with
some of the protesting students at 4:35 A.M. at the Lincoln Memorial.
That the conversations largely reflected Nixon's own interests rather than
those of the students is typical of the way that affiliation-motivated people interact with others of quite different backgrounds and concerns.

(5) Making the tapes was probably an achievement-motivated act. In
his own words, Nixon said, "From the very beginning I had decided that
my administration would be the best chronicled in history." At the same

time, there seemed to be little risk; Nixon said, "I had believed that the existence of the White House taping system would never be revealed." Why, then, didn't Nixon destroy these tapes when (in his own words) it became clear that if "he were to survive, they would clearly have to be destroyed"? In the face of conflicting advice, Nixon came to two conclusions. The first is a conformist reflection of his high n-Aff: He was "persuaded" by Chief of Staff Alexander Haig that their destruction would create an "indelible impression of guilt . . . [worse than] anything I had actually done." The second reflects both his n-Ach and his defensive, "dark" side of his high n-Aff: "The tapes were my best insurance against the forseeable future. I was prepared to believe that others, even people close to me, would turn against me . . . and in that case the tapes would give me at least some protection."

INTRODUCTION

The just-described case of former U.S. president Richard Nixon extends the leadership motivational profile described in Chapter 1 by detailing both the positive, or the "self-healing," and the negative, or the "disease-prone," sides in one eminent leader. Perhaps just as important from the case is a recognition that Nixon's consistently "paradoxical" behaviors, or inconsistencies between his "talk" and his "walk," seemed to become exaggerated during periods of high stress. Nixon's predisposition to be a poor stress-coper did not begin during his presidency, noted researchers Winter and Carlson (1988). Instead, his "vulnerability" was formed in childhood and was never "corrected" by him during adulthood. To make matters worse, Nixon's job as president of the United States seemed to have been a rather poor "personal-job" fit for him, considering his motivational profile and the profile considered by psychosocial experts to be more "appropriate" for such a leadership role. A quick look at Winter and Carlson's "findings" excerpts shows that, throughout his presidency, with the exception of Nixon's "self-healing" manifestations on the n-Ach, on both the n-Aff and the n-Pow, his "disease-prone" manifestations far outweighed his "self-healing" ones. Considering that his "debits" in the role of president seemed to outweigh his "credits," it is little wonder why experts have labeled Nixon "a paradoxical" or "disease-prone" leader.

Studies completed in recent years by Winter et al. (1991a, b) have shown that Nixon is not alone in either his leadership profiling or his "paradoxical" behavioral displays. Other world and corporate leaders with similar motivational profiles have exhibited similar paradoxical behaviors. By accepting that other leaders also high in the n-Ach and in the n-Aff but average in the n-Pow have presented with similar behavioral "paradoxes" during their leadership reigns—and particularly so during periods of high stress—one can better comprehend why George Bush acted the way that he did in the Persian Gulf crisis and why Mikhail Gorbachev acted the way that he did in the Baltic Republics crisis.

Another lesson from the case of Richard Nixon is that there are limitations to just looking at leaders' motivational profiles. Conceptually, as in the preceding case, we have focused on only three of Nixon's motives, and, as Winter and Carlson had pointed out in their 1988 report, motivation is only one aspect of a leader's personality. If we really want to understand Nixon and his "self-healing" potential as a leader, we would have to expand our search to other critical traits, such as his stress-coping abilities and his other personality traits.

Other researchers who have analyzed President Nixon's "paradoxical" behaviors from other theoretical angles have similarly concluded that he was more a "disease-prone" leader than a "self-healing" one, in large part, because he was the wrong person for the job. A stress-inducing job reality seems to have been experienced by Nixon, for according to Mazlish in his 1972 book *In Search of Nixon*, "Nixon himself has commented many times that he is an introvert in an extrovert profession" (p. 55). Mazlish also said that Nixon tended to use national crises as a way of dealing with his own narcissism, his neuroticism, and his death anxiety.

The rest of Chapter 2 looks more closely at how good personal, stress-coping habits increase a leader's success potential. Thus, the first part of Chapter 2 looks at how well Nixon would have fared if he—or any eminent—were to be assessed against a "stress-coping yardstick" instead of a "motivational yardstick." The second part of Chapter 2 looks at the "person-job" fit components that organizational experts say are critical to a successful and stress-reduced career in corporate leadership, in particular. Chapter 2 concludes with some empirical findings reported in recent years on corporate leaders' stress-coping potentials.

COMPONENTS OF THE STRESS C-O-P-EING YARDSTICK

In my 1997 book, *A Self-Diagnostic Approach to Understanding Organizational and Personal Stressors: The C-O-P-E Model for Stress Reduction*, I outlined a four-dimension C-O-P-E model and provided inventories to help readers assess how well they cope with their stressors at work and at home.

C-O-P-E is an abbreviation that stands for the four key types of self and organizational analyses that stress experts believe are essential for understanding and developing stress-coping potentials:

• C: the *control* that people perceive they have over personal and organizational stressors;

• O: the *outward signs* of distress presenting personally and organizationally;

- *P*: the *personality predispositions* and conditioned behavioral patterns contributing to people's overall stress levels; and
- *E*: the *energy expenditures* and *energy returns* of people as a matter of stress buffering or stress disability.

Soon we will return to the case of Richard Nixon and rate him on a four-point, stress-coping yardstick based on the C-O-P-E model. But before we do, let us do a quick review of basic stress terminology and a more thorough review of the stress-coping literature regarding the ingredients for good stress-coping.

Basic Stress Terminology

"Stress" is a natural part of living, but too much of it is costly. Pathological stress levels can cause mental, physiological, and behavioral problems—and even death. No trade or profession seems to be free from stress, and those who are eminent or in highly responsible jobs, such as world and corporate leaders, seem to be especially prone to dealing with higher levels of it. Say the word *stress*, and more working adults than not think of it as something negative and as something to be avoided, but how realistic is this one-sided approach to perceiving stress?

Let's face it, there is no such thing as a "stress-free" life. In fact, the only time that humans are truly stress-free is when they are six feet underground and not moving. Some degree of stress is good. A certain degree of stress makes life interesting and helps adults to self-actualize; that is, to become everything that they are capable of becoming over the longer term. Thus, stress has a positive as well as negative side to it. Let us review for a moment the positive side of the stress equation.

To begin, individuals are born with a finite set of life energy for accomplishing all that needs to be accomplished during their lifetimes. Given that most individuals are programmed by nature to live well into their 70s and beyond, their resourceful spending of their "finite" life energy is critical for long-term survival and for biologically appropriate aging. Resourceful spending of one's finite life energy is good stress management.

Sometimes in life humans need extra bursts of energy, or an extra fuel tank, to accomplish an extraordinary life demand or a set of life demands. Knowing that humans would occasionally need extra fuel, nature supplied all humans with a kind of emergency fuel pack called "the stress mechanism." By definition, the stress mechanism, or general adaptation syndrome (GAS), is a mind-body process that enables individuals to draw on their energy reserves when required, in response to some special energy demand, called "a stressor."

Stressors can be real (e.g., the Vietnam War in Richard Nixon's case) or imagined (e.g., Nixon's believing that others, even people close to him, would eventually turn against him). Energy-draining stressors perceived by the emotional part of the mind to be "undesirable" and "anger-producing" are called "distressors," while the energy-refueling stressors perceived by the mind to be "desirable" and "pleasure-producing" are called "eustressors." By convention, stressors emanating from an organizational environment are called "job stressors," whereas those emanating from the nonwork environment are called "personal stressors."

Regardless of the origin of the stressor, the GAS, once called into action, works something like this. When the mind perceives that the body's "normal" fuel supplies are not adequate for dealing with a stressor (or set thereof), it emits an "alert message" to the body, advising it that extra energy is required. Once alerted, the body instantaneously responds by releasing energy from its body stores through a complex set of biochemical reactions and through coordination of the sympathetic nervous system and the endocrine system. Thus, in this sense, the GAS becomes a very positive survival feature for humans—and places clearly on the positive side of the stress equation.

However, just as few things in life are free, there is a cost associated with GAS usage. This is where the negative side of the equation comes in. Every time that the physiological stress mechanism is called upon, some degree of strain is placed on the human system. By definition, "strain" is the degree of physiological, psychological, or behavioral deviation from the human system's normal life pattern that results from a stressful life event or a series of stressful life events. The degree of energy consumed both in meeting the life demand(s) and in returning the human system to its "normal" state determines the amount of overall strain and, thus, the amount of "bruising" or potential self-destruction experienced by the human system at any time.

Research evidence has shown dramatic, premature aging of human systems placed under excessive, unrelenting periods of strain, called "chronic strain," and excessive GAS usage. By its very nature, aging places the human system at risk for a range of physiological, psychological, and behavioral complications, including reduced immunity to disease, burnout, and a higher propensity to coronary disease and cancer.

To help reduce humans' risk for excessive stress and strain, therefore, nature seems to have stamped on the brain at birth a kind of invisible warning label that reads, "For long-term survival, use the stress mechanism sparingly as well as critically and intelligently." Whether adults attend to this warning over the longer term is what separates the "self-healing" types from the "disease-prone" types. Here is the bottom line to good stress management: *while moderate amounts of stress stimulation are considered to be constructive and necessary for a fulfilling life, too much or too little stress stimulation can be excessively energy-draining, anger-producing, and self-destructive.*

Transferring this learning to corporations and to politics, working adults in any life arena need to be adept at managing their personal and work energy demands to maintain a lifelong level of moderated stress and an adequate supply of finite life energy for accomplishing what needs to be done both on and off the job.

Assessment along a Stress-Coping Yardstick

While most stress clinicians would use a self-report inventory like the Perceived Stress Scale (PSS) (Cohen, Kamarck, & Mermelstein 1983) to assess the amount of distress presenting in clients, we cannot, under the present circumstances, give such an inventory to Richard Nixon to assess his stress-coping ability. Therefore, we shall, like Winter and Carlson, infer from Nixon's behavior his stress-coping abilities, using the four-point stress C-O-P-Eing yardstick.

Control: Q1. *Does the adult manifest being "in control" in the short term and over the longer term?* The psychosocial and organizational literature has many variations on the theme of personal control. Generally, an adult "in control" in the short term is characterized as having the adequate physiological, psychological, and behavioral "adaptive resources" to cope with presenting taxing life events. In contrast, an adult "not in control" or "out of control" in the short term is characterized as lacking the adequate "adaptive resources" to cope with presenting, taxing life events.

When we observe adults at work and comment that they look "in control," what we are suggesting is that they not only look well adjusted but appear to be outwardly "balanced" on the three mind-body health dimensions. That is, there seems to be a kind of invisible "control bridge" connecting these three aspects of their well-being. Moreover, "in-control" adults seem to be able to cope effectively with most presenting life stressors, whether they occur on or off the job. In short, "in-control" adults appear to others to be:

• Relatively free of mind and body disease;
• Emotionally happy;
• Cognitively able to think through life's challenges and opportunities; and
• Productive at work and at home.

In contrast, when we observe adults and comment that they look "not in control" or "out of control," what we are suggesting is that they look less well adjusted or that they seem to be "off-balance." Thus, for these "not-in-control" adults, the control bridge seems to have one or more of its well-being components missing. Moreover, depending on the degree of "imbalance" presenting, these adults seem to be less able, or unable, to cope with their life stressors. In short, "not-in-control" or "out-of-control" adults appear to others to be:

- Physically uncomfortable to physically disabled;
- Psychologically uncomfortable to chronically anxious, depressed, or angry;
- Cognitively less able or unable to think through life's challenges and opportunities; and
- Less productive or unproductive at work and/or at home.

Moreover, when we comment that not-in-control adults think, feel, and behave paradoxically over the longer term, we are, essentially, linking their outside, observable behaviors with their unobservable, information-processing, and feeling capabilities. But are we correct in making this mind-behavior "control" link?

According to U.K. mental health expert Peter Warr (1990), associations between adults' behavior and their mental well-being are likely to be observed in practice, even though behaviors are conceptually quite distinct from the feelings and information processing that are involved in psychological well-being. When adults really are "in control" psychologically, they illustrate this reality to observers through two longer-term behavioral expressions, in particular, competence or mastery and aspiration or self-actualization. When adults are "not in control" psychologically, they illustrate this reality to observers over the longer term by lacking competent and/or aspiring behaviors.

Competence, or mastery, has been widely discussed in the life-coping literature in the past under a number of labels. For example, Jahoda (1958) described competent adults as having mastery over their environment. Bandura (1977) described competent adults as continually building a repertoire of rich, adaptive resources to enable them to cope with, and transcend, their difficulties in living. Moreover, said Bandura, these adults not only believe that they are self-efficacious (i.e., they have the energy to produce desired life effects) but throughout their various life stages maintain *realistic* expectations about their ability to accomplish this mastery. Pearlin et al. (1981) linked mastery with control, saying that mastery refers to the extent to which competent adults see themselves as being "in control" of the forces that importantly affect their lives.

A similarly positive picture has been painted of adults displaying high aspiration or self-actualization (Warr 1990; Maslow 1973). By definition, individuals who display high life aspiration are not only mentally well adjusted but continually interested in, and engaged in, "positive-return" behaviors with people, things, and events in their personal and work environments. Moreover, high-aspiration individuals tend to establish life goals, as well as work and home goals. Because of their strong commitment to their life goals, high-aspiration adults attempt to expend their finite life energy on events that will move them closer to their goals rather than waste it on events that seem contrary to them. In short, high-aspiration adults tend to be good energy managers.

Moreover, high-aspiration (Warr 1990; Maslow 1973) adults seem to be able to adapt to changing environmental circumstances and to move successfully ahead through later life stages because they are able to maintain a sense of cognitive flexibility. They seem to be constantly on the alert for new life opportunities that might result in further cognitive or emotional growth.

Finally, high-aspiration adults (Warr 1990; Maslow 1973) not only make intensive efforts to survive unpreventable life crises but tend to convert life crises into positive life events, if possible, becoming eustressed rather than distressed by them.

Outward Signs of Distress: Q2. Does the adult manifest distress symptomology in the short-term and over the longer term? Short-term and long-term distress and strain present in adults through a variety of outward signs placed along the psychological, the physiological, and the behavioral dimensions. Table 2.1 (Schuler 1980) summarizes adults' common outward signs along these three dimensions, with the behavioral signs further divided into individual and organizational consequences.

For example, when adults are distressed, they will often talk about feeling "anxious" or "depressed." Both of these are psychological outward signs of distress. By definition, "anxiety" is an unpleasant emotional experience varying in degree from mild unease to intense dread, associated with the anticipation of impending or future disaster (Schell 1997, p. 140). To compensate for this feeling of uneasiness, adults defend themselves using a number of psychological mechanisms, including conversion (an unconscious mechanism whereby negative emotion is converted into a motor or sensory activity or a disorder such as ulcers, migraine headaches, asthma, or arthritic pain), dissociation (a "splitting-off" from painful consciousness via loss of memory, loss of sensory function, loss of speech, or loss of muscular function), and anger outbursts and displacements (a conscious or unconscious activity whereby negative emotion is discharged onto a less powerful object for the security of the stressed individual).

"Depression" is a term used by mental health experts in a number of ways (Schell 1997; p. 150), including as a mood, as a syndrome, and as a clinical illness. As a mood, depression is part of the "normal" range of human experience, usually developing in response to some frustrating

Table 2.1
Leaders' Common Outward Signs of Distress

1. Physiological

   Short-term: Heart rate, GSR, respiration, headache
   Long-term: Ulcer, blood pressure, heart attack
   Nonspecific: Adrenaline, noradrenaline, thymus deduction, lymph deduction, gastric acid production, ACTH production

2. Psychological responses (affective and cognitive)

   Flight or withdrawal
   Apathy, resignation, boredom
   Regression
   Projection
   Negativism
   Fantasy
   Expression of boredom with much of everything
   Forgetfulness
   Tendency to misjudge people
   Uncertainty about whom to trust
   Inability to organize self
   Inner confusion about duties or roles
   Dissatisfaction
   High intolerance for ambiguity, do not deal well with new or strange situations
   Tunnel vision
   Tendency to begin vacillating in decision making
   Tendency to become distraught with trifles
   Inattentiveness: loss of power to concentrate

Irritability
Procrastination
Feelings of persecution
Gut-level feelings or unexplainable dissatisfaction

3. Behavior
   A. Individual consequences
      Loss of appetite
      Sudden, noticeable loss or gain of weight
      Sudden change of appearance; decline/improvement in dress
      Sudden change of complexion (sallow, reddened, acne)
      Sudden change in hair style or length
      Difficult breathing
      Sudden change of smoking habits
      Sudden change in use of alcohol
   B. Organizational consequences
      Low performance-quality/quantity
      Low job involvement
      Loss of responsibility
      Lack of concern for organization
      Lack of concern for colleagues
      Loss of creativity
      Absenteeism
      Voluntary turnover
      Accident proneness

Source: Schuler (1980).

37

or disappointing life stressor. The syndrome of depression consists of a depressive mood together with other outward signs of distress, like weight loss, inability to concentrate, and so on. The clinical illness involves the presence of the syndrome of depression and also implies that the state is not transitory and that it is associated with significant functional impairment of the leader. Leaders who are clinically depressed are often unable to work or are able to do so with significantly reduced efficiency.

Also, when adults are distressed, they often speak of experiencing the physiological outward signs of elevated heart rate and rapid respiration.

Finally, when adults are distressed, they often speak of behavioral changes. These include a loss or a gain in appetite, a sudden change in appearance, a sudden change in smoking habits (usually an increase), and a sudden change in substance abuse (usually an increase).

Because substance abuse is thought to be a sign of distress in the eminent, including corporate leaders and politicians, it deserves a bit fuller explanation. Alcohol abusers among the eminent (Ludwig 1990; Rothenberg 1990; Simonton 1994) have been many and have included writers W. H. Auden and Theodore Dreiser, CEO Pierre Peladeau, artists Arshile Gorky and Frederic Remington, composers John Field and Modest Petrovich Mussorgsky, performers Eric Clapton and Robert Mitchum, and world leaders Alexander the Great and U.S. president Ulysses Grant. Given this array, two questions have arisen. Is the incidence of substance abuse more conspicuous among the eminent than among the population at large? If so, is there some viable relationship between the eminents' distress levels and their substance abuse?

Regarding the first question, empirical evidence for excessive alcohol consumption among eminents is sketchy (Simonton 1994). But among creative writers as a subset of the eminent, the rates of alcoholism clearly exceed those found in the general population. While creative eminents in music, in art, and in entertainment also show inclinations to excessive alcohol consumption, business leaders, politicians, and scientists seem to be somewhat less prone to public signs of this disorder, particularly on the job. Exceptions do exist; before his rise to fame in the Civil War, Grant was fired from the military for his excessive drinking.

Regarding the second question, there does seem to be evidence that eminent creators per se consume alcohol as a form of distress "escape." In 1990, Ludwig probed the lives of 34 heavy drinkers of the twentieth century, including distinguished writers, artists, composers, and performers. Because many creative leaders fear that they are only as good as their last accomplishment, their fear of failure along the achievement motive can become an unconscious drive for heavy escapist drinking. Thus lies the stress-induced, stress-coping paradox for these eminents;

fearing failure, creative leaders often bring on their own failure through excessive alcohol consumption. Robert Lowell, an exception to the rule, seemed to think that alcohol not only stimulated his writing potential but helped moderate his manic-depressive symptoms.

Rothenberg's 1990 study found similar results. He further explained why writers and not business leaders tend to drink on the job. Rothenberg said that eminents having the opportunity to drink alone without being discovered are more likely to escape from their distress problems through alcohol consumption. Because writing is best done alone, it is very easy to place a bottle on the desk and continue in one's work. The same holds for artists and composers; they may privately indulge without concern for their reputations. In contrast, corporate leaders, politicians, and scientists are more subject to public scrutiny. Even the threat of having colleagues smell alcohol on their breath acts as a useful daytime deterrent for those in these lines of work. But away from work, they, too, can escape from their frustrated needs by consuming alcohol. In this subset of eminents, a frustrated need for power or a discomfort with having to exert power is often cited as the likely cause for excessive alcohol consumption, followed by a frustrated need for achievement.

Finally, it needs to be emphasized that substance abuse across all areas of eminence is a guise of suicide, gradual but assured (Simonton 1994, pp. 303–304). In such cases, both substance abuse and suicide may be indications of an underlying depressive disorder. In many eminents' lives, alcoholism or drug addiction is clearly a self-chosen means of self-annihilation. A 1991 study by Lester investigating alcoholism in 70 famous American writers found that alcoholism works almost as well as a life shortener as suicide does. Whereas suicides had an average life expectancy 20 years shorter than that of nonsuicides, alcoholics' life expectancies are 14 years shorter than those of nonalcoholics. "We can conclude," says Simonton, "that the lethal efficiency of the bottle is 70% that of the gunshot, bridge jump, car wreck, or drug overdose" (p. 304).

Personality: Q3. Does the adult manifest as a "self-healing" or as a "disease-prone" personality over the longer term? Mental health experts believe that in "self-healers," there is a competence and aspiration carryover effect from one life stage to the next, starting in early childhood and "programmed," in part, by one's parents or guardians. That is, as a result of early childhood patterning and conditioning, self-healers become motivated throughout their life stages to obtain a healthy degree of control or to remain healthily "in control." Thus, the literature consistently notes that self-healers with a high need for being "in control" have an internal locus of control orientation; they feel that they—and not someone else—are responsible for their various life event "wins" and for their life event "losses." In contrast, "disease-prone" individuals with a low need for being "in control" or with an unhealthy fear of being "in control" have an external locus of control orientation; they feel that fate or others are responsible for their various positive and negative life situations.

Because of the internal-locus trait that seems to reside in self-healers throughout their life stages, they tend to make their own decisions and solve their own problems rather than rely extensively on others; they take reasonable, personal actions to avoid a loss of control; they moderate their energy expenditures to accomplish their life goals without infringing on others' abilities to do the same; and they assume "task- and people-balanced" roles in various work and nonwork settings.

Furthermore, self-healers generally like themselves. They reflect in their attitudes and behaviors positive self-esteem. Because of the respect that they have for their own human dignity and for that of others, these "balanced" adults have positive life situations that look, cyclically, like this:

(1) From early childhood onward, even in times of moderated stress situations, self-healers remain relatively realistic and consistent with their cognitive and behavioral potential;

(2) From early childhood onward, even when environmental circumstances become "very taxing," self-healers decide when and how to appropriately expend their life energy so that they can maintain personal control, but they remain aware and respectful of others' needs to also maintain a healthy level of control;

(3) From early childhood onward, as long as "very taxing" life events remain, these self-healers not only are highly motivated to avoid failure but try to resolve the presenting problem by seeking help from professional others, if need be; and

(4) From early childhood onward, as the "very taxing" life events pass or reach some sort of steady state, these self-healers not only credit themselves with their positive life-event outcomes but attribute their negative life-event outcomes to some combination of a lack of personal effort, a lack of personal skills, a lack of adequate resources, or a lack of personal knowledge. In the end, they tend to work on improving their odds of success over the longer term through self-development (Burger & Cooper 1979; Burger 1984).

When self-healers face a chronic series of negative life events or a disastrous life event, it is not uncommon for their roots of competence and self-aspiration to become temporarily bruised or, in severe cases, to become permanently damaged. Stress experts currently believe that the bruising or damaging of these "control" roots is caused by misplaced or inappropriately dealt with pain or anger. Thus, depending on the self-healer's willingness and ability to deal with the presenting pain or anger—which does not include rationalization, displacement, or suppression of such "real" emotions—three outcomes can result. The self-healer under chronic or severe distress can (Burger 1984):

(a) *Stay on the "self-healing" path and healthily and appropriately confront the pain or anger experienced, with or without assistance from others.* Through healthful confrontation, the bruised competence and aspiration roots are able to eventually heal, and the self-healer can go on to mature—mentally and behaviorally—through later life stages, maintaining a positive sense of self along the way; or

(b) *Move onto the "disease-prone" path and avoid confronting the pain or anger experienced by rationalizing it away, by drinking it away, by displacing it onto others at work or at home, or by suppressing it.* Through these pain and anger "escape" tactics, the bruised roots may appear to heal, but they actually develop various degrees of "scar tissue"; thus, depending on the severity of scarring, minor or major problems in the bruised individual's future life-stage adjustment can result. In severe cases, the individual can become attitudinally and/or behaviorally stuck in a given life stage and develop a negative sense of self, presenting thereafter with low self-esteem; or

(c) *Not only avoid constructive confrontation of the pain and anger but ruminate on the negative life event(s) and, by doing so, escalate the amount of anger, pain, and distress experienced over time.* With escalating pain and anger levels, the damaged roots of competence and aspiration eventually atrophy. Thus, the former self-healer is often seen to become increasingly depressed with increasingly unmet personal expectations. The individual may even regress attitudinally and behaviorally to earlier life stages that were emotionally less threatening. In severe cases of competence and aspiration root atrophy, a previous self-healer can develop not only a strong, negative sense of self but a jealousy of, and cynical resentment toward, others perceived by them as being better adjusted and more competent and aspiring. Recent studies have shown that, besides jealousy and cynicism, chronically distressed adults often become clinically depressed and/or substance-addicted (Burger 1984; Burger & Arkin 1980).

Energy Balance: Q4. Does the adult appear to be "energy-balanced" over the longer term? We noted earlier that all humans must maintain an appropriate, finite life-energy "balance" over the longer term to stay mentally, physically, and behaviorally healthy. Failure to do so can result in a condition called "burnout," a condition in which more life energy has gone out than has come in.

Burnout prevention lifestyle habits include getting seven to eight hours of uninterrupted sleep at least three times a week, eating a moderated and balanced diet with fiber, and getting at least 20 minutes of moderated exercise (like walking) daily. Burnout prevention also requires adequate social-emotional refueling, which adds to humans' feelings of self-worth and restores their "emotional fuel." A third burnout prevention strategy includes maintaining an optimistic versus a pessimistic view about life.

Since the landmark work of Lazarus (1966), stress experts have accepted that adults' unique cognitive and emotional appraisals of their life events determine whether they feel "in control," "appropriately stressed," and "in balance" or "out of control," "distressed," and "unbalanced." Lazarus also emphasized that uniqueness in programming and variability in response are the theme to adults' appraisals of their life events in the short term (usually defined by experts to be days, weeks, or several months).

What causes this uniqueness in life-event programming and variability in response for individuals in the short term? Most experts agree that individuals appraise their life events by a dynamic, but past-linked, "standard" that is mood-responsive. Thus, the uniqueness in programming and variability in life-event responding are a function of a complex past-present, mind-behavior control link. At any time, adults' appraisals of, and behavioral responses to, presenting stimuli—be they real or imagined—are a function of many variables, including, but not limited to, their appraised "returns" from recent life events, their past positive or negative meaning assigned to similar or perceived-to-be-similar life events, and their patterned or conditioned responses to the same or perceived-to-be-similar life events.

Over the longer term, adults' informational appraisals are unique but more predictable because they tend to develop "predominantly positive" or "predominantly negative" appraisal and information-processing predispositions. Simply stated, individuals have a sort of "filter" or "lens" on their information appraisal systems that results in their viewing and processing life events as "predominantly optimistic" and "likely refueling" or as predominantly "pessimistic" and "likely draining." By recent convention, the former set of individuals are called "positive affectives," or PAs, while the latter are called "negative affectives," or NAs. High-PAs are excellent stress moderators and energy-refuelers. High-NAs, often referred to as neurotics in the psychosocial literature, are poor stress moderators and energy-refuelers. Thus, high-NAs seem particularly prone to bouts of anger, anxiety, and depression, and, eventually, burnout (Chen & Spector 1991).

As noted in the psychosocial literature (Watson & Clark 1984; Burke, Brief & George 1993) high-NAs tend to dwell on their failures and shortcomings at work and at home rather than accentuate their successes and strengths in both life arenas; focus on the negative side of the world instead of seeing the opportunity for growth and development; view themselves as having low competence and aspiration; have high absenteeism rates at work; report frequent physicians' visits; and complain about many varied symptoms of poor health.

Rating of Nixon on the C-O-P-Eing Yardstick. So how would Nixon likely rate on this four-point C-O-P-Eing yardstick? Answer: not much differently from how he rated on the motivational yardstick. Regarding Q1, most observers would likely say that while in office, Nixon looked more "out of control" than "in control." Safire's statement, "A favorite criticism of Nixon is that he was infuriatingly inconsistent," pretty much sums up this submission. Nixon's "walk" repeatedly failed to speak his "talk"; thus, the "paradoxical" and "tricky Dick" labels given to him by aides close to him seemed fitting. Regarding Q2 on Nixon's outward signs of distress, we are told by Nixon's aides that he tended to avoid confronting his pain from early childhood onward, thus suffering in adulthood from ongoing displays of low self-esteem, bouts of heavy nighttime drinking at Camp David, and displacement of anger onto unsuspecting others. Regarding Q3 on Nixon's personality, we see a number of unresolved "problems" from his early childhood carry over into adulthood, with suppressed rage mounting day by day; Kissinger commented on Nixon's aggressive and antisocial tendencies by noting: "The coarse side of his nature was a kind of fantasy in which he acted out his daydreams of how ruthless politicians behaved under stress. . . . Many people wondered when Nixon would launch one of his characteristically vicious counter-attacks." Finally, regarding Q4, if we had to label Nixon as either a "PA" or a "NA," the latter label would prevail. Witness the emotional pain that "neurotic" Richard Nixon experienced regarding formal dinner menu items and his feared eventual desertion by friends. So, on a scale from 0 to 4, where 0 means "totally distressed" and where 4 means "totally eustressed," we could reasonably place Nixon as a "0" on the stress C-O-P-Eing yardstick during his term in office.

THE PARADOXICAL ROLE OF CORPORATE LEADERS

To this point, we have focused on distress in adults and have focused largely on the paradoxical and pathological levels in Nixon, brought on, in part, by his own personal insecurities and, in part, by the distress of his chief executive role. Let us now move to corporate leaders. What does the organizational literature tell us about the role of present-day corporate leaders? Does a potentially stress-inducing "paradox" of any kind exist for these job incumbents, regardless of their C-O-P-Eing predispositions?

Evidence from the Literature Regarding the Paradoxical Role of Corporate Leadership

Over the past decade, journals and the popular press have highlighted the role of leadership in revitalizing economies and in promoting the success of businesses and government offices. The issue of "corporate" leadership—especially the key role played by an organization's chief executive officer (CEO) or other top manager—has gained increasing notoriety (Grove 1983; Iacocca & Novak 1984).

A review of the organizational literature, however, shows that most empirical work on leadership in the 1980s and 1990s has focused on middle managers. There has been relatively little empirical work done on the corporate elite. This void is troublesome, note Hart and Quinn (1993), because there is much reason to believe that the roles and behaviors of effective top managers differ from those of middle managers. While middle managers tend to focus on work group productivity, CEOs and other corporate elite tend to focus on corporate performance.

Considering the work on CEOs that has been published, the literature remains deeply divided regarding the roles and behaviors required of successful corporate leaders (Zaleznik 1977; Conger & Kanungo 1988; Levinson & Rosenthal 1984; Nulty 1989). To make sense of this mess, Hart and Quinn (1993), Torbert (1987), and others (Bourgeois & Eisenhardt 1988) have begun to posit that successful corporate leadership requires a "balancing" and a "simultaneous mastery" of seemingly contradictory or "paradoxical" capabilities, including decisiveness *and* reflectiveness, broad vision *and* attentiveness to detail, bold moves *and* incremental adjustments, and a task *and* people orientation. Experts Jacques (1986) and Kegan (1982) have stressed the importance of cognitive *and* behavioral complexity for effective corporate leader performance.

Hart and Quinn's Model of Competing Roles for Corporate Leaders

In 1993, Hart and Quinn reported on their Model of Competing Roles for Corporate Leaders. They said that CEOs achieving mastery over diverse and seemingly paradoxical roles will deliver higher firm performance than those with less encompassing approaches to their work. They also maintained that the complexity and multidimensionality of the corporate leader role can be better understood by observing the quadrants in their model (see Table 2.2) (Hart & Quinn 1993, p. 551).

Each of the quadrants in Table 2.2 can be thought of as representing a *domain* of action, entailing a particular *demand* on the firm, with a corresponding *role* for top managers. The four domains—the future, the

Table 2.2
Hart and Quinn's Model of Competing CEO Roles

Executive Leadership: A Model of Competing Roles	
Flexibility	
Domain: The Organization Demand: Commitment ROLE: THE MOTIVATOR **Internal Focus**	Domain: The Future Demand: Innovation ROLE: THE VISION SETTER **External Focus**
Domain: The Operating System Demand: Efficiency ROLE: THE ANALYZER	Domain: The Market Demand: Performance ROLE: THE TASK MASTER
Predictability	

Source: Hart & Quinn (1993).

organization, the operating system, and the market—indicate the four competing demands placed on the firm, which, in turn, become the role and responsibility of the corporate leaders. These four competing demands concern (Hart & Quinn 1993, p. 551):

- *Innovation*: the future positioning of the organization in terms of strategic direction, products, and service.
- *Commitment*: the development and motivation of people and the maintenance of a distinctive identity and value system.
- *Efficiency*: the management of ongoing operations and the critical evaluation of alternative projects and programs.
- *Performance*: the execution of plans and the achievement of results in the marketplace.

To contend with these four competing demands—some requiring flexibility and others requiring predictability—the corporate leader must become proficient in four key roles (see Table 2.2): the Vision Setter, the Motivator, the Analyzer, and the Task Master. Each of these complex roles, having either an external focus or an internal focus, is defined as follows:

The Vision Setter. The Vision Setter role is one of creating a sense of identity and mission—the definition and articulation of the firm's basic purpose and future direction. To fulfill this role a top manager must spend considerable time monitoring and studying emerging social, economic, and technological trends. Analysis of competitors and markets is also critical. In addition, informal contacts, both external (customers, suppliers, competitors, consultants) and internal (functional managers, line workers), are required to sense emerging trends and pick up "weak signals." The future direction of the organization must thus be based upon a mix of disciplined analysis and intuition.

[President] Jimmy Carter provides an excellent example of an executive with a strong orientation toward the Vision Setter role. However, the relative ineffectiveness of his administration reveals how important it is that the vision of the future be compelling and serve to create a sense of identity and collective purpose. This ties directly into the next role—that of the Motivator.

The Motivator. The Motivator role is fundamentally one of the management of meaning. It involves translating the vision and economic strategy of the firm into a "cause worth fighting for"—a core set of concepts and priorities which infuse and mobilize the entire organization. To fulfill this role, the executive must create a sense of excitement and vitality within the organization. Through innovative structures, programs, and processes, the top manager must challenge people to gain new competencies and achieve higher levels of performance. However, it is also essential to provide a sense of permanence and clarity of purpose. Through personal example, metaphor, anecdote, ceremony, and symbol, the executive emphasizes enduring company values.

Seymour Cray, founder of Cray Research, provides an excellent example of an executive strongly oriented toward the Motivator role. The purpose of the company was to build the fastest computer in the world. Cray reinforced this cause through both organizational and personal action. Each year, he would build a new sailboat and then burn it at the end of the summer. This ritual made it clear to employees that what worked in the past will not work in the future. Success in the supercomputer business depends upon the continual reinvention of the product. Such actions, if done well, provide both the spirit of innovation needed to target broad, new strategic goals and the stability and clarity of purpose needed to achieve current objectives.

The Analyzer. In the Analyzer role, the top manager focuses on the efficient management of the internal operating system in the interest of serving existing product-markets. To fulfill this role, the executive leader must stop short of making day-to-day management decisions—this is the role of the divisional and functional managers. Instead, the top manager sets the context and shapes the decisions made by the operating system. This is accomplished through the critical review and evaluation of proposed projects and programs—by asking difficult questions which force business and functional managers to think about their situation in new ways. The executive leader must also have the ability to integrate conflicting functional perspectives in the interest of the total organization.

[The late] Harold Geneen was the quintessential Analyzer during his tenure as CEO of ITT. His orientation toward formal analysis coupled with his active role in decision making epitomized the analytical orientation to management. By insuring that the formal systems of the company facilitated the achievement of the firm's vision, the top manager thus achieves strategic control.

The Task Master. In the role of the Task Master, the top manager is concerned about firm performance and results. In the narrowest sense, this translates into economic performance and the demands of the capital market. In the broader sense, this translates into social performance—serving the full range of external "stakeholders" associated with the organization. To fulfill this role, the executive must not only influence decisions made at lower levels by contributing to specific knowledge and opinions but must also make explicit trade-off decisions and allocate resources to the highest priority activities.

Frank Lorenzo of Texas Air provides a wonderful illustration of an executive consumed with the Task Master role. In the final analysis, the Task Master is a "hands on" role with a strong focus on results—getting the job done today. (pp. 551–553)

Empirical Validation of the Competing Roles Model

Procedure. To empirically validate their model, Hart and Quinn (1993) sent a short questionnaire to the CEO or president of 3,546 firms in a large metropolitan region in the U.S. industrial Midwest, including organizations of nearly all types and sizes. Besides being asked to complete 16 executive leadership role items on themselves, the CEOs/presidents were asked to compare the performance of their company with that of other companies in the same market and at a similar stage of development using a seven-point low performer-to-high performer scale. A total of 916 completed surveys was received, yielding a response rate of 25 percent.

Findings. Hart and Quinn's major study findings were as follows:

(1) The top managers in the sample rated the Task Master role as the one they most frequently played ($M = 3.93$), while the Vision Setter ($M = 3.42$) and the Motivator ($M = 3.40$) roles were the least frequently played. The Analyzer role ($M = 3.70$) was somewhere between the two extremes.

(2) Larger firms demonstrated stronger financial and business performance than smaller firms. As might be expected, firms in munificent environments, those where the CEOs/presidents perceived that the market for their main product would grow in the next year, were also better performers.

(3) Using deductive analysis, Hart and Quinn estimated the degree to which CEOs/presidents could be classified as being "effective" or "successful" on all four corporate leader functions. *Very importantly, the results showed that, at most, only 10 percent of the responding CEOs/presidents could be classified as "highly complex" or "moderately complex" and thus capable of dealing with the multidimensional and paradoxical corporate leader role. The majority, 90 percent, were classified as either "low on complexity" or "unbalanced."* Specifically, these researchers found that:

(a) the "High Complexity" group ($n = 52$), those CEOs/presidents consistently scoring in the upper third percentile on each of the four roles, represented only 8 percent of the respondents; their Vision Setter mean score was > 3.67, their Motivator mean score was > 4.00, their

Analyzer mean score was > 4.00, and their Task Master mean score was > 4.25.

(b) The "Medium Complexity" group (n = 14), those CEOs/presidents consistently scoring in the middle on each of the four roles, represented only 2 percent of the respondents; their Vision Setter mean score was > 3.00 but < 3.67, their Motivator mean score was > 3.00 but < 4.00, their Analyzer mean score was > 3.33 but < 4.00, and their Task Master mean score was > 3.75 but < 4.25.

(c) The "Low Complexity" group (n = 31), those CEOs/presidents consistently scoring low on all of the roles, represented only 4 percent of the respondents; their Vision Setter mean score was < 3.00, their Motivator mean score was < 3.00, their Analyzer mean score was < 3.33, and their Task Master mean score was < 3.75.

(d) The "Unbalanced" group (n = 578), those CEOs/presidents having higher mean scores on the Analyzer and the Task Master roles and lower mean scores on the Vision Setter and the Motivator roles, represented a significant 86 percent of the respondents.

(4) Finally, the study results clearly indicated that the CEOs/presidents of the firms performing above the median on all three performance variables assessed saw their jobs as requiring much greater emphasis on the four leadership roles than did their counterparts in low-performing firms. Neither firm size nor type of competitive environment influenced this outcome.

Consistent with their model projections, these findings indicate that multidimensional performance in corporate leaders seems to be fostered by behavioral complexity, as manifested by a capability to perform effectively on all four leadership roles. Hart and Quinn affirmed:

While the findings tend to support the arguments of the emerging paradoxical perspective, they also suggest an interesting insight about situation and context. *Executives with high scores on all four roles achieve high levels of performance regardless of the nature of their firm's size or competitive environment.* This does not suggest that high performers can arbitrarily move from one firm or industry to another, but it does suggest that high behavioral complexity is a somewhat universal capability. *The capacity to balance competing demands and play all four roles at a high level suggests lengthy experience, hard work, and the development of knowledge and relationships over a long period.* (p. 569)

CORPORATE LEADERS' REPORTED STRESS LEVELS

So, how stressed out are present-day corporate leaders with their "paradoxical" roles? Over the past 20 years, five studies, in particular, have provided useful contributions to this question.

(1) The first study, conducted by Cooper and Melhuish (1980), was

completed in 1980 on a group of 196 male senior managers attending the Administrative Staff College, Henley-on-Thames, U.K. This study's findings indicated that two segments of corporate leaders were particularly "at risk" for physiological and psychological ill health because they were "out of control." Those at risk for premature heart disease seemed to be overly "turned on" by their paradoxical roles; they were the workaholic, task- and perfection-fixated Type A corporate leaders. Those appearing to be at risk for mental ill health experienced a poor personal-organizational fit; like Nixon, these corporate leaders profiled as highly tense, suspicious or paranoid, very intelligent, and quite taciturn—and they worked in organizational situations perceived by them as being "economically vulnerable."

(2) The second study, already alluded to, was Warr's 1990 study on 839 U.K. male and 847 female industrial workers, including top managers. After assessing organizational members' mind-body well-being along nine dimensions, Warr concluded that the higher-level managers reported significantly more job-related "enthusiasm" and job-related "aspiration" than their lower-level counterparts, but they also reported feeling "more job anxious" and "more energy-drained" by the unpredictability and workaholic natures of their jobs. Thus, Warr's study findings indicated some degree of mental health risk for all of those in top leadership functions.

(3) The third study, conducted by Cooper in 1984, assessed 1,065 senior and executive officers in 10 countries around the world on their job satisfaction and mental health risk. The degree of "control" perceived by these global corporate leaders appeared to be a critical factor ensuring greater degrees of job satisfaction and mental health. Examining the data for executives with mental ill-health scores at least 25 percent higher than the "norm" (i.e., scores falling close to those of psychiatric outpatients), Cooper found that in the developing countries and in those with rapid economic change (i.e., Egypt, Brazil, Singapore, Nigeria, and Japan), where "control" at the macrolevel is threatened, over 30 percent of the executives appeared to be "at risk" for stress-induced mental disability. Egypt, for example, "topped" the list, with about 42 percent of the corporate leaders being at risk for mental disability. In contrast, in the developed countries (i.e., the United States, Sweden, and Germany), where "control" at the societal macrolevel is relatively unthreatened, the proportion of executives "at risk" for stress-induced mental disability was markedly less—in the 11–19 percent range. The United States "topped" the latter list.

(4) The fourth study, conducted by Robinson and Inkson in 1994 on 98 male CEOs from organizations in New Zealand, found that while the majority of CEOs—64 percent—felt healthily "in control" and were in good physical health, at least 24 percent of the CEOs were at high risk

for ill health. The latter said they had major concerns about the future of their careers, the economic situation of their country, or a drug or alcohol abuse problem in a family member or close friend.

(5) The fifth study, conducted by Begley and Boyd in 1992 on 235 CEOs in smaller businesses in the New England area of the United States, found that relative to their counterparts in large industry, the corporate leaders in smaller businesses seemed relatively "in control" and mind-body healthy. Their mean scores on a number of inventories indicated high levels of mastery, self-esteem, and levels of optimism. However, cautioned Begly and Boyd, it needs to be emphasized that the CEOs' anxiety and depression scale scores were higher than those reported for 23 occupational groups studied by Caplan's team in 1980 and employing the same measures.

THE BOTTOM LINE

Chapter 2 was all about leaders and eminents being able to obtain and maintain a healthy degree of "control" over their lifetimes to stay moderately stressed and psychologically, physiologically, and behaviorally "healthy."

Thus, Chapter 2 opened with a case on Richard Nixon, a leader who was labeled by his aides and social scientists as being "paradoxical" and "disease-prone." As we looked more closely at the thinking and behaving patterns of Nixon, we concluded that he was at risk for mental and behavioral ill health. This outcome was caused, in part, by his "unbalanced" personality and in part, by the strain placed on him because of a poor personal-job "fit." Whether we assessed Nixon using a motivational yardstick or a stress C-O-P-Eing yardstick, we came to the same conclusion. (Admittedly, we used the same data set.)

The second part of Chapter 2 focused on the "paradoxical" role of present-day corporate leaders. We noted that, like Nixon, it is quite possible that a significant number of corporate leaders are pathologically strained by the poor personal-job "fits" that they find themselves facing daily. Hart and Quinn (1993) estimated the percentage of "unbalanced" and "poor fit" types to be an overwhelming 90 percent, saying that only 10 percent were "balanced" and "fully capable" of doing their jobs.

The third and final part of Chapter 2 focused on the empirical studies that have been done in the 1980s and 1990s regarding the mind-body stress and strain in present-day corporate leaders. After reviewing five key studies completed on corporate leaders around the world, we found that the more "in control" these leaders felt, the better their prognosis for long-term mental, physiological, and behavioral health. Though the studies varied in terms of the percentages of CEOs presently "at risk" for ill health on one of these three dimensions, the findings did seem to consistently indicate that at least 20 percent are, like Nixon, "crying out" for distress help.

REFERENCES

Bandura, A. (1977). Self-efficacy: Toward a unifying theory of behavioral change. *Psychological Review*, 84, 191–215.

Begley, T. M., & Boyd, D. P. (1992). Work stress and health outcomes: The impact of personal orientations among CEOs in smaller businesses. *Journal of Managerial Issues*, 4, 62–83.

Bourgeois, L. J., & Eisenhardt, K. (1988). Strategic decision processes in high velocity environments: Four cases in the microcomputer industry. *Management Science*, 14, 816–835.

Burger, J. M. (1984). Desire for control, locus of control, and proneness to depression. *Journal of Personality*, 52, 71–89.

Burger, J. M., & Arkin, R. M. (1980). Prediction, control and learned helplessness. *Journal of Personality and Social Psychology*, 38, 482–491.

Burger, J. M., & Cooper, H. M. (1979). The desirability of control. *Motivation and Emotion*, 3, 381–393.

Burke, M. J., Brief, A. P., & George, J. M. (1993). The role of negative affectivity in understanding relations between self-reports of stress and strain: A comment on the applied psychology literature. *Journal of Applied Psychology*, 78, 402–412.

Caplan, R. D., Cobb, S., French, J. R. P., Jr., Van Harrison, R., and Pinneau, S. R., Jr. (1980). *Job demands and worker health*. Ann Arbor: University of Michigan Institute for Social Research.

Chen, P. Y., & Spector, P. E. (1991). Negative affectivity as the underlying cause of correlations between stressors and strain. *Journal of Applied Psychology*, 76, 398–407.

Cohen, S., Kamarck, T., & Mermelstein, R. (1983). A global measure of perceived stress. *Journal of Health and Social Behavior*, 24, 385–396.

Conger, J., & Kanungo, N. (1988). *Charismatic leadership*. San Francisco: Jossey-Bass.

Cooper, C. L. (1984). Executive stress: A ten-country comparison. *Human Resource Management*, 4, 395–407.

Cooper, C. L., & Melhuish, A. (1980). Occupational stress and managers. *Journal of Occupational Medicine*, 22, 588–592.

Grove, A. (1983). *High output management*. New York: Random House.

Hart, S. L., & Quinn, R. E. (1993). Roles executives play: CEOs, behavioral complexity, and firm performance. *Human Relations*, 46, 543–574.

Iacocca, L., & Novak, W. (1984). *Iacocca: An autobiography*. New York: Bantam Books.

Jacques, E. (1986). The development of intellectual capability: A discussion of stratified systems theory. *Journal of Applied Behavioral Science*, 22, 361–383.

Jahoda, M. (1958). *Current concepts of positive mental health*. New York: Basic Books.

Kegan, R. (1982). *The evolving self*. Cambridge: Harvard University Press.

Lazarus, R. S. (1966). *Psychological stress and the coping process.* New York: McGraw-Hill.

Lester, D. (1991). Premature mortality associated with alcoholism and suicide in American writers. *Perceptual and Motor Skills, 73,* 162.

Levinson, H., & Rosenthal, S. (1984). *CEO: Corporate leadership in action.* New York: Basic Books.

Ludwig, A. M. (1990). Alcohol input and creative output. *British Journal of Addiction, 85,* 953–963.

Maslow, A. H. (1973). *The farther reaches of human nature.* London: Penguin.

Mazlish, B. (1972). *In search of Nixon: A psychohistorical inquiry.* Baltimore: Penguin.

Nulty, P. (1989). American's toughest bosses. *Fortune,* February 27, 40–54.

Pearlin, L. I., Menaghan, E. G., Lieberman, M. A., & Mullan, J. T. (1981). The stress process. *Journal of Health and Social Behavior, 22,* 337–356.

Robinson, P., & Inkson, K. (1994). Stress effects on the health of chief executives of business organizations. *Stress Medicine, 10,* 27–34.

Rothenberg, A. (1990). *Creativity and madness.* Baltimore: Johns Hopkins University Press.

Schell, B. H. (1997). *A self-diagnostic approach to understanding organizational and personal stressors: The C-O-P-E Model for Stress Reduction.* Westport, CT: Quorum Books.

Schuler, R. S. (1980). Definition and conceptualization of stress in organizations. *Organizational Behavior and Human Performance, 25,* 186.

Simonton, D. K. (1994). *Greatness: Who makes history and why.* New York: Guilford Press.

Torbert, W. (1987). *Managing the corporate dream.* Homewood, IL: Irwin.

Warr, P. (1990). The measurement of well-being and other aspects of mental health. *Journal of Occupational Psychology, 63,* 193–210.

Watson, D., & Clark, L. A. (1984). Negative affectivity: The disposition to experience aversive emotional states. *Psychological Bulletin, 96,* 465–490.

Winter, D. G., & Carlson, L. A. (1988). Using motive scores in the psychobiographical study of an individual: The case of Richard Nixon. *Journal of Personality, 56,* 75–103.

Winter, D. G., Hermann, M. G., Weintraub, W., & Walker, S. G. (1991a). The personalities of Bush and Gorbachev at a distance: Procedures, portraits, and policies. *Political Psychology, 12,* 215–245.

Winter, D. G., Hermann, M. G., Weintraub, W., & Walker, S. G. (1991b). The personalities of Bush and Gorbachev at a distance: Follow-up on predictions. *Political Psychology, 12,* 457–464.

Zaleznik, A. (1966). *Human dilemmas of leadership.* New York: Harper and Brothers.

Zaleznik, A. (1977). Managers and leaders: Are they different? *Harvard Business Review, 55,* 67–80.

CHAPTER 3

The Path to Corporate Success: Strategies for Getting to the Top

If man runs naked down the street proclaiming that he alone can save others from impending doom, and if he immediately wins a following, then he is a charismatic leader. A social relationship has come into being. If he does not win a following, he is simply a lunatic.

—B. R. Wilson (1975)

A CASE IN POINT (COHEN 1997)

On October 19, 1962, the fourth day of the Cuban missile crisis, John Fitzgerald Kennedy was appalled by the options before him. He knew that the Soviet Union had placed nuclear warheads in Cuba, he knew that the United States had to disarm them, and he knew that this clash of interests was pushing the world to the brink of nuclear war.

"If we go in and take them out on a quick air strike, we neutralize the chance of danger to the United States of these missiles being used," the U.S. President said in a recording of a conversation released recently. ". . . [But] there's bound to be a reprisal from the Soviet Union. There always is—their just going in and taking Berlin by force. Which leaves me only one alternative, which is to fire nuclear weapons—which is a hell of an alternative."

The crisis had begun when Soviet Premier Nikita Khrushchev sent offensive nuclear warheads to dissuade the United States from invading Communist Cuba, which lies just 145 kilometers from Florida. The United States demanded that the warheads be withdrawn. After 13 days of high-level negotiation between Washington and Moscow, in which many thought war would break out, they were withdrawn in exchange for a public commitment by the United States not to invade Cuba and a private promise to dismantle obsolete U.S. missiles in Turkey.

Mr. Kennedy's dispassionate analysis, spoken in his familiar cadence, is among hours of taped conversations held between October 13 and October 27, 1962, but declassified only during the winter of 1996. Like Mr. Nixon, Mr. Kennedy taped conversations in his office. Although the taping wasn't illegal, only Kennedy, his secretary and two secret-service agents knew about it. The recordings were never intended to be made public; Mr. Kennedy's purpose for the taping was simply to keep a record for his memoirs.

The last of the 1962 tapes came to light early in 1997. Often inaudible, they were painstakingly transcribed and analyzed by Ernest May and Philip Zelikow of Harvard University. These researchers posit that this authentic, verbatim record of events over that harrowing fortnight shows a firmness, prudence and restraint that will cast Mr. Kennedy, whose record as a leader has been mixed, in a far more favourable light.

"It was the most serious crisis of modern history," Mr. May said in an interview. "He handled it superbly. He walked a fine razor's edge between two pools of fire and survived. It showed just what he could do when he chose to draw on his talents."

More broadly, noted Mr. May, Mr. Kennedy's stamina and judgment as a leader during those 13 days and nights will become an antidote to revisionist criticism of the man and his presidency.

That debate about Mr. Kennedy's influence styles and his morals was reignited in the autumn of 1997, with the allegations of investigative journalist Seymour Hersh. In his 1997 book *The Shadow President: Ted Kennedy in Opposition*, Hersh alleged that organized crime fixed the 1960 election for Mr. Kennedy, that Mr. Kennedy approved the assasination of foreign leaders, and that he entertained prostitutes at the White House.

During the fortnight of the crisis, affirms Mr. May, Mr. Kennedy is seen as resolute, focused and lucid. Facing missiles in his own hemisphere, he sought to forge consensus among his advisers, reassure his European allies, contain hawkish generals and consider the morality of an attack—all the while knowing that a misstep could bring nuclear war to the Northern Hemisphere.

Mr. Kennedy's civil-defense experts told him that 50 million Americans, mostly in rural areas, would die. Mr. Kennedy asked whether there was anything that could be done to protect them. There wasn't, he was told.

From the time that U.S. spy planes discovered the missiles in Cuba, Mr. Kennedy was under pressure to use force: to launch a surgical attack to destroy the missiles; to launch a wider bombing campaign to destroy airfields; or to invade the island, whose Communist leadership under Fidel Castro was seen as an affront to the United States. A year earlier, the United States supported an effort by Cuban exiles to retake Cuba but that failed at the Bay of Pigs.

Mr. Kennedy, fearing that an attack on Cuba could provoke the Russians to take Berlin, played for time. He wanted to give Mr. Krushchev room to manoeuvre. He announced a naval blockade of Cuba.

Mr. Kennedy distrusted his joint chiefs of staff, worried that a trigger-happy field commander could start a war. "We may be attacking the Cubans and a reprisal may come," Mr. Kennedy tells assistant secretary of defence Paul Nitze on the October 22, 1962, tapes. "I don't want those nuclear weapons firing without our knowing." Mr. Kennedy continues: "We've got to make sure these fellows do know, so that they don't fire them off and put the United States under attack . . . I don't want to accept the chiefs' word on that one, Paul."

Mr. Kennedy had grounds for suspicion. General Curtis LeMay, who would later advise "bombing Vietnam into the Stone Age," thought that force was the only recourse at that time. He tells Mr. Kennedy on the October 19, 1962 tapes that a blockade and negotiation "is almost as bad as the appeasement at Munich. [It] would be considered a pretty weak response to this. You're in a pretty bad fix, Mr. President."

On October 22, 1962, Senator Richard Russell visited the White House and also urged force. "The time is going to come, Mr. President, when we're going to have to take this step in Berlin and Korea and Washington, DC, and Winder, Georgia, for the nuclear war. We've got to take a chance somewhere, some time, if we're going to retain our position as a great world power."

When Mr. Kennedy responds that "It's a very difficult problem that we are faced with," Mr. Russell says: "Oh, my God. I know that. A war, our destiny, will hinge on it. But it's coming some day, Mr. President. Will it ever be under more auspicious circumstances?"

Mr. Kennedy remained unconvinced. He was always aware of the moral implications of a surprise attack. On October 18, 1962, Mr. Kennedy listened to undersecretary of state George Ball say: "If we strike without warning, that's like Pearl Harbor. It's the kind of conduct one might expect from the Soviet Union. It is not conduct one expects from the United States."

Attorney-General Robert Kennedy agreed. "I think it's the whole question of . . . assuming that you do survive this . . . what kind of country we are. We did this against Cuba. We do that to a small country. I think it's a hell of a burden to carry."

The tapes crackle and hiss. The tone of the discussions is calm and measured; the debate is respectful and economical. There is little profanity. Mr. Kennedy asks questions often and listens intently. He broadens his circle of advisers and always stays one step ahead of them. When the crisis reached a climax on October 27, 1962, with Mr. Kennedy employing a subtle mix of force and conciliation to get Mr. Khrushchev to back down, Mr. May calls it among "his finest hours in public life."

The conversation is littered with references to Munich and appeasement, characteristic of decision makers of the era. Mr. Kennedy is aware of the dangers of not acting, though he knows well that the 40 missiles in Cuba have little strategic value, given that the Soviets had about 300 other warheads which could have struck the United States.

On October 23, 1962, Mr. Kennedy and his brother were alone pondering the course of a debate that seemed to be leading to an air strike. Mr. Kennedy says: "It looks really mean, doesn't it? But, on the other hand, there wasn't any other choice."

His brother responds: "Well, there isn't any choice. You would have been impeached."

Mr. Kennedy agrees. "Well, I think I would have been impeached."

INTRODUCTION

Both Presidents Nixon and Kennedy had unusual motivational profiles for leaders, with the most unusual trait being their high need for affiliation. Both former U.S. presidents made tapes of conversations held while in office. But according to historical and leadership rhetoric, Nixon was "retired" as the "Watergate president," and his toxic influence tactics while in office earned him the label of "Tricky Dick." Kennedy, on the other hand, was hailed as a "hero" after his assassination, and his trustworthy influence tactics while in office earned him the label of "charismatic."

In recent years, organizational experts have been questioning whether there is a place in the influence strategies of leaders for "emotional" tactics, and, if so, how and where? "The cost effectiveness of emotional intelligence," says Daniel Goleman, author of the 1995 popular book *Emotional Intelligence: Why It Can Matter More Than IQ*, "is a relatively new idea for business, one some managers may find hard to accept"

(p. 149). Goleman goes on to discuss the findings of Michael Maccoby's 1976 study on 250 executives, noting that back in the 1960s and 1970s, most of the executives surveyed felt that their work demanded "their heads but not their hearts." In fact, notes Goleman, many executives said that they feared that feeling empathy or compassion for those they worked with would put them in conflict with their organizational goals. One executive, Goleman emphasizes, even felt that the idea of sensing the feelings of those who worked for him was absurd; it would, he said, "be impossible to deal with these people." Still other executives in Maccoby's study protested that if they were not emotionally aloof, they would be unable to make the hard, critically intelligent decisions that business requires.

Goleman posits that Maccoby's study was done in the 1970s, when the business environment was very different. He argues that such attitudes as espoused by these executives are outmoded—an appropriateness, as it were, of a former day. Now in the 1990s, Goleman adds, and despite what Chusmir and Azevedo found in 1992 (see Chapter 1) about CEOs' having n-Aff mean scores close to zero, a new competitive reality is putting "emotional intelligence" at a premium in the workplace and in the marketplace.

Goleman then quotes Zuboff, a psychologist at Harvard Business School, who pointed out to him in an earlier conversation that

corporations have gone through a radical evolution within this century, and with this has come a corresponding transformation of the emotional landscape. There was a long period of managerial domination of the corporate hierarchy when the manipulative, jungle-fighter boss was rewarded. But that rigid hierarchy started breaking down in the 1980s under the twin pressures of globalization and information technology. The jungle fighter symbolizes where the corporation has been; the virtuoso in interpersonal skills is the corporate future. (p. 149)

Some of the reasons that corporate executives need to be more emotionally intelligent in the 1990s and beyond, says Goleman, are patently obvious. "Imagine the consequences for a working group when someone is unable to keep from exploding in anger or has no sensitivity about what the people around him are feeling. . . . When emotionally upset, people cannot remember, attend, learn, or make decisions clearly. As one management consultant put it, 'Stress makes people stupid' " (p. 149).

"And on the positive side, imagine the benefits for work of being skilled in the basic emotional competences—being attuned to the feelings of those we deal with, being able to handle disagreements [like Kennedy] so they do not escalate, having the ability to get into flow states while doing our work."

Goleman concludes: "Leadership is not domination, but the art of persuading people to work toward a common goal. And, in terms of managing our own career, there may be nothing more essential than recognizing our deepest feelings about what we do—and what changes might make us more truly satisfied with our work" (p. 149).

Could it be, as Goleman posits, that our stereotypic view of the strictly "rationally driven" corporate leader is outdated? Could it be, in fact, that today's successful corporate leaders need to use both rational *and* emotional influence strategies to meet their organizational challenges? If so, how should this "emotion" be constructively released?

To see where the current influence and power strategy evidence lies, we first explore in Chapter 3 the notion of charisma, to get a better understanding of what it is, how it relates to motivation, if there are "seasons" associated it, and how it can best be utilized by organizations. Next, we turn to experts Hambrick and Fukutomi (1991) to better understand how they define the present-day CEO's "paradigm," the "seasons" of a CEO's tenure, and the best way that organizations can utilize their CEO's "tenure" talents. Finally, we close with a discussion of corporate leaders' influence strategies: what is meant by "trustworthy," "transitional," and "toxic" leadership styles and what strategies are likely to be used by such leaders to influence upwardly and downwardly in their organizations.

A FULLER UNDERSTANDING OF, AND APPRECIATION FOR, CHARISMA

Charisma. Besides Kennedy, other leaders have been identified as having it, including Archie J. McGill of AT&T, Dee Hock of Visa, Lee Iacocca of Chrysler, Bill Gates of Microsoft, and Steve Jobs of Apple. But what is it?

Charisma Defined

Interest in the new genre of leadership theory dealing with charisma appeared in the mid-1970s and has continued to grow since then. Originally coined "charismatic behavior" by Weber in 1947, this label included a series of leaders' behaviors perceived by the world as being "inspirational," "visionary," "intuitive," and "symbolic." In the 1980s and 1990s, researchers' attention has been shifted to exceptional leaders who have extraordinary effects on their followers and, eventually, on social systems (such as what was accomplished by Kennedy in the preceding case). House, Spangler, and Woycke (1991) note the emotional significance of charisma:

It is the argument of this new genre of leadership theory that such charismatic leaders affect followers in ways that are quantitatively greater and qualitatively

different than the effects specified by past leadership theories. Charismatic leaders transform the needs, values, preferences, and aspirations of followers. These
leaders motivate followers to make significant personal sacrifices in the interest
of some mission and to perform above and beyond the call of duty. Followers
become less motivated by self-interest and more motivated to serve the interest
of the larger collective. The new theories that describe charismatic leadership
focus on the *emotional attachment* of followers to the leader; the *emotional and
motivational arousal* of followers; identification with the mission articulated by the
leaders; followers' self-esteem, trust, and confidence in the leader; values that are
of major importance to followers; and followers' intrinsic motivation. (pp. 364–
365, emphasis mine)

While House, Spangler, and Woycke recognize that charisma is a sort
of relationship bond between a leader and followers, and although they
do not define charisma as a personality trait of specific successful leaders,
they do maintain that certain leader personality characteristics contribute
to the formation of a charismatic relationship with followers. First, charismatic leaders tend to have the leadership motive profile described in
Chapter 1: they are high on the n-Pow, high on the n-ActI, and lower
on the n-Aff. Second, charismatic leaders tend to have a stronger n-Ach
that manifests itself in overt behavior; "pure charismatics," affirmed Weber (1947) achieve over and over again in their lifetimes—instead of
resting on their laurels or relying on some formal or hereditary position.

The test for charisma, suggest House, Spangler, and Woycke (1991), is
when followers say that it exists, or when followers behave in specific
ways. These ways include the followers' performing tasks beyond most
leaders' expectations; having a change in fundamental values and beliefs—often for the betterment of themselves, of society, or of the organization; showing a devotion, a loyalty, and a reverence toward their
leader; having a sense of excitement about, and enthusiasm for, the tasks
conducted for and with their leader; and having a willingness to sacrifice
their own personal interests for the sake of the "collective goal."

Three environmental variables tend to interact with the personality
characteristics of leaders, say House, Spangler, and Woycke, to bolster
the emergence of the leader's behavioral charisma (1991, pp. 389–390).
These pertain to presidential and corporate leaders. First, the social value
system surrounding the leader is critical. For example, the American
presidency of the eighteenth century was a very different institution from
that of the late twentieth century. Back in the eighteenth century, the
"ideal" president for the U.S. society, as personified by Washington, was
the virtuous statesman who resisted the personal use of power. Under
eighteenth-century social conditions, it would have been difficult for a
president with charismatic potential to emerge. But in the twentieth century, where institutional and family values are daily being challenged in

society, a "family-man" president like John F. Kennedy could charismatically fill a gaping void. Second, an environmental factor that either facilitates or retards the emergence of charisma in leaders is the level and intensity of societal crises existing during their terms. Basically, crises facilitate the emergence of charisma by providing opportunities for leaders to take bold, forceful actions—often causing followers to do much the same. Third, the mass media may provide either negative or positive "exposure" opportunities for charisma to surface. In the case of President Kennedy, for example, the media acted as a positive force. Even the coverage surrounding the assassination of President Kennedy increased his charisma rather than downplayed it.

Finally, note House, Spangler, and Woycke (1991), while the followers, the organizations, and society often benefit from having charismatic leaders during particularly "straining" social and economic times, there can be considerable personal costs to the charismatic leaders themselves. Simonton (1976, p. 130) says that there is a sort of "paradoxical" relationship between the charismatic leaders' high n-Pow and their skillful ability to get the attention that they deserve—but do not always necessarily want. Charismatic presidents, as a case in point, says Simonton, probably know better than their noncharismatic counterparts how to use the press to convey an image of dynamic leadership and achievement. Although this "image of personal magnetism" helps ensure their popularity with the masses, it is not without personal costs. In particular, experts have noted that the higher a presidential leader's power drive, the greater the likelihood that he or she will become the target of an assassination attempt. In short, notes Simonton, a powerful, charismatic president like John F. Kennedy attracted the attention of one-too-many deranged personalities. His conspicuousness was accentuated all the more by his tendency to be forceful, aggressive, radical, impulsive, and temperamental. In contrast, a below-average power-motivated president would present as far too timid, conciliatory, conservative, methodical, and moderated to provide an inviting target for a shattered ego with a gun.

How Charisma Relates to the Motivational Profiles of Leaders

We have already outlined some motivational components of charismatic leaders. But an interesting question that needs to be answered is: If Nixon's and Kennedy's motivational profiles were high on the n-Aff, which is uncharacteristic of the charismatic's motivational profile, then how was it that Kennedy presented as charismatic to his followers, while Nixon did not?

House, Spangler, and Woycke (1991) attempted to answer this question. Using a technique similar to that used by Winter and Carlson in 1988 (see Chapter 2), this research team compiled the motivational profiles of 31 U.S. presidents from Washington to Carter. George Washington served as the "baseline" for these comparisons.

After their data analysis, House, Spanger, and Woycke concluded that Nixon's motivational profile was incongruent with that found for charismatics, while Kennedy's was more prototypical. As noted already, both Nixon and Kennedy had two of the highest n-Aff scores of all presidents, which may reflect their ability "to get emotional" with minimal provocation. For example, compared to "baseline" George Washington, whose n-Aff score was 54, Nixon's n-Aff score was a high 76, and Kennedy's n-Aff was an even higher 85. So in terms of n-Aff, said this research team, Nixon and Kennedy were similar in that they were both highly "emotionally charged." But, on the n-Pow, which is considered to be an essential component of charismatic leaders, "baseline" Washington obtained a very low score of 41, Kennedy received a characteristically high n-Pow score of 77, and Nixon received an uncharacteristically moderated n-Pow score of 53. Thus, on this critical n-Pow dimension, Nixon and Kennedy differed considerably. Third, on the n-Ach dimension, which is also associated with charismatics in stronger, but not in exaggerated, degrees, "baseline" Washington had a low n-Ach score of 39, Kennedy had a characteristically strong n-Ach score of 50, and Nixon had an uncharacteristically high n-Ach score of 66. Finally, regarding n-ActI, on which charismatics present very highly (as illustrated by scores below 1), "baseline" Washington had an uncharacteristically low n-ActI trait (i.e., a score of 3.01), Nixon had an even lower n-ActI trait (i.e., a score of 4.74), and Kennedy had a characteristically high n-ActI trait (i.e., a score of 0.79). Thus, concluded House, Spangler, and Woycke, charismatic leaders seem to need two motivational traits, in particular, to catalyze the "followership" reaction: a high n-Pow, balanced by a high n-ActI. Thus, when it is needed to motivate others to commit to some goal, "emotion" seems to be channeled by charismatic leaders through these two critical outlets.

The "Seasons" for Charismatics

A number of researchers since the 1970s have emphasized that all leaders, even charismatic ones, have "seasons" in their leadership tenure that affect their popularity. This "seasonality" has been particularly noted in political leaders. In 1973, for example, Mueller tried to discover the factors responsible for the "ups" and "downs" in U.S. presidential popularity from Truman to Johnson. One factor, he found, was the tendency for a president's approval rating to decline during the course of his term, from the "ups" of "the honeymoon" immediately after the election to the doldrums some four years later. If a president is reelected, Mueller noted, his popularity resurges upon the second inaugural, only to fall again. So inexorable is this tenure pattern that some political researchers, such as Stimson in 1976, suggested that approval ratings may not depend at all on a president's actual performance while in office but upon the "seasonality" of his term.

Closely related to the "seasons" issue, a number of researchers since the 1970s have argued there are events in society that cause the leader's popularity to shift either up or down. That is, charismatic leaders have shifts in popularity, due, in part, to changing "political winds." For example, in 1975 Bloom and Price and in 1977 Kenski reported that international crises, in particular, can either boost or kill a charismatic leader's popularity. In short, the "crisis" outcome as perceived by the people—positively or negatively—results in major gains or major losses for the charismatic leader. While the Bay of Pigs fiasco of 1962 actually raised President Kennedy's standing with the U.S. people, Truman's engagement of American forces in the Korean War caused his approval ratings to plummet.

Moreover, in 1978 Kernell argued that seasonality, political event crises, and presidential performance are all integrally related. That is, a leader's popularity in politics does not simply decline after election or reelection, but rather an apparent loss or gain in popularity is caused, in part, by how society perceives the outcomes of key societal events and, in part, by how the leader makes critical decisions and behaves while in office. Kernell found that a president's approval rating in one popularity poll has a positive autocorrelation with ratings in previous and in later polls. That is, there is a certain inertia that seems to prevail in public opinion about how well the president is doing while in office, an opinion that, for the most part, changes gradually rather than furiously. While the worst-rated presidents have been those whose administrations were plagued by major scandals—namely, Grant, Harding, and Nixon—Nixon was the only president who was able to score, through a combination of his own paradoxical behaviors and administrative scandals, enough negative points from his American people to be forced to resign.

Along the latter lines, in 1980, Grush noted that for charismatic leaders, in particular, their initial pushes into power and their continued popularity while in power positions hinge, in large part, on their "critically intelligent" use of their cognitive, emotional, and behavioral gifts, especially in a marketing sense. Grush studied the determinants of success in the 1976 Democratic presidential primaries and found that almost 80 percent of the variance in voting outcome could be attributed to just three predictor variables: the candidate's previous regional exposure, with such exposure providing "an edge" over the competitors; a "bandwagon carryover" effect, with a victory in one primary significantly improving the odds of winning in the next primary; and the degree of marketing engaged in by the candidate, with a greater degree of exposure through newspaper, television, or radio spots optimizing the candidate's chances of winning.

There is little reason to doubt that such macro- and microsystem "seasonal" forces would similarly affect charismatic leaders' successes in the corporate world.

Implications of Charisma for Organizations

House, Spangler, and Woycke (1991, p. 391) expound on three implications of charisma for organizations:

(1) *Organizational Members' Commitment to Organizational Goal.* To the extent that the leader's goals and values are congruent with the goals and values of the organization, charismatic leadership provides a strong link between organizational goals and members' commitment to such goals. To the extent that the leader's goals and values are in conflict with those of the organization, as when leaders represent a challenge to the status quo, charismatic leadership is likely to induce negative attitudes toward the organization and resistance to directives from management by organizational members. Thus, charismatic leadership is a strong force for or against members' commitment to organizational goals.

(2) *The Importance of the Early Detection of Charismatic Potential in Leaders.* The early detection of "self-healing" leadership potential is critical for organizations. Charismatic potential is part of such a package. The finding that exceptional presidential performance per se has been shown to be related to the motivational needs for power (n-Pow), power inhibition (n-ActI), and achievement (n-Ach) suggests that charismatic leaders in organizations may be identified at relatively early ages and career stages on the basis of their motivational and personality profiles. The sooner that these valuable organizational members are identified, the sooner the organization can begin to "hone" their skills so that they can be used, when needed, to save the organization—or to move it ahead of its competitors.

(3) *The Conditions under Which Charismatic Leadership Is Most Likely to Be Required and Effective.* It would be naive to think that charismatic leaders work effectively at all times and in all circumstances. The "seasonality" of charisma tells us otherwise. That is, the organizational conditions have to be "right" in order for charismatic leaders' skills to be optimized. The findings from a number of studies completed since the 1970s suggest that charismatic leadership is required or, at least, is more appropriate in situations requiring a combination of highly involved and active leadership and emotional commitment and extraordinary effort by both leader and followers in pursuit of some ideological

goals. Under conditions requiring routine, but reliable, performance in the pursuit of pragmatic goals, charismatic leadership is less likely to be required and may even be dysfunctional. Furthermore, charismatic leadership seems most likely to emerge under conditions of crisis, in organic and in decentralized, rather than in mechanistic and bureaucratic, organizations and in the context of value systems that allow for the emergence of personal power.

Like Goleman, these researchers believe that there is a constructive place for "emotion" in the influence strategies of modern-day corporate leaders. House, Spangler, and Woycke (1991) conclude:

Complexity and change characterize the modern world. Leaders of large enterprises and nation states cannot rely solely on traditional face-to-face encounters, direct supervision, and rules and regulations. Modern organizations need cohesion, inspiration, and basic values. Effective leaders provide these through their own values, their personal example, their enthusiasm, and their confidence in themselves and in others. They [like John Kennedy in the opening case] are effective because they are charismatic. (p. 391)

Before leaving this section, Adler (1997, p. 154) points out that while North Americans, in particular, value charisma in their leaders, the Germans, as a case in point, do not particularly value charisma in their contemporary leaders, apparently because they associate it with the negative charismatic displays carried out by Hitler during World War II.

THE PRESENT-DAY CEOS' PARADIGM

To this point, we have been discussing how charismatic leaders become motivated to "influence" others either within their organizations or within their societies to move closer to some worthwhile cause. But how do present-day CEOs, especially those without the charismatic gift for influencing others, stay motivated to their "corporate leader paradigms," given the changes that occur over their tenures? In 1991, in a critical study, Donald Hambrick and Gregory Fukutomi of Columbia University attempted an answer to this question.

The "CEOs' Paradigm"

As posited by Hart and Quinn in 1993 (see Chapter 2), present-day CEOs' jobs are complex, ambiguous, and information-overloaded at times. Because CEOs cannot comprehend all of the relevant stimuli that are available, they must operate within a finite model, or paradigm, of how the environment behaves, what options are available, and how the organization should be run. The "CEOs' paradigm," note Hambrick and

Fukutomi (1991), is based, at a minimum, on two conceptually distinct, but related elements: (1) their cognitive schema and (2) their skill-based behavioral repertoires.

By definition, a "cognitive schema" is the preexisting knowledge that corporate leaders bring to an administrative situation and includes their conscious and unconscious preconceptions, beliefs, inferences, and expectations. As such, a schema is much like the personal "givens" that top managers interject into their decision making. This schema is derived from cultural and family experiences in early childhood, from business experiences and networks in adulthood, from formal education, and from incidental observations.

The corporate leaders' behavioral repertoires are a variable supply of skills, devices, or expedients possessed by them to accomplish what needs to be accomplished. For example, some CEOs have substantial experience in negotiating acquisitions, whereas others have the ability to give charismatic speeches before large audiences. Still others have the ability to quickly analyze and digest complex numerical reports. As with cognitive schemas, behavioral repertoires are derived from the CEOs' prior experiences and personal aptitudes. In fact, CEOs' perceptions of their behavioral repertoires form part of their cognitive schema and include a sense of their strengths and weaknesses, of what is "comfortable" or "straining," and of what is the most appropriate approach for running their organizations. CEOs have varying personal resources for conducting business, and over time they consider some elements of their behavioral repertoires to be proven and reliable, other behavioral elements to be available but not very familiar or previously tested, and still other behavioral elements to be weak suits that should be avoided. Finally, some of the CEOs' potential available resources may lie undetected or untested for long stretches of time. Thus, whereas the CEOs' cognitive schemas serve as perceptual and interpretive apparatuses for them to be successful in their jobs, the CEOs' behavioral repertoires represent their tangible abilities to apply their schemas in a social and economic context, with varying degrees of discretion. Generally, the more open the organizational climate, the greater the degree of discretion given the corporate leaders to motivate upwardly and downwardly.

The CEOs' cognitive schema and behavioral repertoires, combined, form the "CEOs' paradigm," as noted, which is simply a model of the CEOs' cognitive and behavioral self, the environment, the organization, and the interconnections among these elements. As complex as this model appears to be, it is exceedingly limited, incomplete, and idiosyncratic, caution Hambrick and Fukutomi (1991). Importantly, "the CEOs' paradigm" forms the basis for CEOs' motivations, actions, and inactions. Like their moods, the CEOs' paradigm is dynamic, changing over the course of their tenure in the organization, particularly as new learning occurs. Moreover, the CEOs' commitment to their paradigm varies in strength across their tenure; that is, CEOs may be more "learningful" or "open-minded" and less committed to the paradigm at certain phases of tenure.

How Entry Conditions Define the CEOs' Paradigm. It would be naive to think that all CEOs engage in the same sequence of activities and emphases during their tenures or that "the particulars" surrounding CEOs' entry conditions are similar. As Gordon and Rosen discussed in their 1981 synthesis of the literature on leader succession, a set of interrelated forces greatly determines CEOs' initial orientation and initiatives, from which later motivational phases derive. For example, the performance and problems of the organization prior to succession largely determine "the experiences" and "inclinations" of the successor who is sought; in turn, these inclinations greatly influence the actions taken by CEOs during their terms of office. Moreover, CEOs are under political and social pressure to display "the orientation" for which they were initially selected. Contrary to what many people in society may think, even CEOs are not the masters of their own universe; they must communicate frequently with those on the board and with those at all levels within the organization. Simply put, corporate leaders are accountable to, and must influence, others both upwardly and downwardly. As Gordon and Rosen emphasized, "Newly appointed leaders do not function totally independently of their sponsors and of how those around them expect them to function" (p. 239). Hambrick and Fukutomi provide an example:

[I]n 1981 General Electric was extremely profitable, but had a very low growth rate and was weighted down with primarily mature businesses. Among several contenders to replace Reginald Jones as CEO, Jack Welch, the person picked by the board, was known for his impatience and track record of innovation and growing businesses. Even his demographic profile lined up with what seemed to be needed: youth, advanced education in technology, and experience in R&D. There seems little question that Welch had a mandate to inject youth and dynamism into GE; he was picked precisely because it was thought that his paradigm—his schema and repertoire—would make the growth and dynamism occur; he was under pressure to behave in line with such expectations. It was not surprising that Welch immediately sold off numerous low-growth businesses, put major resources into high-growth businesses, and sought technological advantage in industries that had never been considered in "technological" terms, such as appliances and lighting. (1991, p. 722)

Thus, note Hambrick and Fukutomi, CEOs' mandates, their inclinations, their paradigms, and their initial actions after entry on the job align in such a way that allows a concise conceptualization of the starting point in CEOs' tenure—a reference point for considering subsequent trends during their tenure.

Research over the past 20 years has indicated that changes on five variables occur over the course of CEOs' tenure, thus impacting on their long-term motivations, behaviors, and upward and downward influence styles: (1) their commitment to their paradigms, (2) their task knowledge, (3) their information diversity, (4) their task interest, and (5) their power. The confluence of these trends gives rise to five discernible CEO seasons, the next major topic to be discussed. But, first, let's review these five variables of interest.

How Commitment Affects the CEOs' Paradigm. CEOs' commitment to their paradigm changes over time. Two explanations for why this change occurs have been described in the organization literature, with Hambrick and Fukutomi (1991) favoring the second. The first view, espoused by Salancik (1977) and Staw (1976) and others, is that the commitment of CEOs to their paradigms gradually increases over their tenures; that is, CEOs are most open-minded about how the organization should be run at the outset of their tenures and then become increasingly close-minded and committed to their own modus operandi as their tenure increases. Such a notion rests on the assumption that CEOs enter the job with few preconceptions of the decisions that should be made or the behaviors that should be undertaken; then, after a fact-finding and diagnostic period, CEOs undertake actions that result in the "tendency to repeat"— that is, doing within their behavioral repertoires what they do best.

The second view, espoused by Vancil (1987), Gabarro (1987), and others, is that the commitment of CEOs to their paradigms starts out high initially, decreases during a period of open-mindedness and experimentation, and gradually increases toward paradigm recommitment or toward revised paradigm commitment. Initial paradigm commitment likely results from the CEOs' believing that they were selected for the job because of the "fit" between organizational requirements and their schema and repertoires. Then, a period of careful diagnosis, fact-finding, and "immersion" into the organizational culture leads to some experimentation on the part of the CEO. Finally, there is a recommitment to the original paradigm or to some revised version of it. This recommitment appears to be a function of three primary factors: the energy and psychological investments already made in that mode of operating, the visibility and public acceptance of that "known" mode of operating, and the belief that a relatively "fixed" mode of operating signifies "correctness" and "adequacy." In short, because CEOs are allowed to remain in their jobs only as long as their performances are satisfactory, their tenure tends to equate with a validation of their paradigm: the longer that the CEOs' approaches to running the firm have met with acceptable performance, the greater the CEOs' convictions in the enduring correctness of their approaches (Miller & Friesen 1984). This commitment is typically accentuated by praise and congratulations by board members and organizational members alike for a job well done.

In short, on the matter of paradigm commitment, Hambrick and Fukutomi (1991) believe that most CEOs may start their tenures with remarkably strong commitments to their paradigms, but, like presidential leaders, after gaining a performance and political foothold, they experience a brief period of broadening their mind-sets—which leaves them more firmly believing in their original paradigms or motivates them to revise their paradigms for a better "fit." Beyond this rather limited period of flexibility, however, each passing year in the job tends to bring CEOs to a heightened sense of correctness in their established ways of operating and of viewing their organizations.

How Task Knowledge Affects the CEOs' Paradigm. Although new CEOs may be in a slight task knowledge disadvantage early in the game if they were brought in from outside the company, research has shown that new CEOs tend to overcome this handicap by quickly acquiring a great deal of "critically intelligent" knowledge early in their tenure. Gabarro (1987) emphasizes the importance of this early learning phase for long-term survival, referring to it as an "orientational immersion." However, the accumulation of task knowledge, notes Gabarro, tapers off after some period in the job, eventually reaching a point of only incremental advance. Based on his studies of general managers, Gabarro estimates that for corporate leaders, the critical "incremental advance" period comes after about 2.5 to 3 years on the job.

How Information Diversity Affects the CEOs' Paradigm. Just as CEOs' task knowledge increases during their tenure in a first-rapidly, then-slowly pattern, the information source diversity attended to by CEOs starts out broader and becomes increasingly narrow. Aguilar (1967), Katz (1982), and others have found that new general managers tend to gather environmental information in roughly even proportions between "external" and "internal" sources. However, as they develop more comfortable and reassuring internal networks, these managers tend to sharply reduce their use of external information sources in favor of internal conduits. Hambrick and Fukutomi (1991) maintain that as a CEO's tenure extends, a similar reliance on internal, rather than external, information sources is further influenced by the tendency for internal sources to have learned how to cater to their CEOs' information preferences. That is, with time and experience, key subordinates and staff come to know the format, the timing, and even the content of information that their CEOs will likely accept. This pattern of "conditioned catering" becomes obvious in the Kennedy case, with the upward-influence quotes of General Curtis LeMay and Senator Richard Russell. However, caution Hambrick and

Fukutomi, the CEOs, in the end, are the ultimate filterers and molders of their information. If, like John Kennedy, CEOs decide that the information given by internal sources either does not "fit" into their known acceptance zones or runs counter to their paradigms, the CEOs will take their own preferred course of action. In short, given a clearer sense of the quality, content, and dependability of internal sources' information over time, CEOs tend to rely on narrower and more finely filtered information as their tenure advances.

How Task Interest Affects the CEOs' Paradigm. Given that CEOs, like other professionals, find themselves facing job repetition and relative mastery over their tasks over the course of their tenure, there is no reason to believe, note Hambrick and Fukutomi (1991), that they are immune to strain caused by job boredom. In fact, major parts of the CEOs' job recur with a certain sameness from one period to the next: reviewing business unit plans, making ceremonial visits to outlying facilities, preparing for annual stockholder meetings, reviewing detailed capital allocation requests, courting and reassuring board members, and so on. Though at first CEOs may find these demands to be stimulating and novel, after performing these tasks a few times, the novelty is reduced, and CEOs' interests start to wane. Depending on the personality factors of the CEOs, they may come out of this period feeling eustressfully ensconced and content, or they may come out feeling strained, less responsive, and even burned out. In the latter circumstances, what occurs is a dulled acuity in CEOs, resulting in an eventual uncoupling of executive leadership from the organization's competitive environment (Romanelli & Tushman 1988).

How Power Affects the CEOs' Paradigm. As in any new job, new CEOs face relative job security vulnerability. This early lack of power and vulnerability, notes Vancil (1987), is reflected in the disproportionate number of CEOs whose tenures last three years or less, about 19 percent. With time in office, however, CEOs' power and influence tend to mount. In the absence of mandatory retirement policies, note Hambrick and Fukutomi (1991), each passing year in office brings a greater likelihood of the CEOs' continuing tenure and power. Of course, there are exceptions to the rule. For example, "turnaround" CEOs might be brought into a troubled company by the board and given immense initial power to make changes. Or, "midtenure" CEOs could experience poor performance and reduced organizational power, but not such poor performance as to result in their departure. Finally, CEOs approaching mandatory retirement may be perceived by their boards as being "lame ducks" and having a diminution of power.

For CEOs who, for a combination of reasons, are able to remain beyond the critical three-year "test period," the prognosis for growth in power and influence is positive, affirm Hambrick and Fukutomi. This increase in power can come from a variety of forces, including CEOs' opportunities to reconfigure their boards with their sympathetic and supportive appointees; their abilities to create a charismatic mystique, drawing unquestioned deference or loyalty from their organizational followers; their abilities to create "cumulative success" track records; and, from a purely legal angle, their abilities to accumulate stock and stock options that can enhance their influence over the publicly held firm (Gabarro 1987).

Summary of Variables Affecting the CEOs' Paradigm. In short, five critical variables can be expected to affect the CEOs' paradigm over the course of their tenure. (1) The CEOs' commitment to their paradigm begins at a relatively high level, decreases briefly during a period of relative open-mindedness, and then increases steadily throughout the remainder of tenure. (2) The CEOs' task knowledge increases at first quickly, and then it slows down. (3) The CEOs' information diversity begins with external and internal sources, then reduces primarily to internal sources and becomes increasingly selective. (4) The CEOs' task interest is initially very high, then tapers off, and in some CEOs, may even become pathologically "straining." (5) Considering no unforeseen organizational disasters or marked downturns in productivity, the CEOs' power generally increases after a vulnerable three-year test period until retirement or until such time as they choose to leave.

The Five Seasons of CEOs' Tenure

When the just-cited variables are considered as an interrelated set of dynamic flows, Hambrick and Fukutomi (1991) suggest that five discernible "seasons" exist in CEOs' tenure—each placing its own set of demands and stress and strain on CEOs. These seasons include (1) the response to mandate, (2) experimentation, (3) the selection of an enduring theme, (4) convergence, and (5) dysfunction.

(1) *The Response to Mandate Season.* When entering their jobs, CEOs focus their finite life energy on responding to the mandate for which they were hired. Early on, then, CEOs' actions are very much a reflection of their going-in mandate. According to Vancil (1987), this mandate is usually more implicit than explicit; thus, CEOs must determine the magnitude, direction, and pace of change that their boards are expecting. To cope with this rather anxiety-producing demand, CEOs tend to decide to have either a mandate of continuity and minimal change (resulting in generally lower stress levels for the CEOs and their organizational members alike) or a mandate of dramatic innovation and change—involving the more stressful options of cutting costs, innovating, expanding globally, resolving litigation, and so on. According to Gabarro (1987), regardless of which option is chosen (that of lower or of higher risk), CEOs

tend to focus their energies on their strongest going-in credentials; thus, they tend to make changes—if they are needed—in the functional areas in which they have the most skill and experience. As a generalization, note Hambrick and Fukutomi (1991), "outsider" CEOs tend to undertake to make more changes than "insiders." Finally, this first "mandate" season is characterized by the CEOs' high commitment to their paradigm, relatively low task knowledge, relatively high use of diverse information sources, relatively high level of task interest, and relatively low level of power.

(2) *The Experimentation Season.* After attending to their going-in mandate and after having achieved some early successes, the CEOs then start a season of cognitive, emotional, and behavioral experimentation. For CEOs who are flexible in temperament and mind-set, this potentially "eustressing" phase involves a relaxation in the CEOs' commitment to their previous paradigm. Finite life energy is spent on attempting new approaches to running the enterprise and generally trying broader-gauged methods than were earlier tried.

Not only is this season the least reported in the organizational literature, caution Hambrick and Fukutomi (1991), but there are obvious exceptions to the experimentation rule. Dogmatic dictators may, at times, find themselves in top executive suites; however, quite unlike their more flexible "experimental" peers, these corporate leaders are not only totally convinced of the enduring correctness of their initial paradigm but very comfortable in pursuing their original paradigms indefinitely.

In accepting that more research needs to be done on the experimental CEO season, Hambrick and Fukutomi conclude that with the evidence reported to date (Gabarro 1987), between the second and the third year in office, the "experimental" CEOs tend to have acquired a great deal of knowledge from diverse information sources and tend to have an ongoing high level of task interest. Given their performance track records, the CEOs may now have the established credibility to consider and implement new or revised corporate directions.

(3) *The Selection of an Enduring Theme Season.* In the third season, CEOs tend to select a theme for how the organization should be configured over the longer term. At this time, posit Hambrick and Fukutomi (1991), CEOs may reflect on the strategies that they have tried during the first two stages of tenure. In the end, the CEOs tend to rely upon those elements that seem to work best and that seem to be the most comfortable and eustressful. That is, at this point in tenure, the CEOs begin to recrystallize their paradigm for running the enterprise. What emerges may largely reflect the CEOs' original paradigm, a revised paradigm from the CEOs' experimental season, or some combination of the two.

(4) *The Convergence Season.* After selecting a theme for long-term, finite life energy commitment, the CEOs tend to begin to reinforce and bolster

the theme through a stream of relatively incremental actions. These moderately straining actions typically relate to organizational structure, staffing, processes, and functional area initiatives. Hambrick and Fukutomi's label (1991) for this fourth convergence season was adopted primarily from Romanelli and Tushman (1988) and from Miller and Friesen (1984) during the 1980s. Romanelli and Tushman found that organizations alternate between relatively brief spurts of major change and long periods of incremental change, or convergence. Major change tends to coincide with CEO succession, whereas convergence tends to occur in subsequent years of CEOs' tenure. Similarly, Miller and Friesen found in a study of quantified business histories that companies generally are affected by momentum, whereby a change in an organizational attribute is three times as likely to be followed by further change in the same direction than by a reversal in direction. Although Miller and Friesen did not provide explicit data about executive tenures, they concluded that these rare reversals tend to be associated with new CEOs and that momentum is nearly a universal phenomenon among longer-tenured CEOs. Moreover, such a conclusion is consistent with Gabarro's (1987) observation that almost all the actions taken by new corporate leaders occur in their first 2.5 years in office. After that, a period of incremental refinement occurs in which only a few changes are typically made by corporate leaders—and those only to fine-tune the organization.

In the convergence season, the CEOs' commitment to their paradigm is strong and getting stronger, task knowledge not only has increased greatly since their tenure initiation but has reached a plateau, exposure to information is even narrower and more filtered than in previous seasons, task interest has started to wane, and power is relatively great and projected to continue increasing. Sooner or later, however, the CEOs' fifth and final season begins.

(5) *The Dysfunction Season*. At some point in tenure, the CEOs' positives are outweighed by their negatives. Thus starts the CEOs' season of psychological and perhaps behavioral dysfunction. Commonly, job mastery gives way to job boredom; job exhilaration gives way to fatigue, sometimes subtle and sometimes pronounced; and organizational strategizing gives way to habituation. Oddly, note Hambrick and Fukutomi (1991), CEOs in this high-stress stage tend to show few outward signs of distress because they are well socialized in the importance of maintaining solid corporate impressions and appearances. However, inwardly, the CEOs' motivational sparks for performing are dimmed, and their openness and responsiveness to organizational stimuli are generally diminished. Thus, if the CEOs covertly suffer from high-to-pathological levels of distress at this stage, the continuing incumbency of these CEOs becomes dysfunctional for the corporate leader as well as for the organization.

As a means of coping with the experienced distress, the CEOs often tend to engage in fewer and fewer substantive initiatives, even of actions that would reinforce the enduring theme. Their decision making becomes increasingly slower and based on highly distilled information (Hambrick & Fukutomi 1991). The CEOs tend to become increasingly involved in ceremonies that are comfortable and relatively eustressful and become less involved in the more straining acts of organizational substances (Romanelli & Tushman 1998). To compensate for this significant, finite life energy drain, the CEOs' outside interests may increase as they search for more fulfilling life energy investments. Overall, as a result of these dysfunctions, the organization's adaptive properties are placed at risk and often wane. In 1988, Miller, for example, found in a study of Canadian companies that environment-organization alignments were observed for companies whose CEOs had been in office for a moderate or a brief period but were not observed when CEOs had been in office for 10 years or more.

Paradoxically, posit Hambrick and Fukutomi (1991), though during this final season CEOs appear to be quite disengaged or trapped psychologically, if not behaviorally, their power is at an all-time high. That is, these corporate leaders may have appointed many board members, selected and retained loyal coworkers, developed a charismatic aura, and even secured a sizable block of the company's stock. But in the absence of a mandatory retirement provision, the chances of their choosing to voluntarily depart from the organization may be very limited. For such CEOs, noted Vancil (1987), even though some or most of their job excitement is gone, giving up their jobs altogether is generally an unappealing alternative. As a result, the duration of the dysfunctional season can sometimes be quite long, mood-disrupting, and consciously "closeted." Corporate leaders' subtle "cries for help" at this stage often fall on deaf ears.

Implications of the Five-Season CEO Model for Boards and Corporate Leaders

A number of practical implications for the five-season CEO model can be foreseen, affirm Hambrick and Fukutomi (1991). These are as follows:

(1) While it is reasonable to ask what the average duration of each season is, existing empirical data do not allow for any particularly defensible estimates. For the sake of argument, however, the following estimates are likely quite typical: response to mandate season: one to two years; experimentation season: one to two years; selection of an enduring theme season: one to two years; convergence season: three to five years; and dysfunction season: all remaining years. Depending on the makeup of the CEO and on the organizational climate, variations along these estimates could be substantial.

(2) The CEO seasonal model has practical implications for boards. If

the model is valid, then companies need to be alert to the dangers of their CEOs' staying too long in office. While U.S. presidents and other world leaders have terms lasting 4 years or so, some CEOs can practice for stretches exceeding 10 years. Thus, the mandatory retirement policies that many firms have for their top officers seem to be well advised. However, it may well be that these mandatory retirement policies should be based on the CEOs' years in office rather than on their age. For example, a person who becomes CEO at age 45 may have a greater likelihood of clinging to an obsolete paradigm and being at risk for losing sharpness on the job by age 55 than a CEO at age 65 who has held the CEO position for only 5 years. Because the CEO usually accumulates power and influence as a function of time in office, a strong mandatory retirement policy at the outset of the CEOs' tenure may be one realistic way of ensuring that the corporate leaders leave office before their performance and psychological motivation deteriorate.

(3) Conversely, boards need to be similarly cautious about releasing CEOs from office before they are reasonably "seasoned." Because of the learning and experimentation process associated with the CEO role, corporate leaders who leave prior to four or five years in office (and possibly even a shorter time in dynamic industries) tend not to have had a chance to achieve peak cognitive, emotional, and behavioral performance on the job. Organizations that have a tendency to "CEO houseclean" often may be without the payoffs of the wisdom that seems to come from moderated, but not overly lengthy, tenures on the job.

(4) Moreover, boards need to be wary of selecting CEOs whose repertoires are well suited to a pressing initial mandate, such as cost-cutting measures, but who do not have the emotional, cognitive, or behavioral depth to pursue other themes during their tenures. That is, boards should have 5- to 10-year horizons in mind when they select their CEOs, not 2-year, "potentially blinding," and "organizationally bankrupting" horizons.

(5) Finally, the model has important implications for corporate leaders themselves, particularly with regard to how they can maximize both their organizational contributions and their mind-behavior balance. One of the most perplexing questions is whether the dysfunction that comes with an extended tenure can be forestalled or minimized. The answer seems to lie strictly in CEOs' renewal, their open-mindedness, and their "self-healing" potentials. One of the most important contributions for reducing corporate leader dysfunction and burnout may be the talent and diversity of the management team that the CEOs assemble, as well as their ongoing willingness to listen to, and not censor, that team's divergent insights. Furthermore, the CEOs' ongoing repertoire development through formal educational programs, sabbaticals, retreats, executive development programs, stress management programs, and so

on may simultaneously influence the CEOs' open-mindedness and reduce their stress levels.

Ultimately, as Hart and Quinn posited in 1993 (see Chapter 2) and as
Goleman posited in 1995, functional and effective present-day CEOs
must retain an emotional capacity for dealing with uneasiness and strain,
a skepticism about the status quo, and an ongoing curiosity about their
coworkers' diverse points of view "to surmount the very human tendency to cling to formulas that have worked well in the past" (Hambrick
& Fukutomi 1991, p. 739). When the job involves international management competence, as Roth (1995) posits, present-day CEOs need to rely
upon a complex cognitive schema, an ability to get "emotional" and
"persuasive" when necessary, and a behavioral repertoire that includes
some paradoxes. Thus, both rational and emotional proficiencies seem
critical to successfully performing today's CEO function.

CORPORATE LEADERS' INFLUENCE STRATEGIES

Whicker's Definitions for Trustworthy, Transitional, and Toxic Leaders

Obviously, not all corporate leaders are as trustworthy and charismatic
as Kennedy or as paradoxical and "tricky" as Nixon when influencing
upwardly and downwardly in their organizations. Some corporate leaders, rather, would fall somewhere between these two extremes.

Over the past two decades, a number of researchers have attempted
to classify the influence strategy styles of leaders. One of the most interesting recent attempts was completed by Marcia Whicker and detailed
in her 1996 book *Toxic Leaders: When Organizations Go Bad*. Whicker defined three main types of "influencers" in organizations and in politics
and placed them along a self-healing-to-disease-prone continuum: (a) the
trustworthy leaders, (b) the transitional leaders, and (c) the toxic leaders.
Though Whicker did not estimate the percentage of each of these types
in the corporate leader population, her definitions for the three types are
useful:

(a) *The trustworthy leaders* are the self- and other-healing, good, moral,
prototypically high n-ActI leaders. Not only can they be trusted to put
the goals of their organization and the well-being of their followers first,
but they value their own self-esteem and the esteem of others. Furthermore, they seek their own self-actualization and try to help their organizational members obtain the same. Utilizing a "trusting" command,
coordinating, consensus, or persuasive style, trustworthy leaders like
John Kennedy and Lee Iacocca are "green-light" leaders, meaning that
countries and organizations with such leaders at the helm have a "green
light" to progress in productivity and growth. Iacocca's style of "trustworthy" command influence reflects this green-light phenomenon:

Likened to a field marshal, Iacocca's leadership style was to surround himself with loyal supporters who were bright but not "yes" men, "car guys open to new ideas." His management techniques were described as "hard-nosed." He controlled the personnel reporting to him directly by keeping tabs on them in his "black book," and instructed them to keep tabs on their subordinates in a similar fashion. Through the process of quarterly grading and reviewing of subordinates, Iacocca implemented his philosophy that "if you can't grade a man, you can't follow him at all." Iacocca contended that his system of quarterly reviewing and reporting—a process that takes place annually in most corporations—forced managers to be accountable, rewarded productive employees, increased motivation, and stimulated problem-solving. Nor was Iacocca afraid of wielding the ax when he felt it was called for. His "command" leadership lifted Chrysler from the brink of death by bankruptcy, just as earlier it had built up Ford. (p. 42)

(b) *The transitional leaders* are not as self- and other- healing as trustworthy leaders, primarily because they are narcissistic and quite self-absorbed rather than other- and company-absorbed. They are neither uplifting in their long-term impact on others nor purposefully malicious toward them. Rather, they are focused on the approval of others and are overly concerned with their personal role as leaders. Utilizing an "absentee" consensus or "busybody" coordinating or "controller" command leadership style, transitional leaders like Michael Milken, Donald Trump, and Ross Perot are "yellow-light" leaders, meaning that they have a cautionary "yellow light" to organizational growth and productivity. Perot's style of "controller" command influence illustrates this yellow-light phenomenon:

Perot's energy and extensive schedule of appointments caused one news magazine to depict him as the energizer bunny, a pop culture icon used in advertising and known for its capacity to keep on going and going and going. A billionaire by age thirty-eight, Perot's power came from his great wealth, which he attributed to luck. Yet close associates credit his extraordinary energy and shrewdness, which he used to maintain tight command and control of the organization he built. This characteristic was first exhibited in his actions at Electronic Data Systems (EDS), the company that brought his initial wealth, and continued throughout his aborted presidential campaign in 1992. Perot clung rigidly to a "Norman Rockwell" view of how the world and especially his organizations should be run, even hanging original Rockwell paintings in his Dallas office. To assure this view, he exerted command by involving himself in all aspects of decision making. . . . Perot, for example, wanted his employees and recruiters to present a certain image—one reflecting conservative and even militaristic values. Not trusting his workers to select their own wardrobes, he created a company dress code that dictated dark suits, white shirts, narrow ties, and shined shoes. . . . [Moreover, Perot tried to avoid disorder] for EDS by recruiting only married white men with a military background and at least five years of work experience. Yet he demanded eighty-hour work weeks from them for "niggardly" salaries, and work often involved substantial travel. . . . Perot's clear sense of mission dissipated when he moved from the profit oriented world of business to the messier world of national politics. He correctly sensed that the national mood was one of increasing populist individualism, including a rejection of both mainstream political parties. Yet he offered up no clear vision of where the nation should be going, beyond pithy statements and criticisms of other plans. These pithy aphorisms worked well initially in the evolving world of talk show politics but ultimately failed Perot on the campaign trail. (pp. 100–102)

(c) *The toxic leaders*, representing the dysfunctional or "disease-prone" end of the leadership continuum, are maladjusted, malcontent, often malevolent, and even malicious or antisocial. Not only do they succeed by tearing others down, but they glory in turf protection, fighting, and controlling followers rather than in uplifting them. Utilizing an "enforcer" consensus, a "street-fighter" coordinating, or a "bully" command leadership style, toxic leaders like Richard Nixon, John Dean, Bob Haldeman, John Ehrlichman, Donald T. Regan (former head of the giant financial investment company Merrill Lynch and secretary of the Treasury during Ronald Reagan's first term), Herbert Hoover, Ross Johnson (former CEO of RJR Nabisco), and Jimmy Jones are "red-light" leaders. The red-light designation means that their leadership style plummets productivity and applies brakes to organizational growth, causing progress to screech to a halt. With a deep-seated, but well-disguised, sense of personal inadequacy, a focus on selfish and narcissistic values, and cleverness at deception, these antisocial leaders are toxic, indeed. Jimmy Jones's "bully" command leadership style illustrates this red-light phenomenon:

Bullies are not self-revealing, unlike street fighters who will pal around as buddies, so the source of their anger may be deeply hidden. More likely it is many sources, but all of the sources can be traced back to a massive sense of personal failure. The source of the sense of inadequacy of . . . toxic leaders is much more likely to be traced back to system problems, childhood family circumstances, or factors beyond the toxic leader's control. . . . Jim Jones was born to a semi-invalid father injured by mustard gas in World War I and an ambitious mother who worked a depressing job in a factory. In his Indiana town where many residents were of German descent, Jones looked dark and almost Asian, later claiming he had some Indian blood. Jones was ashamed of his family and their lack of normality, and perhaps of his role in it, since his mother worked at a poorly paid job to earn money for his college education. By age four, he was swearing profanities as entertainment before town men to earn money for sodas. According to Reiterman, Jones internalized the shame and pain of being alone most of the time and an outcast, reporting later: "I was ready to kill by the end of the third grade. I mean, I was so fucking aggressive and hostile, I was ready to kill. Nobody gave me any love, any understanding. In those days a parent was supposed to go with a child to school functions. . . . There was some kind of school performance, and everybody's fucking parent was there but mine. I'm standing there. Alone. Always was alone."

... Bullies that charge others with acting unethically and unprofessionally may be acutely aware of the lack of ethics in their own behavior. Bullies that threaten to fire others may have on earlier occasions been fired themselves, sometimes more than once.... Bullies are not limited by normal moral boundaries. Unlike absentee leaders, busybodies, and controllers, bullies will knowingly engage in unethical behaviors that border on or cross over into malfeasance. Despite their lip service to the importance of the law, they will hide, manipulate, and manufacture evidence if they need to do so to get at a target. They will manipulate and manufacture personnel records, placing great emphasis upon the personnel file as a substitute for more concrete measures of productivity and performance and regard placing negative letters and memos in the personnel files of targeted employees as great personal victories.... Jones left the country with his flock, in part, to get away from the reaches of U.S. law. (pp. 154–157)

Kipnis and Colleagues' Definitions for Tacticians, Bystanders, and Shotguns

During the early 1980s, the team of Kipnis, Schmidt, Swaffin-Smith, and Wilkinson assessed the upward and downward influence styles of first- and second-line managers from many firms in England ($n = 121$), Australia ($n = 126$), and the United States ($n = 113$), using their inventory called the Profile of Organizational Influence Strategies (POIS).

The current POIS measures how managers attempt to influence their superiors (form 1), their coworkers (form 2), and their subordinates (form 3). In all, six influence styles are assessed: (1) *reasoning*: the strategy involving the use of facts and data to support the development of a logical argument; (2) *friendliness*: the strategy involving the use of impression management, flattery, and the creation of goodwill; (3) *coalition*: the strategy involving the mobilization of other people in the organization; (4) *bargaining*: the strategy involving the use of negotiation through the exchange of benefits or favors; (5) *assertiveness*: the strategy involving the use of a direct and forceful approach; and (6) *higher authority*: the strategy involving gaining the support of higher levels in the organization to back up requests.

In this cross-cultural managerial sample, the research team found essentially no difference among countries in how managers exercised influence. When seeking to influence their superiors, managers reported that they relied most often on reason, followed by coalitions, and then by friendliness. Resorting to higher authority was the least often used strategy to influence superiors.

The rank order of preferred strategies was somewhat different when influencing subordinates. Once again, the managers reported that the most frequently used strategy was reason. The second most popular strategy was assertiveness. While perhaps not surprising, this study result supports the belief that managers can assert themselves aggressively when they demand compliance from their subordinates but not when they are seeking compliance from superiors.

Moreover, the study findings indicated that managers' selection of influence strategies varied with power, with their objective for wanting to use influence, and with their expectation of the target's willingness to comply. Assertiveness strategies were generally used when the managers' objectives were to benefit the organization, when expectations for success of compliance were low, and when the managers' organizational power was high. Reason strategies were used when the managers' objectives were to benefit the organization, when expectations for success of compliance were high, and when the managers' power was high. Friendliness strategies were used when the managers' objectives were to benefit themselves, when expectations for success of compliance were low, and when the managers' power was low.

To further determine if managers vary the "mix" of influence strategies used, the research team used cluster analysis to determine patterns of managerial influence in each of the three countries. The findings revealed that managers in all three countries fell into one of three groupings, placeable along a self-healing-to-disease-prone continuum:

(a) *The tactician cluster* of self- and other-healers used a judicious and deliberate selection of strategies. Reasoning was used first, and other strategies followed. The tacticians were identified by a high score on reasoning and average scores on the other influence strategies. Unlike their less self-healing counterparts in the other two clusters, managers in this cluster had power in their organizations. They managed work that required considerable planning before it could be carried out; they had considerable influence over setting budgets, influencing company policy, and dealing with personnel matters; and they expressed satisfaction with their ability to perform their work.

(b) *The bystander cluster* lacked the selection of any one strategy for influencing others; they had low scores on all of the influence strategies. Although they held power positions, these leaders exercised little influence in their organizations. Instead, they directed large units of subordinates and carried out routine work. In each country, those in this group tended to be in the same job for the longest time. In short, these bystander managers seemed to mark time in mundane jobs and saw themselves as having little or no organizational impact. They suffered from low job satisfaction, seemed to have a low n-Pow, and illustrated the phenomenon social psychologists call "learned helplessness."

(c) *The shotgun cluster*, the most disease-prone of the three, relied on a nonjudicious selection of strategies to influence others. They had high scores on all six influence strategy scales, particularly assertiveness, which was the preferred first-attempt strategy. These managers reported having many unfulfilled objectives in terms of being able to sell their ideas, obtaining personal benefits, or getting others to work more effectively. In each country, they were the ones with the least organizational experience. In short, shotgun managers were inexperienced and probably ambitious, and they seemed to have great expectations. To this end, they openly attempted to obtain what they wanted through the indiscriminate use of influence strategies.

In summarizing their research results, Kipnis, Schmidt, Swaffin-Smith, and Wilkinson (1994) noted:

It is our experience that effective managers are flexible and are able to identify and use the most appropriate strategy in a given situation. The Tactitian profile best exemplifies this approach. The question for managers to consider is how satisfied they are with the way influence is used in their organization. . . . In organizations whose culture does not encourage vigorous expression of ideas upward, managers may become apathetic and lapse into a bystander pattern. Such an organization may be easy to control; however, we suspect that pressure for innovation and change would also be at a minimum. (p. 186)

Later, in 1988 Kipnis and Schmidt further investigated the upward influence attempts of 87 hospital CEOs and the relationship between their upward influence styles, their stress levels, and their salaries, using their earlier developed POIS scales. Consistent with their previous study findings, Kipnis and Schmidt hypothesized that the use by CEOs of the self-healing tactitian cluster would result in the lowest job tension and stress and would reap the largest salary. Their hypothesis was fully supported by their study findings. Kipnis and Schmidt concluded "[T]he present findings raise many questions that require further study. For example, it is well documented that stress is caused by significant life events at work and at home. Based on the findings of this study, one wonders whether individuals experience added stress as a result of the influence styles they use" (p. 540).

THE BOTTOM LINE

Starting with the case of Kennedy, who was labeled as a charismatic leader, we spent the bulk of Chapter 3 trying to get some insights about successful influence strategies in organizations and in politics. Consistent with Hart and Quinn's 1993 assertions (see Chapter 2) and Goleman's assertions (1995), we discovered that successful leaders in today's "challenging" societies and corporations need to have honed a complex set of cognitive, emotional, and behavioral gifts. Moreover, there must be a good person-job "fit" and a good corporate leader-organizational "fit" to optimize profits and job satisfaction. Corporate leaders and their boards must also be cognizant that these "fits" are dynamic rather than static and that for charismatic leaders and those less gifted in this regard, "seasons" occur during leadership tenures. Finally, we noted that at least three main leader influence styles occur in organizations and in politics, ranging from the self-healing, trustworthy, tactician style to the disease-prone, toxic, shotgun style. Each has its personal and organizational costs and benefits.

In closing, I'd like to present a short article that illustrates well what we discovered in this chapter: modern-day corporate leaders need to be rationally *and* emotionally balanced *and* behaviorally flexible to cope with today's organizational challenges. Otherwise, "unsuccessful" corporate leaders are shown the door. Willis's (1997) piece follows:

Chief executives at broadly held Canadian companies used to have it made. With no controlling shareholder to crack the whip, these executives could post relatively ordinary performance numbers, yet seldom experience the wrath of their owners. Institutions that got frustrated tended to sell their stakes and move on. As Paul Gagne can attest, it's now a different world.

Mr. Gagne, aged 51, departed the CEO's slot in forest products giant Avenor last Thursday after 21 years with the company. He joins a rapidly growing club of corporate leaders who have found themselves out of work after failing to deliver on promises, a club that's welcomed Moore Corp.'s Reto Braun and Mac-Millan Bloedel's Robert Findlay in recent weeks.

Institutional investors, particularly activist pension funds, are showing a decidedly un-Canadian lack of patience with CEO strategies that don't work. In Mr. Gagne's case, his sin was to aggressively back a merger with Repap Enterprises that scared the heck out of Avenor's shareholders. Mr. Gagne's proposal, shot down by a shareholder vote, would have loaded Avenor with debt.

When the Repap merger cratered, Mr. Gagne didn't have another trick up his sleeve. He'd also made some powerful enemies by publicly rebuffing the idea of a merger with rival Domtar, a concept backed by the mighty Caisse de depot et placement du Quebec.

With Mr. Gagne gone, Avenor's board of directors is likely being overwhelmed by investment bankers with ideas on how to "maximize shareholder value" by selling the company. Street sources say the only thing clouding Avenor's future is the murky, interlocked world of finance and government that continues to make takeovers in Quebec a unique part of the Canadian experience.

What's becoming clear is that CEOs who survive and prosper these days need more than just the vision thing. They need the wisdom to recognize when their best-laid plans just aren't working and a new approach is required. (emphasis mine)

For example, contrast Mr. Gagne's harsh treatment to the warm endorsement the market gave Nova Corp. CEO Ted Newall's admission two weeks ago that his cherished corporate structure wasn't working and his promise that it would be replaced. Assuming Mr. Newall delivers, he'll have justified the faith of investors who pushed Nova's stock up 17 percent in recent weeks. If he doesn't, there's a comfy fireside seat waiting at the ex-CEO's club. (p. B2)

REFERENCES

Adler, N. J. (1997). *International dimensions of organizational behavior*. Cincinnati: South-Western College Publishing.

Aguilar, F. J. (1967). *Scanning the business environment*. New York: Macmillan.

Bloom, H. S., & Price, H. D. (1975). Voter response to short-run economic conditions: The asymmetric effect of prosperity and recession. *American Political Science Review*, 69, 1240–1254.

Cohen, A. (1997). Tapes show JFK weighing war risk. *The Globe and Mail*, October 20, pp. A1, A13.

Gabarro, J. J. (1987). *The dynamics of taking charge*. Boston: Harvard Business School Press.

Goleman, D. (1995). *Emotional intelligence: Why it can matter more than IQ*. New York: Bantam Books, pp. 148–150.

Gordon, G. E., & Rosen, N. (1981). Critical factors in leadership succession. *Organizational Behavior and Human Performance*, 27, 227–254.

Grush, J. E. (1980). Impact of candidate expenditures, regionality, and prior outcomes on the 1976 Democratic presidential primaries. *Journal of Personality and Social Psychology*, 38, 337–347.

Hambrick, D. C., & Fukutomi, G. D. S. (1991). The seasons of a CEO's tenure. *Academy of Management Review*, 16, 719–742.

House, R. J., Spangler, W. D., & Woycke, J. (1991). Personality and charisma in the U.S. presidency: A psychological theory of leader effectiveness. *Administrative Science Quarterly*, 36, 364–396.

Katz, R. (1982). The effects of group longevity on project communication and performance. *Administrative Science Quarterly*, 27, 81–104.

Kenski, H. C. (1977). The impact of economic conditions on presidential popularity. *Journal of Politics*, 39, 764–773.

Kernell, S. (1978). Explaining presidential popularity: How ad hoc theorizing, misplaced emphasis, and insufficient care in measuring one's variables refuted common sense and led conventional wisdom down the path of anomalies. *American Political Science Review*, 72, 506–522.

Kipnis, D., & Schmidt, S. M. (1988). Upward-influence styles: Relationship with performance evaluations, salary, and stress. *Administrative Science Quarterly*, 33, 528–542.

Kipnis, D., Schmidt, S., Swaffin-Smith, C., & Wilkinson, I. (1994). Patterns of managerial influence: Shotgun managers, tacticians, and bystanders. In L.A. Mainiero & C. L. Tromley (Eds.), *Developing managerial skills in organizational behavior*. Englewood Cliffs, NJ: Prentice-Hall, pp. 182–187.

Maccoby, M. (1976). *The gamesman: Winning and losing the career game*. New York: Bantam.

Miller, D. (1988). *Stale in the saddle: CEO tenure and adaptation*. Working Paper. Montreal: McGill University.

Miller, D., & Friesen, P. H. (1984). *Organizations: A quantum view*. Englewood Cliffs, NJ: Prentice-Hall.

Mueller, J. E. (1973). *War, presidents, and public opinion*. New York: Wiley.

Romanelli, E., & Tushman, M. L. (1988). Executive leadership and organizational outcomes: An evolutionary perspective. In D.C. Hambrick (Ed.), *The executive effect: Concepts and methods for studying top managers*. Greenwich, CT: JAI Press, pp. 129–140.

Roth, K. (1995). Managing international interdependence: CEO characteristics in a resource-based framework. *Academy of Management Journal*, 38, 200–231.

Salancik, G. R. (1977). Commitment and the control of organizational behavior and belief. In B. M. Staw & G. R. Salancik (Eds.), *New directions in organizational behavior*. Chicago: St. Clair Press, pp. 1–54.

Simonton, D. K. (1976). *Greatness: Who makes history and why*. New York: Guilford Press.

Staw, B. M. (1976). Knee-deep in the big muddy: A study of escalating commitment to a chosen course of action. *Organizational Behavior and Human Performance*, 16, 27–44.

Stimson, J. A. (1976). Public support for American presidents: A cyclical model. *Public Opinion Quarterly*, 40, 1–21.

Vancil, R. F. (1987). *Passing the baton: Managing the process of CEO succession*. Boston: Harvard Business School Press.

Weber, M. (1947). *The theory of social and economic organization*. M. Henderson and T. Parsons (Trans.); T. Parsons (Ed.). New York: Free Press.

Whicker, M. L. (1996). *Toxic leaders: When organizations go bad*. Westport, CT: Quorum Books.

Willis, A. (1997). Pushy funds stock ex-CEO's club. *The Globe and Mail*, November 11, p. B20.

Wilson, B. R. (1975). *The noble savages: The primitive origins of charisma and its contemporary survival*. Berkeley: University of California Press, p. 7.

CHAPTER 4

The Path to Corporate Success: Personality Traits and Behavioral Profiles of Those Who Have Made It to the Top

Harry Rosen is a retailer in what may be the stress capital of Canada—Toronto—and he knows a thing or two about pressure. He has prospered in the volatile business of high-end men's wear, and he says that is partly because he views stress in two ways. "There is a high you get from the achievement that stressful times can bring," he says. "But it's paradoxical—you experience elation at the same time you experience tension." Rosen keeps stress in check by starting his day with a one-hour workout that includes running, weight training and stretching. "It's nice to know you can touch your toes at 64," he says. He restricts alcohol to the occasional shot of 100-proof vodka, and unwinds by reading or watching what he calls "rubbish" videos. And he tries to be philosophical. "I'm a veteran of many wars and when things aren't as buoyant as I'd like, I remind myself that I've been here before."

—P. Christopher (1996)

A CASE IN POINT

Some leaders have what psychosocial scientists call "predominantly disease-prone" personalities and behavioral traits. Other leaders have, in contrast, "predominantly self-healing" personalities and behavioral traits. Somewhere in-between, say these experts, lie the rest of our leaders' personalities and behavioral traits.

Case A (Kets De Vries 1993)

Harry Langner [name disguised] came to me for therapy, suffering from severe depression and a number of stress symptoms following his forced resignation after only five years as president of the Telar Corporation [name disguised], an established company in the brand-name foods business. His appointment to the presidency in his early forties had been the climax of a dazzlingly high-flying career. His predecessor had personally picked and groomed him for the job, with the general approval of the Board and company executives. What had gone wrong in the intervening period? Why had Langner fallen from grace so hard and so fast?

The qualities that the outgoing president and other company executives had particularly admired in Langner—his talents as a team player and his professed commitment to participatory management—had melted away the moment he became CEO. Many of those who had known him before his appointment said that he seemed to change into a different person overnight. He was universally criticized for increasingly following his own path and no longer listening to what others had to say.

As CEO, Langner immediately embarked on a number of expensive projects. His first scheme was to relocate the head office of the corporation from the north to the east of the country, ostensibly to be nearer the market. However, cynics within the company suggested that the real reason behind the move was Langner's desire to be nearer his country estate. A series of luxurious purchases followed, including two company jets to fly Langner and his top executives around the world, and a custom-designed yacht allegedly to be used to entertain business associates. In fact, the boat was used by Langner and his friends mainly to go deep-sea fishing.

Stating that the purpose was to streamline the company, change its rather traditional image, and make it more of a trendsetter, Langner undertook two major reorganizations within four years. The only visible results of the work of the armies of consultants hired during this time were a serious destabilization of the company, the loss of a number of valuable long-term employees, and significant problems with morale. A number of questionable, extravagant acquisitions followed without much thought to their fit with other parts of the company. Telar Corporation began to have losses for the first time in years, and its stock value declined rapidly.

In spite of the company's going into "the red," Langner's salary and considerable perks remained unaffected. He appeared to be unperturbed by the downward slide in profits, enthusiastically organizing a planning conference in a chateau near Paris when the company was in increasing financial difficulty. No expense was spared, including the chartering of helicopters to transport company employees and guests, excessive speaker fees for a number of politicians, and the hiring of a three-star French chef to supervise the catering. By this time, Langner's autocratic style and imperious way of acting had completely alienated the few of his original supporters who still remained with the company. Any illusions of frank interchange had disappeared; good ideas were ignored and withered away. Several high-level resignations were given, stock was selling at an all-time low, and a funereal atmosphere pervaded the organization. Langner was unapproachable, as impervious to the problems within his company as he was deaf to those executives who tried to reach him. The crisis came when Langner approved a low-interest loan to a company of which he was part owner. This conflict of interest gave the Board the excuse it needed to ask for his resignation. Despite his protestations that he did not see any potential conflict because he did not occupy a management position in the second company, Langner was forced to resign.

Some weeks after, with his morale at an all-time low, Langner came to see me. It was his first experience of therapy, and he armed himself beforehand by reading fairly extensively on the subject. He made an immediate impression as he entered the room. Good-looking and meticulously dressed, wearing an Armani suit, Gucci shoes, and a Patek Philippe watch, he wasted no time in demonstrating his familiarity with clinical terminology. One of the first things he did was to pull out of his briefcase a number of newspaper clippings showing him photographed with well-known people from the worlds of politics and the arts. He had no reservations about talking about himself.

Langner recalled that he was always the center of attention while he was growing up. His parents showed off his looks, dressed him up, made him sing songs and recite when they had visitors. He retained vivid memories of people sitting around, watching and encouraging him to perform. He was always considered very talented, destined to have a great future. His mother persuaded his teachers to allow him to skip a year in high school. In retrospect, Langner sometimes wondered whether that had been a wise move because it put a lot of pressure on him and he lost friends as a result. He complained that his parents never seemed to care much about his own personal desires; they were more interested in outward symbols of success, like academic achievements and good looks.

Langner was a very good high school student and at graduation was listed in the yearbook as the person most likely to succeed. He went on to study at an Ivy League college, where he was shocked to discover that things no longer came so easily to him. To obtain good grades, he had to work hard for the first time in his life—a task made more difficult by the amount of time he spent with women. After receiving his M.B.A. degree, Langner's major problem was choosing one job from among the many he was offered. He was a most successful interviewee, finding it extremely easy to charm recruiters. His interest in the media and taste for glamor led him naturally toward advertising. He initially joined a subsidiary of Telar Corporation, where his contagious enthusiasm and self-assurance led to a series of rapid promotions.

After gentle prompting, Langner acknowledged some of the darker [disease-prone] aspects of his personality. He recognized that his relationships had probably always been somewhat lopsided. He took admiration for his work for granted, feeling he was entitled to it. However, he found it difficult to show real rather than pretended interest in the work of others. Lower-level executives who failed to show enthusiasm for his ideas quickly found themselves out of favor. Langner admitted that rousing his anger could be dangerous for someone's career. He mentioned two occasions when he had gone out of his way to put rivals in a bad light. Although he knew how to be subtle, he could also be vindictive. Langner elaborated at length on his talent for charming his superiors. He was good at displaying his best side, at playing political games. It had paid off. He had obtained the top job—for a while, at least. However, with the top job he lost his sense of boundaries. Somehow he had slid into believing that the normal rules of conduct no longer applied to him, that he would get away with any transgression. "The game" got out of hand. The havoc his attitude brought to the organization, where people felt damaged and diminished, resulted in its near bankruptcy.

Case B (Stinson 1997)

Joy Calkin, the new president of Extendicare Inc, sees big opportunities for Canada's largest nursing home operator in the greying of baby boomers. But Ms. Calkin isn't dreaming about bricks-and-mortar nursing homes. The former nurse also wants to capitalize on demand for in-home services from an elderly, but still vigorous population.

"Why would Extendicare build for a wave when there's a trough coming?" says Ms. Calkin, 59, pointing out that educators went on a big building boom in the 1960s, only to end up with a longer-term glut of schools. Most elderly people are healthy, she explains, such as her 90-year-old father who walks five kilometers daily, campaigns in municipal elections, and lives in his own apartment. For this group, carefully targeted housekeeping and therapy services provided in the home enable them to remain living in their own residence and lower health care costs, she says.

Extendicare Inc, based in Markham, Ontario, Canada, already has a foothold in the home care market through its Para-Med Health Services division, which provides a wide array of nursing, physiotherapy and housekeeping services in Ontario, Alberta, and British Columbia. Although a small part of the company, it is growing rapidly, with revenue up 19% in the nine months ending September 30, 1997.

Ms. Calkin, a specialist in health systems management, joined Extendicare Inc as president and CEO in August, 1997, from an administrative post at the University of Calgary in Western Canada. She takes over a company whose growth is taking place largely south of the Canadian-U.S. border. Extendicare Inc purchased Arbor Health Care Co. of Lima, Ohio, in the fall of 1997 for $325 million (U.S.). Once the offer is completed, Extendicare will add 31 nursing homes, 4 institutional pharmacies and 10 outpatient rehabilitation operations, most of them in Ohio and Florida.

Arbor Health specializes in providing acute care for seriously ill patients. Many of Extendicare's other U.S. facilities are retirement homes that provide housing and meals for people who need minimal care.

Ms. Calkin replaces former CEO Fred Ladly, who remains with Extendicare Inc as Deputy Chairman. A native of Kentville, Nova Scotia, Ms. Calkin has put her stamp [of moderation] on the corporate leader office, rearranging the furniture, adding a music stand where she stands to read corporate reports, and spending $400 (Canadian) on new area rugs.

She says her first business experience came at the age of 12 when she began working in her family's hardware store. As a nurse, she specialized in helping chronically ill children learn to care for themselves, and she taught nursing at several Canadian and U.S. universities.

A director of Extendicare Inc for the past two years, she became intrigued by boardroom discussions that considered the impact of decisions on employees, quality of care, shareholders, and the bottom line. She says that she's interested in issues "with a lot of staying power" in terms of service and investment, a view that seems to fit well with Extendicare's reputation as a conservatively managed company. Through carefully leveraged expeditures, Extendicare Inc can respond to population shifts, she says, but to be effective, spending has to be carefully targeted. "You don't build forever—you build for need and you move with the needs."

Mr. Fred Ladly, who was on the search committee for his replacement, found Ms. Calkin to be "a very bright woman" and was drawn by her ability to work with people and make tough decisions. "We're a service organization with a lot of employees," [said Ladly]. "We pride ourselves on how we work with people." Her contribution to the Board showed "she can get things done, without a lot of bureaucracy and red tape."

Ms. Calkin's previous job was Vice-President Academic at the University of Calgary, where she grappled with budget cuts imposed by the Alberta provincial government. Despite the downsizing, she is credited with helping create a positive relationship among faculty, support staff, and students.

"She could be tough when she needed to be, and she didn't shy away from making decisions," says Dr. Howard Yeager, University of Calgary's Associate Vice-President Academic of the three years he worked for her. "Unlike many senior administrators, she was not particularly interested in wielding power, but in getting the job done." At the university, she played a key role in implementing the budget cuts and helped put the university on a firm footing for the future, he emphasized.

Now Ms. Calkin turns her attention to helping Extendicare Inc find ways to provide health care into the 21st century. As people get older, she believes that they are investing for future needs and considering various housing arrangements, such as sharing homes or buying condominiums to reduce maintenance needs. Even with alternatives to nursing homes, Ms. Calkin knows that some people will always be so ill as to require institutional care. Her goal, therefore, is to make sure nursing homes are like "an extension of home" and "a place where you get respect and assistance when you need it." The new corporate leader concludes: "In the real world I want a place that's clean and accessible, in both physical and financial terms for a significant number of the population, not just the rich."

INTRODUCTION

Harry Langner and Joy Calkin are two corporate leaders with two very different styles of managing their firms. The leadership style of Harry Langner seems to characterize "predominantly disease-prone" behaviors and traits, while the leadership style of Joy Calkin seems to characterize "predominantly self-healing" behaviors and traits. Let's look more closely at this labeling.

When fired from his position at Telar Corporation, Harry Langner was in the fifth year of his leadership tenure, placing somewhere in the convergence phase of Hambrick and Fukutomi's CEO tenure model. Thus, according to expectations, Langner should have selected "a theme" for Telar's and his own energy commitment, and he should have been daily reinforcing and bolstering this theme through a stream of "relatively incremental" actions. In most firms at this stage of CEO tenure, actions typically undertaken relate to moderated changes in organizational structure, staffing, processes, and functional area initiatives. It seems, from reading Case A, that a "moderated" stream-of-things is what the Telar Corporation Board expected from Langner's leadership behavior. The board, in fact, apparently selected Langner for the CEO spot because they saw him as a task-and-people-balanced leader who preached participatory management and team cooperation in his earlier corporate leader history. But what the board got once Langner walked into the top position was a Type A leader whose style was narcissistic, extravagant, and status-fixated. Contrary to his board's expectations, Harry Langner did not practice either participatory management or finite resource moderation when he became CEO. Instead, in an extremely self-centered, low n-ActI, and high n-Pow way, he spent big bucks on personal pleasures, treated organizational members callously and aggressively, and forced Telar Corporation into a state of near-bankruptcy in a short amount of time. Regrettably for him and his organization, Langner's leadership style, once "talked" and "walked" in a relatively self-healing manner as he worked his way up the corporate ladder, became pathologically self-, other-, and company-destructive almost overnight. In the end, Harry Langner's leadership style eventually left him jobless and depressed—and the company barely functioning.

Joy Calkin, in contrast, is a new CEO who has been in her leadership position for only three months. According to Hambrick and Fukutomi's model, Calkin is in the first phase of her CEO tenure, and she seems to be aware that her actions must reflect the conservative-but-growing mandate for which she was hired. Extendicare Inc. seems to have invested in a leader who, at least initially, appears to be task-and-people balanced, understands the image of her company, is low-to-moderate in her spending patterns, can make tough decisions when she needs to, and envisions nursing homes as an extension of home—a place where clients can get the respect and the assistance they need when they need it. Seemingly motivated by a "balanced" n-Pow and n-ActI, Joy Calkin appears to be utilizing her previous practical and moderated University of Calgary leadership style by not offending the people she works with and by taking calculated financial risks. The positive outcomes of her short tenure as corporate leader are obvious: not only have Extendicare's revenues been up in recent months, but the company seems to be showing growth in the U.S. marketplace. A predominantly "self-healing" Type B leader, Joy Calkin seems to be able to make the kind of decisions when she needs to that will keep her organizational members' morale solid and her company's competitiveness in the marketplace alive and well.

These two cases on Harry Langner and Joy Calkin emphasize the importance of the corporate leaders' need to effectively manage not only their finite life energy over the longer term but the finite resources of their organizations. Too often, say the psychosocial experts, the higher-degreed, "disease-prone" corporate leaders erroneously choose one objective over the other and suffer the consequences. Psychosocial scientists suggest that a corporate leader's ability to successfully accomplish this bifold feat is a function, in large part, of the leader's previously conditioned cognitive and behavioral tendencies, which started in childhood and continued—often unchallenged—through adulthood. These "enduring cognitive and behavioral tendencies" are called "personality predispositions" in the psychosocial literature. The latter can be subdivided into the "self-healing" and the "disease-prone" types, as well as other recognized categories.

Chapter 4 continues to look more fully at the traits of "predominantly self-healing" and "predominantly disease-prone" corporate leaders by building on the stress-coping, energy conservation, and strategy-building principles outlined for "self-healers" in earlier chapters. Accordingly, Chapter 4 begins with a brief discussion of the different kinds of classifications reported in the psychosocial literature on disease-prone types. The bulk of Chapter 4 details the "self-healing" Type B profile and the "disease-prone" Type A (i.e., cardiovascular-prone) and Type C (i.e., cancer-prone) profiles. Chapter 4 closes with a summary of findings regarding the empirical studies completed on the personality predispositions of present-day corporate leaders. Chapter 5 continues on this self-healing and disease-prone theme, describing some of the more common personality and mood disorders allegedly found in today's corporate leaders.

SOME SIGNIFICANT POINTS ABOUT PERSONALITY PREDISPOSITIONS IN THE PSYCHOSOCIAL LITERATURE

Let us review, for a moment, some significant points about personality predispositions in the psychosocial literature. As a starting point for Chapter 4, we accept that two dimensions of personality affect corporate leaders' behavior on and off the job: their cognitive or information-processing sides and their emotional sides. When we get into the topic of "disease-prone" personalities, we must accept that "faulty" cognitive and affective tendencies can be exacerbated by "faulty" environmental circumstances, thus placing the affected corporate leaders and their organizations at risk for all sorts of problems, as evidenced in the case of Langner.

Some of the cognitive and affective "faults" found in corporate leaders have been attributed by mental health experts to (1) genetic and biochemical sources—the endogenous factors—and by others to (2) parental conditioning and ongoing life-event programming sources—the exogenous factors.

Before getting into the details of "self-healing" and "disease-prone" personalities, it is useful to recognize that any classification regarding type is controversial, with experts positing that there are few "pure" types, regardless of which classification schema one uses to make type distinctions. Stated simply, corporate leaders tend to self-report at any point in time a certain percentage of self-healing traits along with a certain percentage of disease-prone traits. As in Nixon's and Kennedy's cases, the "predominant" traits perceived by the experts as existing in each case protagonist determine the "self-healing" or "disease-prone" label assigned to that individual.

Constraints in Personality Classification

Too, we need to emphasize that the boundaries between "normal" and "abnormal" personalities and between the different personality types are, to a large extent, arbitrary, although latent class variables may underlie some of them (Widiger et al. 1988). Moreover, we need to accept that there are many different systems for classifying personality traits and personality disorders, with varying numbers of categories existing within them. Even in the late 1990s, experts agree that the optimal number of categories needed to partition the mental health and ill-health domain remains unclear (Widiger et al. 1988). The reality is that the number of items in the personality taxonomies has ranged considerably, from small numbers, such as Hippocrates' four temperaments, to large numbers, such as Fourier's 810 character types. Although a low number tends to result in failure to represent clinically important personality descriptions, increasing the number tends to result in overlapping categories.

Three Major Types of Personality Classification: The Psychoneuroses, the Psychoses, and the Personality and Mood Disorders

Recognizing the classification constraints just described, the late mental health expert H. J. Eysenck identified three broad categories (Leigh, Pare, & Marks 1977, p. 257) that he posited encompass psychological ill health: neuroticism (N), psychoticism (P), and extraversion-introversion (E-I). On these three broad dimensions, noted Eysenck, may be constructed a grouping of the common behavioral disorders found in adults and described in the psychiatric and personality literature (pp. 301, 302, 303). These include the psychoneuroses, the psychoses, and the personality and mood disorders.

(1) *The Psychoneuroses*, which are primarily exogenous factor-based, are quite common in working adult "normals" (including corporate leaders) and include the anxiety reactions, the depressive reactions, the anger reactions, dissociative or hysterical reactions, phobic reactions, obsessive-compulsive reactions, and the Type A (cardiovascular-prone) and the Type C (cancer-prone) physiological reactions.

(2) *The Psychoses*, which are endogenous factor-based, include the more severe schizophrenia, schizoaffective, and delusional disorders.

(3) *The Personality Disorders and the Mood Disorders*, which can be endogenous factor-based, have features that are relatively enduring. Ten personality disorders are commonly described in the psychiatric literature (American Psychiatric Association 1994), including the narcissistic personality, the antisocial or psychopathic disorder, and the borderline personality. In the personality disorders, the enduring patterns of "inner experience" and behavior deviate in varying degrees from the expectations of one's culture, they generally have an onset in adolescence or in early adulthood, and they tend to lead to distress or impairment in the individual. Six mood disorder classes are commonly described in the psychiatric literature, whereby an enduring disturbance in mood is the predominant feature. The mood disorders include the unipolar and the bipolar depressive disorders. In the unipolar depressive disorders, there is no history of ever having had a manic episode, whereas in the bipolar disorders, both mania and depression are felt to some degree.

Details on the Psychoneuroses

Chapter 4 focuses on the Type A and the Type C psychoneuroses because along with the self-healing Type B predisposition, they are found in working adults and, presumably, in corporate leaders on a large-scale basis. In general, the psychoneuroses may be distinguished from the more severe psychoses by the fact that in the psychoneuroses, emotional experience and behavior are quantitatively, rather than qualitatively, different from "normal," insight about one's orientation is usually present in varying degrees, and the working adult's relation to, and sense of, reality are generally unimpaired (Leigh, Pare, & Marks 1977, pp. 301–302).

Further, personality deterioration, disorders of concrete thinking, disorientation, and loss of contact with reality do not usually occur in the psychoneuroses (Leigh, Pare, & Marks 1977, pp. 301–302). What does occur over the longer term, however, is a greater risk for poorer mental and physiological health, with the Type As theoretically being at particular risk for premature cardiovascular disease and with the Type Cs theoretically being at particular risk for cancer.

In short, the Type A and the Type C behavioral patterns are seemingly common psychoneurotic reactions to life events in which anxiety, generated by the conflict between the working adult and his or her life stressors, is "defended against" by such varied psychological coping mechanisms as those earlier described in Chapter 2: repression, conversion, and anger outbursts or anger displacement.

While Freud's ideas on the etiology of the psychoneuroses are based on the individual's fixation at certain levels of development (i.e., the oral, anal, or phallic stages), the Pavlovian concepts regarding etiology are centered on the idea that both the Type A and the Type C "disease-prone" patterns are actually learned behavior patterns, reinforced by continuing stress. From a clinical point of view, this is relatively good news. Because the psychoneuroses are, for the most part, learned, they are capable of being "reprogrammed" or even extinguished by modern-day cognitive and behavioral therapy (CBT) techniques. According to estimates, the prevalence of neurotic ill-health is high, with at least 15 percent of the adult working population being significantly incapacitated by their psychoneurotic symptomology (Leigh, Pare, & Marks 1977, pp. 301–302).

RECENT DISCOVERIES OF PERSONALITY PREDISPOSITIONS ASSOCIATED WITH PHYSIOLOGICAL HEALTH

Several times throughout *Management in the Mirror*, we have expressed the concern that there have been few empirical studies completed on corporate leaders' personalities, primarily because of their inaccessibility to researchers. Similarly, physiological experts over the past three decades have had considerable difficulty unraveling the mysteries behind personality predispositions and physiological ill health, in large part because they cannot use conventionally sound experimental methodology to assess personality-physiological disease presentations. That is, they cannot randomly assign certain types, say the coronary-prone Type As, to high-stress and low-stress work and personal life conditions and then wait to see if these subjects develop cardiovascular disease. Given these real-world shortcomings, most of what researchers have discovered about personality predispositions and physiological disease-proneness has come from inferences drawn from various kinds of theoretical assumptions and "after disease manifests" lines of evidence.

After decades of research investigating the predictors of premature cardiovascular disease (CHD), North American mental and cardiovascular health experts Chesney and Rosenman (1983) have painted in the literature a picture of the non-coronary-prone working adult, called "the Type Bs." Seemingly like Calkin, they are not provoked to become excessively competitive, aggressive, or impatient when "taxing" personal or organizational demands present. Rather, these physiologically "self-healing" Type B adults maintain an optimistic, moderated, task-and-emotional-balanced style of responding to life's various stressors and challenges.

Similarly, after decades of research investigating the predictors of premature cancer onset, European mental health experts Grossarth-Maticek and Eysenck (1991) have painted in the literature a picture of the "self-healing" working adult, called "the autonomous self-healer," described by these experts as having the ability to:

- correct exaggerated environmental expectations by recognizing the actual consequences of their own behavior;
- regulate their "nearness to," and "distance from," particularly distressing persons or things;
- not expect unrealistic satisfaction of their most important emotional needs from other people or things in a passive, helpless, and dependent position but be able to achieve their desired emotional consequences through their own well-planned activities, their own positive or corrective self-evaluations, and their own moderated behavior patterns; and
- over the longer term, correct or abandon unhealthy and potentially destructive object-dependent patterns of behavior by seeing the potentially negative personal and work-life consequences of such dependencies.

According to psychosocial experts, a large part of the self-healing process is due to the unique information processing and psychological noise reduction that go on within the minds of these working adults and corporate leaders. Their reaction to "taxing" work and home stressors is distinct. Basically, they see challenges, rather than threats, in their environments, they are cognitively adaptable to change, they remain optimistic when others fall to pessimism, and they are on a lifelong search for mental and behavioral growth, dogmatically opposed to stagnation or regression. In short, as outlined in Chapter 2, the self-healers perceive that they have a great sense of control over what occurs in their lives, and they feel committed to the various areas of their lives—including work and nonwork activities.

Experts Friedman and VandenBos (1992) further suggest that a number of manifest verbal and nonverbal behaviors, many of them unconsciously driven, distinguish self-healing working adults and corporate leaders from their disease-prone counterparts. Specifically, the self-healers' constellation of verbal and nonverbal traits include:

- A "natural" smile, such that the individual's eye movements, eyebrows, and mouth are synchronized, not forced, into producing a warm, inviting smile when interacting with others in the work and home environment;

- A calm and conscientious appearance, not prone to fidgeting or aggressive gestures;

- Balanced body movements and speech, with body gestures that tend to move away from the body and with vocal tones that sound at peace and moderated; and

- An overtly emotionally intact but not overcontrolled mind, as reflected in few speech disturbances—even in stress-producing work and home situations.

Moreover, add Friedman and VandenBos, from an interpersonal perspective, PA-driven self-healers attract others to themselves in the workplace and in other social settings because they tend to make the best out of a not-so-perfect situation, and they have a remarkable, often charismatic sense of bringing the best out in others. Self-healing working adults and corporate leaders tend to have an optimistic growth orientation, are interpersonally spontaneous and creative, are good problem solvers, have a sense of humor that is philosophical rather than hostile, and are generally concerned with issues of beauty, justice, ethics, and understanding others. Because of their "upbeat" way of coping with life's challenges and their uncanny ability to socially and emotionally refuel themselves and others, self-healers have significantly fewer stress-related mental and physiological disorders than their more disease-prone counterparts. Simply put, they derive much eustress (or positive energy returns) from their home lives, their leisure pursuits, and their jobs.

Like Joy Calkin and her father, the self-healers seem to be habituated to moderated and healthy lifestyles. They are able to build into their daily regimens the time and the means for social and emotional refueling, self-introspection, and psychological noise venting with minimal self- and other-denigration. Though self-healers are adequately n-Ach- and n-Pow-driven—liking to do their jobs very competently and successfully—they are not obsessed to the extreme with task perfection or organizational profits, especially not at the expense of people. In short, self-healers realize the basics of self-preservation—for themselves and for others with whom they relate, both on and off the job.

RECENT DISCOVERIES OF PERSONALITY PREDISPOSITIONS ASSOCIATED WITH PHYSIOLOGICAL ILL HEALTH

The Physiological "Disease-Prone" Described

Accepting the preceding descriptions for the physiological "self-healers," it should be emphasized early on that the findings that currently prevail in the 1990s regarding personality predispositions and physiological ill health have been challenged and critiqued by experts around the world. Thus, the findings remaining in considerable favor have shown that there are groups of adults who are physiologically and often psychologically "disease-prone" by virtue of their:

- inability to express appropriately and assertively their negative emotions and frustrations,
- failure to cope with interpersonal stress in an appropriate and constructive fashion, and
- overreaction to work and home stressors by way of high degrees of expressed anger and aggression (i.e., "anger-out") or by way of anger denial and suppression (i.e., "anger-in") (Eysenck 1985; Friedman & Booth-Kewley 1987).

In terms of labeling, the cardiovascular-prone types, often called "the anger-out" types, are known as the Type As, with there being a further subdivision into the "fully-developed, pronounced Type A1s" and the "less fully developed Type A2s." The cancer-prone types, often called "the anger-in" variety, are known as the Type Cs, with there being a further tentative subdivision into the "emotionally dependent Type Cs" and the "antiemotional and overrational (poker-faced) Type Cs."

Moreover, there is a sort of consensus among present-day mental and physiological health experts that, unlike the self-healing, autonomous Type Bs, the Type As and the Type Cs do not have adequate degrees of autonomous self-regulation, internal control, or positive affect (PA). Rather, in varying degrees, they seem to be characterized by "outside" or "exogenous control" and negative affect (NA), and for this reason they place in the psychoneurotic class. Their high-NA characteristic, say the experts, seems to be the result of, in smaller part—about 25 percent—heredity and, in larger part—about 75 percent—faulty early childhood conditioning and ongoing "faulty" socialization (Grossarth-Maticek & Eysenck 1991; Price 1982).

In short, the physiologically disease-prone Type A and Type C corporate leaders do not become diseased overnight; instead, they tend to develop poor stress-coping habits in childhood and carry these forward into adulthood, accumulating costs along the way. Left unchallenged, these poor stress-coping habits can eventually lead to premature cardiovascular disease or to cancer.

Moreover, say the experts, because of their chronic NA predispositions, physiologically disease-prone corporate leaders often suffer from bouts of anxiety and depression from one life stage to another, beginning in childhood and continuing through adulthood. Then, once in a depression, these individuals tend to further increase their distress levels and NA by dramatically inhibiting their healthful cognitive and behavioral tendencies that could guide them to a positive light in terms of probable, realistic, and possibly eustressful work and home outcomes. Regrettably, their previously rooted disease-prone cognitions supersede their positive "could-bes"; thus, disease-prone corporate leaders, like Harry Langner, become increasingly angry and frustrated with their lot in life.

Further Details on Early Conditioning Patterns of the Disease-Prone Type As and Type Cs

Although Type As and Type Cs have various degrees of emptiness and lack of self-respect at the root of their mental and eventual physiological dilemmas, their outward appearances and manners of coping with work and home stressors vary (Grossarth-Maticek & Eysenck 1991; Price 1982). But before examining these differences in outward mannerisms and stress-coping, we need to explore more fully the "empty" childhood conditioning that exists in Type As and Type Cs, noting slight variations.

Starting in early childhood, say the experts, the Type As and the Type Cs are conditioned by significant others—usually their parents, their guardians, their early educators, and their sport coaches—to become either "achievement-dependent" or "person-dependent." Thus, from an early age, Type A and Type C children become "regulated" from the outside rather than from the inside. By the child's being repeatedly encouraged through verbal, nonverbal, and behavioral means to make his or her need-satisfactions very dependent on the behavior of particular persons (for the Type Cs, often the parents themselves) or on achievement (for the Type As, often in terms of high marks or sport competition wins), the patterns of disease-proneness become indelibly marked at an early age. Certainly by age five, the experts note (Grossarth-Maticek & Eysenck 1991; Price 1982), both the Type A and Type C child's need satisfactions become contingent upon playing an externally driven role, where autonomous self-regulation becomes an almost nonentity; such was obvious in the case of Langner.

In later childhood, through adolescence, and through later adult life stages, these Type As and Type Cs continue to live the conviction that they are incapable of achieving need-satisfying situations and need-satisfying reactions through their own adaptive resources. In this fashion the likely high-degree Type A and the likely high-degree Type C corporate leaders move into organizations, searching for some "all-powerful" achievements or persons to make their lives "complete." Sadly, the contribution of their own "self-healing" autonomy becomes, often without their consciously being aware of it, increasingly nonsignificant and unimportant.

Particulars of the Type C Stress-Coping Style. This continued "passivity" of coping with life's work and home stressors constitutes the essential personality and behavioral predispositions of the emotionally dependent adult Type C (Grossarth-Maticek & Eysenck 1991). Throughout their adulthood, Type Cs fulfill their emotional needs—at least the way they see it—through a series of "symbiotic" relationships. But true symbiosis does not exist, for the emotionally dependent Type Cs see some all-powerful and need-satisfying other or others as determining their primary behaviors and emotional reactions to work and home situations. Ironically, the antiemotional and overrational strain of Type C denies this emotional dependency. If the "other" or "others" decline or fail to satisfy the Type C's needs and wishes, then hopelessness, agitation, helplessness, and anxiety, in various degrees, result. Though in their minds, their n-Aff remains poorly sated, the Type Cs' dependency on their chosen others at work and at home escalates rather than de-escalates with time. Because of this paradoxical reality, Type Cs are typically viewed as being "experts" in psychological noise denial and suppression rather than as being constructive agents who work through what is really at the root of their childhood problem. Nixon serves as such a noise suppressor case.

As is probably already obvious, unsated Type Cs seem not to learn over their life spans from their painful relationship outcomes the importance of their own self-healing cognitions and behaviors but instead enter into a habit of chronic self-blame, self-denigration, and negative escapist stress-coping. High-degree Type Cs rarely, if ever, place themselves in a position of correcting their feelings of low self-worth; therefore, they tend to set themselves up for a lifetime of distress. Over the longer term, these emotionally dependent, but emotionally starved, Type C adults often complain of emotional exhaustion. Their inability to make themselves independent and self-autonomous leads to increasing passive acceptance of a rather unfulfilling life situation, to overuse of their parasympathetic stress-response systems (and thus to reduced immunity), to hopelessness, to despair, and to depression. Eventually, typically following a high-stress period, posit Grossarth-Maticek and Eysenck (1991), Type Cs often are diagnosed with cancer.

Particulars of the Type A Stress-Coping Style. The Type A child's reactions to life's stressors are somewhat different from those of the Type C child. Whereas the same nonautonomous pattern of thinking is conditioned early on by parents and guardians in Type A children, they react to rejection by others or to losses of desired "objects" (such as game or mark losses) with anger, some of it buried deeply inside and some of it openly expressed (Price 1982).

This same "anger-out" stress-coping is later seen in the Type A corporate leader, when rejection by significant others or when losses of desired "objects" (including profits, business acquisitions, munificent compensation, or job prestige) are perceived. Thus, adult Type As commonly experience a lifetime of psychological and social-emotional emptiness, frustration, and disappointment—in large part, caused by their own unpleasantness and aggression, which were rooted in childhood. Sadly, Type A corporate leaders tend not to openly admit such empty feelings to others—or even to themselves. Instead, they bury their social-emotional emptiness in task perfection and profits, desperately trying to get some "conditional" approval from significant others for tasks well done, the "real" indicator, in their minds, of their self-worth.

Moreover, when Type As lose in the corporate arena or at sport competitions, they are not particularly "good sports" about it. As Harry Langner suggested, it is more likely for Type As to project the blame for their losses onto others and onto "the system" rather than onto themselves. Type As, in fact, work hard at maintaining self-control by becoming psychologically and/or physically "controlling" over others. Moreover, like Harry Langner during his high-stress years as CEO, it is rare for Type A leaders to seek "self-healing" rehabilitation until some life crisis manifests—such as their being fired from work or their cardiovascular disease being medically confirmed. Until such time, Type As typically think that others—not themselves—have "the problem."

Given their relatively easy provocation to anger, workaholic and perfection-fixated Type As are notorious for overworking their sympathetic stress response systems. Eventually, note the cardiovascular experts (Chesney & Rosenman 1983; Price 1982), with the biochemical war raging within them and with the premature aging of their systems that thus results, coronary heart disease can and often does get diagnosed at early ages.

Projected Type A and Type C Inoculations. Despite the childhood "nonautonomous root" similarities between Type As and Type Cs, Eysenck and his colleagues (Grossarth-Maticek & Eysenck 1991) have suggested that because of their vastly different stress-coping styles, Type As should be inoculated against getting cancer prematurely, and Type Cs should be inoculated against getting cardiovascular disease prematurely. However, at this stage of empirical research, such assertions remain highly tentative.

Consistently Reported Research Findings on the Disease-Prone Type As

On face, Type A corporate leaders tend to walk fast, talk fast, think fast, have relatively loud voices, are workaholics, are perfection-fixated, often use sarcasm to "covertly" express their anger or antagonism, have forced rather than "natural" smiles, and talk over others if others take too long to come to a point. There is very little lag time between Type As' processing of stimuli and their responding to them. Because Type As desire rapid closure and "ROI" (return-on-investment) feedback on their energy expenditures, they tend to be very action-oriented (Tang 1986). Meditation is generally not on their daily agenda. Moreover, because of their heavy reliance on their sympathetic stress response systems, Type As commonly appear to be somewhat anxious, hyperactive, and ready for fight or flight.

The primary traits associated with Type A predispositions in working adults and corporate leaders (Price 1982; Friedman & Rosenman 1974) include: (1) competitive achievement-striving: Type As work hard, determined to win at almost any cost; (2) a heightened sense of time urgency: by their own admission, Type As seem fixated on time and are often adamant about being on time for appointments; (3) easily aroused impatience and anger: by their own admission, Type As get easily aroused when others interrupt them in their task progress or get in their way as they devotedly make their way to the top of their organizations; and (4) excessive job involvement: organizational members, in describing their Type A leaders, are apt to see them as workaholics obsessed with task perfection and profits, often at the expense of people and their needs.

Furthermore, according to the psychosocial literature, Type A predispositions are especially common among working adults and corporate leaders in highly urbanized settings, where a demanding external environment catalyzes both the genetic predispositions and the hyperactive stress responses of individuals attracted to this type of setting. The Type A predisposition is said to be present to some degree in about half of today's employed males and females, especially in the early career stages (Thurman 1984; Schell & Deluca 1991). While there were once thought to be gender differences in Type A propensities, with women having significantly lower propensities for being Type A than men, recent reports from the 1990s indicate that there are few male-female differences when upward-striving occupations as a whole are analyzed. That is, Type A female corporate leaders, like their Type A male counterparts, can boast of having large quantities of incomes and assets, of being in executive positions, and of obtaining considerable formal education (Thoreson & Low 1990). Quite like Harry Langner, the more ostentatious

Type As of both genders can often be spotted in organizational crowds, sporting Armani suits, Gucci shoes, and a Patek Philippe watch.

Over the past few decades, a variety of epidemiological and physiological research studies have reported that the unidimensionally focused, workaholic Type As may be twice as likely as their moderated and more "task-and-people-balanced," assertive Type B counterparts to suffer from premature CHD (Jenkins 1976). Age is also a factor in Type A presentation. Recent research findings suggest that the Type A pattern in adults begins to diminish gradually after age 55–60, because of eventual insights gained by Type As about the self-destructiveness of this lifestyle pattern, because of a declining life-energy pool (Moss et al. 1986), or because of a combination of the two.

Finally, the "irrational" cognitions that seem to drive Type As and keep them "pumped up" for hyperactivity and high energy expenditure are summarized in Table 4.1 (Thurman 1984). If Type As find their cognitions challenged—which to them are perfectly rational, reasonable, and worthy of keeping (Westra & Kuiper 1992)—they reportedly get anxious, turning to the common anxiety-reduction strategies.

Consistently Reported Findings on the Disease-Prone Type Cs

On face, Type Cs have softer voices and more moderated behavioral patterns than Type As. In fact, verbally and nonverbally, Type Cs appear to be much more Type B than Type A in outward character. Meditation may even be on their daily agenda. The emotionally dependent strains of Type C tend to be outwardly sensitive to others at work and at home, while the antiemotional and overrational strains of Type C often appear to be "poker-faced" in their outward appearances, telling others that they are not stressed.

According to behavioral oncologists, the emotionally dependent Type Cs suppress and/or have an inability to express their negative emotions, particularly anger and frustration. Concerned that they may hurt other people's feelings or that they may jeopardize their interpersonal relationships, the emotionally dependent Type Cs, in particular, are "expert" at not asserting their negative feelings and at not giving negative feedback to others at work or at home. Other characteristics of the emotionally dependent Type Cs include their appearing to be overly patient, conflict-avoidant, and group-harmonizing in work and nonwork environments. The emotionally dependent Type Cs are often seen as being quite socially desirable individuals, complying with the wishes of others (Grossarth-Maticek & Eysenck 1991).

The Type Cs' stress-coping style is thus generally characterized as abrogating one's own needs in favor of others' needs (i.e., the emotionally

Table 4.1
Irrational Beliefs Associated with the Type A Behavior Pattern

Quantity of output is more important than quality of output.
Faster is always better.
It is horrible when things are not done on time.
Winning or losing a competition is a reflection of one's worth as a person.
One is only as good as his/her accomplishments.
Most events that slow one down are avoidable.
An endless string of accomplishments ensures that one will like oneself.
Nonachievement-oriented activities are a waste of time.
One can have complete control over one's life if one just tries hard enough.
Speeding up the pace of one's activities is the best way to keep or regain control.
Being perfectionistic is the best way to ensure high quality achievements.
Openly expressing anger and hostility makes other people pay for getting in my way.

Source: Thurman (1984).

dependent strain) or as suppressing one's negative emotions (i.e., the antiemotional and overrational strain). Despite what they may think about themselves, the stress-coping pattern of both strains of Type C is "noise-filled" and "bottled-up," a volcanic-eruption-to-be that is literally "burning" at the Type C from inside. This noise-escalating pattern, concealed behind a facade of pleasantness for the emotionally dependent strain or behind a poker face for the antiemotional and overrational strain, appears to be effective as long as the Type C's work and home homeostasis remains intact and relatively low-stressed (Baltrusch, Stangel, & Waltz 1988). However, studies have shown that the chronic blockage of the expression of the Type C's needs and the chronic blockage of negative affect, in particular, have destructive psychophysiologic consequences for both strains.

Not only do Type C corporate leaders (like Ben Webster?) likely suffer from bouts of hopelessness, helplessness, and depression over their lifetimes because of an inability to handle interpersonal conflicts at work and at home, but their parasympathetic stress-response systems are likely put into heavy use, resulting in high plasma cortisol levels and immune deficiencies (Baltrusch, Stangel, & Waltz 1988).

Using a cognitive diathesis-stress theory framework, Grossarth-Maticek and Eysenck (1991) posited that depression bouts in Type C working adults are likely caused, in large part, by their own self-defeatist attitudes. That is, Type Cs come to believe that highly desired relationship outcomes in the home and in the workplace are unlikely to occur or that highly aversive relationship outcomes are likely to occur and that no response in their somewhat limited cognitive and behavioral repertoire will change the likelihood of these outcomes. Cancer patients on medical wards have been clinically observed to utilize this type of self-defeatist coping strategy as a means of dealing with their experienced anxieties.

A summary of the literature findings on the Type C profile is given in Table 4.2.

Measuring the Type A, the Type B, and the Type C Predispositions

Giving working adults and corporate leaders feedback on their Type A and Type B propensities is considerably easier than giving them feedback on their Type C propensities, because many more inventories exist for the former as compared to the latter.

First, regarding accurate assessment of Type A-Type B patterning, both face-to-face structured interview methods and self-report inventories exist. Reviews completed over the past 20 years have consistently indicated that the structured interview (SI) is the most accurate way of assessing coronary-proneness, or Type A patterning. However, this method requires a trained professional to accurately assess clients' Type A predispositions (Rosenman et al. 1964).

Because of the expense and relative inconvenience of engaging in SI assessments, clinicians and industrial psychologists have often chosen to rely on clients' self-report scores obtained from the popular Jenkins Activity Survey (JAS) (Jenkins, Rosenman, & Zyzanski 1974), the Framingham Type A Scale (Haynes et al. 1978), the Bortner and Rosenman Scale (Bortner & Rosenman 1967), or the more recent Survey of Work Styles (Gray, Jackson, & Howard 1989) (developed on a sample of male business managers).

Although all of the these instruments purportedly assess the primary Type A traits existing in working adults (i.e., competitive achievement-striving, a heightened sense of time urgency, excessive job involvement, and easily aroused impatience and anger), experts continue to debate which of the Type A traits are the most destructive and which of the self-report instruments best "predict" coronary-proneness (Gray, Jackson, & Howard 1989).

Regarding the first debate issue, experts seem to be consistently reporting that anger/hostility is the trait most likely causing premature

Table 4.2
Summary of Type C Characteristics

Genetic and Early Childhood Factors: - Genetic Predispositions - Unfavorable family interaction patterns (i.e., lack of closeness to parents during childhood and youth) - Early losses and separations
Behavioral Features: - Overcooperative - Appeasing - Unassertive - Over-patient - Overly rational and anti-emotional at times - Avoidance of conflicts; exhibits "harmonizing behavior" - Unexpressive of negative emotions; in particular, anger - Compliant with external authorities - Defensive response to stress (i.e., high on social desirability and anxiety)
Medical Findings: - Type C is a prognostic indicator in patients with malignant melanoma, significantly associated with thicker and more invasive tumors - Breast cancer patients score higher than healthy controls on measures of social desirability, emotional suppression, and state anxiety - Significantly higher suppression of anger using the Courtauld Emotional Control Scale in cancer patients, compared to healthy persons

Source: Baltrusch & Waltz (1988).

CHD (Smith & Leon 1992). If inventory usage by clinicians is any settlement of the second debate issue, then the JAS is clearly the winner of the contest. Again, caution experts Byrne, Rosenman, Schiller, and Chesney (1985), if the JAS or any other self-report inventory is alternatively chosen to the SI to assess clients' Type A propensities, clinicians should be aware of obtaining some degree of false CHD "risk" readings.

Within the past decade, experts from Europe have suggested that measuring only Type A-Type B propensity is too narrow a focus and that inventories more broadly assessing mental and physiological self-healing and disease-proneness should be used by clinicians. Accordingly, Grossarth-Maticek and Eysenck (1990) developed a self-report inventory that purportedly assesses in an individual the Type A (Type 2), the Type B (Type 4), the Type C (Type 1 and Type 5), and the narcissistic and antisocial traits (Type 3 and Type 6).

EMPIRICAL FINDINGS ON THE PERSONALITY PREDISPOSITIONS OF CORPORATE LEADERS

Without exaggeration, over the past 20 years, just about all of the investigations on corporate leaders' personality predispositions have focused on Type A, coronary-proneness. Several of these studies have already been discussed in Chapter 2. To date, no study has examined the Type C predispositions of corporate leaders.

When it comes to Type A and Type B predispositions in corporate leaders, the research findings in North America over the past 20 years seem to indicate a rather consistent picture for lower and middle managers. In short, there seems to be a preponderance of Type As drawn to managerial careers, especially at the middle and lower levels, where most of the type assessments have been made.

For example, the 1989 Canadian study completed by Gray, Jackson, and Howard on a sample of 163 male, middle-level managers drawn largely from manufacturing and financial businesses indicated Type A and Type B proportions of about 67 percent and 33 percent, respectively. The positive feature of this study was the methodology used to assess organizational clients, given that the researchers obtained scores using the SI, the Jenkins Activity Survey (JAS), the Framingham Type A Scales, and the Survey of Work Styles (SWS). This research team cautioned, however, that the proportion of Type As found in their study sample of male, middle-level managers was likely an inflated result for Type A propensity, due to the overclassification of men as Type As.

The consistency in findings for Type A-proneness for leaders at higher levels is much less solid. In their 1976 review of earlier completed studies, Cooper and Marshall noted, for example, that in a 1958 longitudinal study by Pell and D'Alonzo on Dupont organizational members, the incidence of myocardial infarction was inversely related to salary level. Cooper and Marshall also noted the 1960 study of Stamler, Kjelsberg, and Hall and the 1963 study of Bainton and Peterson reporting contradictory findings on cardiovascular disease-proneness in upper management ranks.

THE BOTTOM LINE

This chapter opened with two cases on corporate leaders who had two very different styles of managing their firms. Harry Langner came across as a big-spending, status-conscious corporate leader who seemed to have little regard for many people below him or for the firm's scarce resources once his feet were planted in the "top office." Joy Calkin came across, in contrast, as a very moderated spender who, as a corporate leader, seemed to have high regard for people both within her firm and within North American society.

Following a somewhat exhaustive search on the self-healing Type B and on the disease-prone Type A and Type C traits of working adults, we concluded that Harry Langner could best be described as a likely disease-prone Type A and that Joy Calkin could best be described as a likely self-healing Type B.

We discovered, too, that reports over the past 20 years or so indicate a rather consistent propensity for lower- and middle-level managers in North America and elsewhere to be predominantly Type A in nature, as compared to Type B. However, we qualified our acceptance of this finding for top corporate leaders, noting that some reviews completed over the past 20 years have reported Type A patterning exceptions. Finally, we noted that although no studies have been completed on the Type C predispositions of corporate leaders, it would be naive to think that only Type As and, to a lesser degree, Type Bs are drawn to careers in business.

I would like to close this chapter on self-healing and disease-proneness with a rather humorous piece recently written by Margaret Wente in *The Globe and Mail* (1997). Called, "Why I'll Never Be CEO," this article gives some interesting insights into why self-healers (men and women alike) may choose to have shorter, rather than longer, tenures as CEOs:

The day I realized I wasn't cut out to be a CEO was the day my own CEO (who has since gone on to greater glory) burst into my cubicle in the midst of some corporate crisis or other. He was there to raise the alarm. To make sure I got the point, he pounded his fist on my desk and declared, "Our balls are on the line here!"

That was when I knew I just didn't have the equipment for the job.

Counting up the female CEOs has become a staple of business and popular journalism. The tone is always chirpily upbeat. *Maclean's* did its women CEOs cover a couple of weeks ago and concluded there are more than before, but it's still tough to get ahead. *Fortune* did its cover a couple of months ago. Its spin was that there are more than before, and, guess what! A lot of them wear nail polish!

In fact, nearly 30 years after the feminist revolution, there are still no, zip, zero women leading large corporations like GM, Coke, IBM or Exxon. Half of *Maclean's* cover women (an extremely accomplished bunch, no question) run the Canadian division of American companies, which is about equivalent in the great scheme of things to being in charge of California. They are not really at the top.

Will they get there? Probably not.

The CEO of a major corporation must have many attributes, most of which are available equally to men and women. But two are not. One is the drive for dominance. The other is an irrationally obsessive [Type A] focus on the business.

The dominance trait is the reason why the top monkey in the jungle is usually a male. It's the reason why warriors and fighters are generally men. It's also one reason why the chief executive officer of IBM is Louis Gerstner, and not you. He's got more of it than you do.

It's no accident that the prevailing metaphors of business are borrowed from the battlefield. Your competition is the enemy, and your job is to grind them to dust. Takeovers are battles. Marketing is warfare. This language was not invented by journalists to brighten up dull business copy. It's the way people actually talk and think.

"You gotta draw blood to win," says an advertisement in our paper for a conference entitled "Retail on the Cutting Edge." "You need a battle plan to thrive."

So whatever happened to empowerment, team-building, and all that softer, relationship-oriented [Type B] stuff that every manager must take courses in these days and that women are alleged to be so good at? That stuff has its place. Its place is to empower you to beat your enemies to a pulp.

"What do you do when your competitor's drowning? Get a live hose and stick it in his mouth," said Ray Kroc, the founder of McDonald's. If you find that attitude congenial, you are CEO material. If, in addition, you are willing to devote your heart, mind, soul and your every waking moment to the battle, you are CEO material. Balance? That's for wimps.

Consider the parallel careers of Douglas Ivester and Brenda Barnes, two extremely smart people in that most capitalist of businesses, soft drinks. Mr. Ivester has worked his whole life for Coke. Ms. Barnes has worked her whole life for Pepsi.

Mr. Ivester was rewarded this week with the CEO job at Coke, where he takes over from the legendary Roberto Goizueta. He is described as a pugnacious, brutally competitive [Type A] workaholic. During a keynote speech to the soft-drink industry a few years ago, he quoted his hero Ray Kroc, and brandished a garden hose to show he meant it. "I want your customers. I want your space on the shelves. I want your space of the consumer's stomach," he told the audience, who applauded wildly. In the past little while he has spent 200 days on the road in 46 different countries. "His work is his play," says a friend, or, more accurately, a business associate. Mr. Ivester doesn't really have time for friends.

Brenda Barnes has also been in the news. As head of Pepsi's North American beverage business, she was one of the world's top-ranking women in business. Her life, too, was marked by constant travel and long separations from her husband and three kids. After 22 years of gruelling hours and missed birthdays, Ms. Barnes realized her life was miserable and decided to call it quits, even though the company was grooming her for higher things. The main difference between her conditions of work and Mr. Ivester's is that he enjoys them.

It's silly to imagine that life at the top will change soon. Not all chief executives are as nasty as Mr. Ivester, but they do all have an insatiable drive for dominance, and they are all consumed by their work. That is why the shareholders pay them extremely handsomely: they pay them to win.

Human males are aggressive, hierarchical and territorial. That so many of them channel their energies into selling Coke, instead of bashing each other over the head with clubs, is remarkable testimony to the progress of civilization. Human females have other strengths. They know, for example, that Coke isn't It. They know that channeling all your life's energies into selling sweetened fizzy water is, on some level, ludicrous. That's the main reason why neither Ms. Barnes nor I will ever be CEO. (p. D7)

REFERENCES

American Psychiatric Association. (1994). *Diagnostic and statistical manual of mental disorders. Fourth edition. DMS-IV* Washington, DC: American Psychiatric Association.

Baltrusch, H. J. F., Stangel, W., & Waltz, M. E. (1988). Cancer from the biobehavioral perspective: The Type C pattern. *Activas Nervosa Superior*, 30, 18–20.

Bortner, R. W., & Rosenman, R. H. (1967). The measurement of pattern A behavior. *Journal of Chronic Disorders*, 20, 525–533.

Byrne, D. G., Rosenman, R. H., Schiller, E., & Chesney, M. A. (1985). Consistency and validation among instruments purporting to measure the Type A behavior pattern. *Psychosomatic Medicine*, 47, 242–259.

Chesney, M. A., & Rosenman, R. H. (1983). Specificity in stress models: Examples drawn from Type A behavior. In C. L. Cooper (Ed.), *Stress research*. New York: John Wiley & Sons, pp. 21–34.

Cooper, C. L., & Marshall, J. (1976). Occupational sources of stress: A review of the literature relating to coronary heart disease and mental ill health. *Journal of Occupational Psychology*, 49, 11–28.

Eysenck, H. J. (1985). Personality, cancer and cardiovascular disease: A causal analysis. *Personality and Individual Differences*, 5, 535–557.

Friedman, H. S., & Booth-Kewley, S. (1987). Personality, Type A behavior and cardiovascular disease: The role of emotional expression. *Journal of Personality and Social Psychology*, 53, 783–792.

Friedman, H. S., & Rosenman, R. H. (1974). *Type A behavior and your heart*. New York: Alfred A. Knopf.

Friedman, H. S., & VandenBos, G. R. (1992). Disease-prone and self-healing personalities. *Hospital and Community Psychiatry*, 43, 1177–1179.

Gray, A., Jackson, D. N., & Howard, J. H. (1989). Validation of the survey of work styles: A profile measure of the Type A behaviour pattern. *Journal of Clinical Epidemiology*, 42, 209–216.

Grossarth-Maticek, R., & Eysenck, H. J. (1990). Personality, stress and disease: Description and validation of a new inventory. *Psychological Reports*, 66, 355–373.

Grossarth-Maticek, R., & Eysenck, H. J. (1991). Creative novation behaviour therapy as a prophylactic treatment for cancer and coronary heart disease: Part I—Description of treatment. *Behavioral Research Therapy*, 29, 1–16.

Haynes, S., Feinleib, M., Levine, S., Scotch, N., & Kannel, W. (1978). The relationship of psychosocial factors to coronary heart disease in the Framingham Study, II: Prevalence of coronary heart disease. *American Journal of Epidemiology*, 107, 384–402.

Jenkins, C., Rosenman, R., & Zyzanski, S. (1974). Prediction of clinical coronary heart disease by a test for the coronary-prone behavior pattern. *New England Journal of Medicine*, 290, 1271–1275.

Jenkins, C. D. (1976). Recent evidence supporting psychological and social risk factors for coronary disease: Part II. *New England Journal of Medicine*, 294, 1033–1038.

Kets De Vries, M. F. R. (1993). *Leaders, fools, and imposters*. San Francisco: Jossey-Bass, pp. 29–33.

Leigh, D., Pare, C. M. B., & Marks, J. (1977). *A concise encyclopedia of psychiatry*. Lancaster, U.K.: M.T.P. Press.

Moss, G. E., Dielman, T. E., Campanelli, P. C., Leech, S. L., Harian, W. R., Von Harrison, R., & Horvath, W. J. (1986). Demographic correlates of 51 assessments of Type A behavior. *Psychosomatic Medicine*, 48, 564–574.

Price, V. A. (1982). What is Type A? A cognitive social learning model. *Journal of Occupational Behavior*, 3, 109–129.

Rosenman, R. H., Friedman, M., Straus, R., Wurm, M., Kositchek, R., Hahn, W., & Werthessen, N. T. (1964). A predictive study of coronary heart disease. *Journal of the American Medical Association*, 189, 15–22.

Schell, B. H., & DeLuca, V. M. (1991). Task-achievement, obsessive-compulsive, Type A traits, and job satisfaction of professionals in public practice accounting. *Psychological Reports*, 69, 611–630.

Smith, T. W., & Leon, A. S. (1992). *Coronary heart disease: A behavioral perspective*. Champaign, IL: Research Press.

Stinson, M. (1997). Extendicare extends its reach beyond nursing homes. *The Globe and Mail*, November 18, p. B20.

Tang, T. L.-P. (1986). Effects of Type A personality on task labels (work vs. leisure) on task preference. *Journal of Leisure Research*, 18, 1–11.

Thoreson, C. E., & Low, K. G. (1990). Women and Type A behavior pattern: Review and commentary. In M. J. Strube (Ed.), Type A behavior. [Special Issue]. *Journal of Social Behavior and Personality*, 5, 117–133.

Thurman, C. W. (1984). Cognitive-behavioral interventions with Type A faculty. *The Personnel and Guidance Journal*, 62, 358–362.

Wente, M. (1997). Why I'll never be CEO. *The Globe and Mail*, October 25, p. D7.

Westra, H. A., & Kuiper, N. A. (1992). Type A irrational cognitions and situational factors relating to stress. *Journal of Research in Personality*, 26, 1–20.

Widiger, T. A., Frances, A., Spitzer, R. L., & Williams, J. B. W. (1988). The DSM-III-R personality disorders: An overview. *American Journal of Psychiatry*, 145, 786–795.

CHAPTER 5

The Path to Corporate Success: Normal Moods and Mood Disorders Accompanying Those Who Have Made the Climb to the Top

> Worshipping a dictator is such a pain in the ass. It wouldn't be so bad if it was merely a matter of dancing upside down on your head. With practice anyone could learn to do that. The real problem is having no way of knowing from one day to another, from one minute to the next, just what is up and what is down.
>
> —C. Achebe (1987)

A CASE IN POINT (LEVINSON, SABBATH, & CONNOR 1992)

When asked to consult with a company whose CEO's erratic, impulsive behavior threatened to destroy the firm, consultants Harry Levinson, PhD (L), Joseph Sabbath, MD (S), and Jeffrey Connor, PhD (C) had to make a differential diagnosis of the CEO and respond to his behavior based on that assessment. Developing a relationship that was immune to his attacks enabled the consultants to structure recommendations that recognized his talents and opened avenues for organizational survival and the CEO's continued growth. The following case speaks to the usefulness of psychological theory in managing "difficult people" problems, especially when they involve corporate leaders.

The director of human resources of a high-tech company in a Chicago suburb called L to ask for consultation on behalf of her chief executive. She said that he was concerned because their recent turnover of upper middle-management and officers was 35% higher than their norm. The president of the company had been a participant in an executive seminar conducted by the senior author some years before, and had recommended to him that he call for consultation. The call was precipitated by the unexpected loss of another senior officer.

S and C accompanied L to the meeting in the office of the chief executive, G. The office was in a three-building corporate complex, to which admission was controlled by security agents, because some of the company's work had to do with national defense. G welcomed us to his second floor office. He was a tall, athletically built, casually dressed 55-year-old man. His large office was decorated with a variety of paintings, sculpture, prints, and plants, as well as samples of the company's products. A large emblem of his military service decorated the wall behind him.

G sat behind an outsized desk. We three sat in front of the desk: L in the center, S on the left, and C on the right. G put his stockinged feet up on the desk and proceeded to address us rapidly, including liberal quotations and metaphors, frequently in military language with such terms as "triage," "troops," and "trenches." From time to time, he would offer a homily; for example, "If you want to eat raisins, you have to spit out the seeds." He repetitively offered coffee from what seemed to be an inexhaustible pot.

G launched into a self-description:

I am an aggressive and abrasive person. I am an entrepreneur. I have been diagnosed as Manic-Depressive and, up till a few years ago, took lithium. I have been seeing a psychiatrist, and am not taking any medication now. You can call him if you want to. I've changed; I have learned a lot. My family made money illegally. I got into trouble as a kid. In those days, I didn't know what the truth was, but later on found people along the way that I admired and changed my mind. Two years ago, I separated from my wife. Now I want to know the truth about what's going on in my company. Whatever it is, I want to know, and want the people here to know it. You can interview whoever you want, as many as you want, including any other consultants.

G indicated in his discourse that his father had been arrested many times and that he had been reared in a difficult environment. He did not specify what his own brushes with the law had been, except to say that he had once been arrested as a suspect in a murder he did not commit and was released. He had overcome the handicaps of his upbringing to achieve a graduate degree. He had seen not one, but two psychiatrists, and a clinically trained management consultant.

L told him that S and C would conduct a series of one-to-two-hour interviews with people who would represent a cross section of the staff from the president down, including a few of the officers who had left the company, as well as some members of the Board of directors. The purpose of the study, namely to try to understand the reasons for the high turnover, would be explained to each of the executives, managers, and employees before each interview. They would be told that the interviews were voluntary and confidential, and that a summary would subsequently be prepared for G. G agreed.

Diagnostic Hypotheses

We were concerned in our post-meeting discussion with how we should deal with G. We were impressed in our first meeting with the Hypomanic, Paranoid, and Narcissistic features in his self-description, his denigrating view of others, and the clues to omnipotent strivings that we inferred between the lines of his comments. The risk was high that he might abort our efforts, or impulsively intrude into our work, or reject us altogether. If he were indeed in a Manic phase and no longer taking lithium, there might well be no holding him down, and there was the risk that the ultimate feedback would precipitate the Depressive aspects of his cycle. If the Paranoid features were strong enough, then he might experience our feedback report as an attack and perceive us as enemies who were out to destroy him. The Narcissistic features indicated that we must be unusually careful to support his self-image.

Clearly, he was not Psychotic. Though he could be harsh to people, as he himself told us, and he had an adolescent record as an Antisocial person (primarily stealing), he was not a classically Antisocial personality. In fact, he had built this successful organization over 15 years, which was now doing $25 million in sales. He seemed to have considerable ego strength, despite his limited anxiety tolerance and impulse control. Although the elements of omnipotent striving and devaluation of others are prominent features of the Borderline personality, he seemed, in the first interview, at least, to be able to be warm and concerned and able to relate to some people on a long-term basis. He seemed closer to the Narcissistic personality.

Ours was not to be a therapeutic intervention. We were not here to treat G. Yet, clinical insights would be important both to understand what was happening in the organization, particularly, as was now apparent, as a product of G's personality, and what could be done about it. . . .

Expressive psychotherapy was clearly out of the question; nor could we resolve his managerial problems by recommending that he take his lithium again, although that might well be indicated. Given the nature of his behavior, we would have to maintain a firm, consistent reality boundary and maximize the positive transference by demonstrating that we had our own strength and were not frightened of him. As Kernberg suggests, our supportive effort would require helping him recognize the boundaries of reality and understanding the effects of his behavior without judging him or moralizing about them. Kernberg points out that the therapist must "tactfully, yet consistently, confront the patient with how he contributes to his own difficulties. . . ."

The Process Joined

When G himself was scheduled for an individual interview with S, he sent a message through his secretary that he was "tied up" and did not know when he would be available. S, he said, should interview some of the other people. His secretary mentioned in an aside that he had remarked that he did not like the idea of spending two hours in an interview. By this time, he himself had already abruptly called several of his top officers out of their interviews with S and C without explanation. S decided to go to his office anyway.

S asked G's secretary to call him at his meeting. G was incensed that S had called and said, "Listen, my friend, I have the right to change the time when I want to. I am speaking to someone about an acquisition, and I'll be tied up for an hour or so." S asked what other time could be arranged. G replied, "Well, maybe I'll see you tomorrow or next week." S confronted him with his prior remark about being finished in an hour and said that he would be waiting for him in his office. After a long pause, G said, "Okay, around 11:00 A.M."

G arrived exactly at 11:00 with eyes blazing. His first remark was, "You've got one hell of a nerve interrupting me. I was arranging to acquire this company in the South." S responded that we had an appointment and had work to do. G replied, "Don't give me that bullshit—all right now, come into the office. Don't worry, you'll get paid for your time. I resent intensely being interrupted. Sit down, and I'm taking five."

After returning from his private bathroom . . . G was thanked by S for the arrangements he had made and for the excellent cooperation on the part of the employees, executives, and managers. S reported that they had been very helpful in the consultation so far. G settled down quickly, saying, "Okay." He then started to ramble about these problems:

1. Because of the growth of the company, he cannot now know and communicate with everyone. "It is no longer like a family."
2. Some of his people are afraid of him. He does not know why. Some cower and whimper. He does not like that; he feels they must misunderstand or not hear correctly; some of his officers do not hear. He added, "I know I fire people on the spot, but I call things as I see them. Some people are serfs; they should only be emptying wastebaskets."
3. He did not want his company to grow bigger as long as people were troubled and problems were unresolved. "I've been through a lot myself, but now have never felt stronger or better."
4. "I want a fit between myself and the staff and the organization."
5. "I want to choose people who are loyal. How can we do that? Genetic engineering, maybe. There are 48 chromosomes; maybe we can splice a few good ones." He referred to one of the vice-presidents who left as "a consummate paranoid."

During the interview there was a telephone interruption, after which G said, "I chewed that guy's ass out so hard he won't be able to sit down for a week." The interview ended with his stating that he hoped the consultants would not just be scribes, and that he would be told something that would be of use.

Meeting Afterthoughts

This interview with G confirmed our diagnostic hypothesis that we should maintain ego boundaries in a supportive context and see the Paranoid features as typical of those more likely to be found in a Narcissistic character disorder. Despite the evidence for sadistic control and for the projection of rage, there was evidence of some soft, sentimental, and tender feelings, as reflected in his yearning for a family. His insistence on high standards of production, on orderliness, precision, clarity, and control are consistent with the product and the need to maintain exacting production and clean work areas. That these obsessive-compulsive features reflect severe unresolved sadism and controlling, vengeful behavior that drives people away seemed to be secondary to the basic Narcissism.

G's History

G had let everyone in the company know about his background, that he had grown up in a deprived environment. His parents separated early, his father was a gambler, and his mother was uninterested in him. He was reared by relatives, and in his high school years got into trouble with the law for stealing from supermarkets. He entered military service by lying about his age and then worked his way through college. During the summers of his college years, he became a research assistant to a professor with whom he is still close. He then became a salesman for a chemical company from which he was fired because he "didn't do well in a structured environment." He and two others then formed the present company in 1962. By 1972, there were 70 employees and the company was striving for $3 million to $4 million in sales.

One informant reported that the management group would come in on a Sunday, throw a case of beer on the counter, and, with G in stockinged feet, would talk about things. G became the leader, as the other two pulled back, and was made president in 1968. He is reported to have a good deal of concern about the families of others. He himself married in 1965. Subsequently, he and his wife had four children. Through 1978 the company was run by consensus. Eight people decided everything.

The research department evolved a new device which had a wide range of potential uses. It became an instant success and a new plant had to be found for production. The company began to expand at the rate of 70% a year and was cited in a magazine as one of the 100 fastest growing companies in America. It attracted a wide variety of young, ambitious engineers.

About this time (1981), G's mood swings became a concern for his family and colleagues. He agreed to see a psychiatrist and was put on lithium.

Serious business problems then began to develop. The new plant, which was several hundred miles away from the present headquarters, had production and labor problems, and could not keep up with the demand. It had to be sold to a conglomerate. Unfortunately, a number of key personnel who had been involved in that project went with the division. Apparently, that was a significant psychological loss for G. He was also in the process of separating from his wife.

The rate of growth fell from 70% to 20%. The generous price paid by the acquiring corporation was insufficient to support the number of ambitious plans that G had initiated impulsively. He embarked on rapid expansion by recruiting engineers and manufacturing personnel, and by acquiring competitors. When people left his organization and tried to compete with him, he sued them for patent infringement, so that neither they nor smaller competitors dared to compete. He built two new buildings, bought a company airplane, and became involved in a variety of real estate deals. For three years, he would not leave his office building at night, sleeping during the day and working at night during the period of extended growth.

He saw another psychiatrist who stopped his lithium. He continued to dress informally in Pendleton shirts and Levis. His mood swings moderated. His goals were to grow 20% to 30% a year and to reach $100 million in sales with a pretax profit of 20%. He met another woman and then began to take better care of himself. He remarried in 1984.

He agreed to his Board's request that he hire a chief operating officer. Nevertheless, the strain on the company increased to the point where employees left in large numbers and morale was poor. The Board and the stockholders felt that they had bet on a wild man and were willing to ride with him until, in 1984, for the first time, the company failed to show a profit. G had said that his goals were to make his company a fun place and to make money. Neither was happening. Several top officers left and it was at this time that he was asked to consider consultation.

What Other Organizational Members Said about G (excerpts)

G is not willing to accept the fact that he is not a manager. He is task-oriented, not goal-oriented. He wants immediate solutions. If someone does a snow job on him, he will change his mind. That means there is a constantly moving set of priorities. He is impulsive, a one-man company, a gunfighter. He goes off at the least sign of a challenge.

When his officers are away, he finds things are wrong, and then justifies his intervention. He undercuts his officers' authorities, therefore, and puts them in a bad light with their subordinates. The top management group is seen as performing on demand and loyal to him, but some think that they have no experience running anything. Despite working 50 to 60 hours a week, the responsibilities of managers are not clear and that contributes to the high turnover.

The climate is abrasive and the casualties are high. Said one, "When he gets upset, he takes no prisoners." At a meeting, he can go from being the kindest person to being the cruelest. He can call people names and fire them on the spot. One former employee said, "G was nice to me when I was ill, then later he fired me without an explanation. . . . He has a shit list; he chews people out in front of others. He makes you feel guilty if you take a vacation. He will call you at any hour of the night and has nighttime and early morning meetings. It is better to admit a mistake. He thinks people are stupid and says so. If you walk slowly, it indicates to him that you think slowly. Everything is blame; no one wants to be held responsible for not achieving, not pleasing G. You never know when you are doing good, only when you're not doing good. Even when you are told you are doing well, you get only a token raise."

Few people can go toe to toe with him. For many it is not worth the fight, so issues are not dealt with. He categorizes people into tigers and turkeys. His attitude is, "What did you do for me this week?" Alternatively, "If you don't like it here, leave. You're lucky to have a job."

Other informants complain: when they talk with him, they will always come away feeling they are wrong. He decides without facts that the other person is wrong. He publicly excoriated a consultant who had been called in to speak to the group on better communications. He looks for signs of weakness in people, signs of uncertainty and fear. He believes black and white about people: they are good or no good. People are accused of "masturbating in the corner" or "playing with themselves." He is demoralizing and degrading. If you make the least mistake, he shakes you like a tiger—turns you into a wet rag. Once a person's name is paged over the intercom, there is a fear of what he is going to be subjected to. Some people see his car in the lot and feel intimidated.

Some believe he wants to be Number One because it is good for him, not for the company. They report he buys out competitors, trying to secure 100% of the market share, even though after having 80%, it is too expensive to try to get more. They say, he has a need for something successful. The company is his own baby. *He wants to do so much, so it will allow him time to do things for society*. It is something he does not share. [emphasis mine]

They see him as fierce and fearless in turning on the opposition and getting to the heart of a matter. Regardless of how painful it is, he exposes people. They say, he will relentlessly track you down if you are disloyal. He spent hundreds of thousands of dollars trying to sue someone who left the company for another similar type of organization. In his fights with other people and customers, he goes through things from the sewer to the heavens. He is concerned about failure. He wants odds less than zero. For him, failure is not an option.

But, they add, he has no tolerance for training people, for building them from within, or developing a management organization. Women are viewed as dumb broads who have no place in management.

What are the consequences? Costs are out of control. There is no organized market research, for G has no tolerance for numbers and details. It is a good place for confident, competent, iconoclastic people. "You do things here to please. You modify a forecast or try to read through G's bluster. You talk about things here that are safe: topics like baseball. In order to stay, you become invaluable or adoring. Everyone is busy covering themselves instead of using energy to brainstorm for the common good. Headhunters refuse to send people here anymore. You need a thick skin to survive. We do a lot of things three or four times over."

The interviewees use these words to describe G: "He's wacko." "He's like a time bomb." "Certifiably crazy." "This place is run by a wild man." "He is a wild-assed entrepreneur." "He lacks control." "He's sensitive to any allusions to his integrity because of his background."

INTRODUCTION

Harry Langner and G seem to be corporate leaders who, despite the fact that one wears Armani suits, and the other wears Levis, are, in many ways, "cut from the same cloth." Both are described by the consultants who were called in to deal with them as highly self-centered and narcissistic workaholics who work incessantly and who expect others under their control to do the same. At times, they are paranoid in their dealings with others, are antisocial in the sense that their rage is projected onto others in the workplace, are inconsistent in their treatment of organizational members, and are particularly sensitive about rejection and failure. Maybe because we are provided with more information on G than on Harry, G presented as a somewhat more severe and disease-prone case. Yet, despite these shortcomings, one thing became abundantly clear about Harry Langner and G: both are go-getters. Failure, in terms of business deals, seemed not to be an acceptable outcome for either of them.

How many Harrys and Gs are walking about present-day corporate hallways? While hardly any estimates exist regarding the prevalence of narcissists, manic-depressives, and antisocial personalities within the corporate leader population, recently, a number of popular media reports (Tillson 1996; Mc Farland 1996) have suggested that the numbers may actually be larger than most adults would think.

While Chapter 4 explored some mental and physiological costs of the psychoneurotic Type A and Type C behavioral patterns, in particular, Chapter 5 explores more fully the personal and organizational costs (and, in some cases, benefits) affiliated with narcissicim, mood disorders, and antisocial personality. Besides defining these terms and giving their etiology, references to the prevalences of these disorders in the corporate leader population as well as in the general population are offered. What becomes obvious at the end of this discussion is that all three of the just-cited personality and mood disorders involve some element of "controlled rage," and all three, for a variety of reasons, meet with resistance to professional interventions that are aimed at getting clients back on the self-healing path.

Before getting into the details on these three disorders, a return to an overview of the personality and the mood disorders is in order.

AN OVERVIEW OF THE PERSONALITY AND THE MOOD DISORDERS

Details on the Personality Disorders

As noted in Chapter 4, the personality disorders are wide-ranging and generally encompass 10 disorders (Leigh, Pare, and Marks 1977, p. 629). The definitions and the prevalence rates for the general population (if known) (American Psychiatric Association 1994) follow. The disorders identified as likely occurring in G, in varying degrees, are described first.

1. *Narcissistic Personality Disorder*: a pattern of grandiosity, need for admiration, and lack of empathy (prevalence 2–16 percent in the clinical population and less than 1 percent in the general population).

2. *Antisocial Personality Disorder*: a pattern of disregard for, and violation of, the rights of others (prevalence 3 percent in males and 1 percent in females in community samples).

3. *Paranoid Personality Disorder*: a pattern of distrust and suspiciousness such that others' motives are interpreted as malevolent (0.5 percent–2.5 percent prevalence in the general population).

4. *Borderline Personality Disorder*: a pattern of instability in interpersonal relationships, self-image, and affects, with marked impulsivity (prevalence 2 percent in the general population, but prevalence ranges from 30 percent to 60 percent among clinical populations with other co-occurring personality disorders).

5. *Obsessive-Compulsive Personality Disorder*: a pattern of preoccupation with orderliness, perfectionism, and control (prevalence 1 percent in community samples).

6. *Schizoid Personality Disorder*: a pattern of detachment from social relationships and a restricted range of emotional expression (prevalence unknown).

7. *Schizotypal Personality Disorder*: a pattern of acute discomfort in close relationships, cognitive or perceptual distortions, and eccentricities of behavior (3 percent prevalence in the general population).

8. *Histrionic Personality Disorder*: a pattern of excessive emotionality and attention-seeking (prevalence 2–3 percent in community samples).

9. *Avoidant Personality Disorder*: a pattern of social inhibition, feelings of inadequacy, and hypersensitivity to negative evaluation (prevalence 0.5–1 percent in the community population).

10. *Dependent Personality Disorder*: a pattern of submissive and clinging behavior related to an excessive need to be taken care of (actual prevalence unknown but among the most frequently reported of personality disorders in mental health clinics).

The personality disorders have been further grouped by mental health experts into the following three clusters, based on descriptive similarities (American Psychiatric Association 1994, pp. 629–630):

- Cluster A includes the paranoid, the schizoid, and the schizotypal personality disorders. Working adults with these disorders often appear to others to be "odd" or "eccentric."

- Cluster B, of particular interest to us regarding corporate leaders, includes the antisocial, the borderline, the histrionic, and the narcissistic personality disorders. Working adults with these disorders often appear to be dramatic, overly emotional, easily angered, or erratic. In their attempts to release anger, the narcissistic and the antisocial types are apt to lash out at others through verbal and physical aggression, while the borderline types are apt to lash out at themselves through self-mutilation and threats or attempts of suicide. Also, while the antisocial personality disorder is more common in men than in women, the borderline, the histrionic, and the dependent personality disorders are more common in women.

- Cluster C includes the avoidant, the dependent, and the obsessive-compulsive personality disorders. Working adults and corporate leaders with these disorders often appear to be "anxious" or "fearful."

On a final note regarding personality disorders and clustering, it should be recognized that this three-pronged system, although useful in some research and applied situations, has limitations and has not been consistently validated. Moreover, it needs to be emphasized, as is obvious in the cases of Harry Langner and G, that it is not uncommon for several of the disorders from the clusters to co-occur. The difficulty for many clinicians, as was obvious from the quotes of the consultants called in to help G and his organization, is which disorder to attend to first in dealing with such complex people problems. When mood disorders present at the same time, as was the case with G, the problem becomes especially complex.

Details on the Mood Disorders

The bipolar I and bipolar II mood disorders have variations along the manic and the depressive episode theme. As noted in Chapter 4, the unipolar label is generally reserved for adults suffering from depressive episodes without a history of mania, whereas the bipolar label is reserved for adults suffering from both manic and depressive episodes. In the bipolar I disorders, manic episodes prevail, whereas in the bipolar II disorders, depressive episodes prevail.

While several mania-related types are recognized (Leigh, Pare, and Marks 1977, p. 226), manic episodes are characterized, in varying degrees, by elated and unstable mood, flight of ideas, and increased psychomotor activity. In severe cases of manic episodes, clouding of consciousness and disorientation may occur, as well as hallucinations and delusions. However, the latter are transitory, occur at the height of the illness, and do not have the ominous significance of the more firmly held delusions or persistent hallucinations occurring in schizophrenia. Manic episodes almost always have a rapid onset measured in days or weeks and are frequently preceded by, or are followed by, depressive episodes—thus earning the bipolar label.

Depressive episodes consist of a depressive mood with some or all of a number of other symptoms (Leigh, Pare, and Marks 1977, p. 117): insomnia, weight loss, inability to concentrate, suicidal ideation, and so on. Depressive illness in working adults is common, ranking close behind CHD as one of the major causes of serious morbidity. As noted in Chapter 2, depressions vary widely in their symptomology, in their course, and in their response to treatment, and although numerous attempts by mental health experts have been made to classify them, none of the many suggested schemata have won universal acceptance. Experts, as noted, often claim that there are two types of depression: the endogenous type, which is found in manic-depressive disorder, and the neurotic or reactive or exogenous type, which is primarily stressor-related.

The definitions for the six classifications of the mood disorders based on the bipolar I and bipolar II theme are given here (American Psychiatric Association 1994). They are further defined in Chapter 9.

1. *Negligible bipolar I, bipolar II, or likely bipolar I and II tendency*: Defined as negligible behavioral tendencies relating to Bipolar I and Bipolar II and being of insufficient number, severity, pervasiveness, or duration to meet full criteria for a Manic or a Depressive Episode.

2. *Bipolar I, hypomanic tendency*: Defined as a distinct period of abnormally and persistently elevated, expansive, or irritable mood and behavior that lasts *at least 4 days*. A hypomanic episode typically begins suddenly, with a rapid escalation of symptoms within a day or two. Symptoms include grandiosity, a decreased need for sleep, an increased need for goal-directed or creative output, and an excessive involvement in "high-risk" pleasurable activities. Episodes may last for several weeks to months and are usually more abrupt in onset and briefer than Major Depressive Episodes. The Manic or Depressive phases are not severe enough to cause marked social or occupational functioning. (pp. 335–338)

3. *Bipolar I, manic tendency*: Defined by a distinct period of an abnormally and persistently elevated, expansive, or irritable mood and behavior. This period of abnormal mood and behavior must last *at least 1 week* and must be accompanied by at least three additional symptoms from a list that includes inflated self-esteem or grandiosity, decreased need for sleep, pressure of speech, etc. Manic Episodes begin suddenly, with rapid escalation of symptoms over a few days. Frequently, Manic Episodes occur following psychosocial stressors. The episodes usually last from a few weeks to several months and are briefer and end more abruptly than Major Depressive Episodes. In many instances (50%–60%), a Major Depressive Episode immediately precedes or immediately follows a Manic Episode. (pp. 328–332)

4. *Bipolar I, mixed episode tendency*: Characterized by a period of time lasting *at least 1 week* in which the mood and behavior criteria are met both for a Manic Episode *and* for a Major Depressive Episode *nearly every day*. The individual experiences rapidly alternating moods (sadness, irritability, euphoria) accompanied by symptoms of a Manic Episode and a Major Depressive Episode. Mixed Episodes can evolve from a Manic Episode or from a Major Depressive Episode or may arise *de novo*. Mixed Episodes may last weeks to several months and may remit to a period with few or no symptoms or evolve into a Major Depressive Episode. (pp. 333–335)

5. *Bipolar II, major depression tendency*: Defined as a period of *at least 2 weeks* during which there is either depressed mood or the loss of interest or pleasure in nearly all activities. The individual must also experience at least four additional symptoms drawn from a list that includes changes in appetite or weight, sleep, and psychomotor activity; decreased energy; difficulty thinking; or recurrent thoughts of death or suicidal ideation. *To count toward a Major Depressive Episode, a symptom must either be newly present or must have worsened compared with the person's pre-episode status. The symptoms must persist for most of the day, nearly every day, for at least 2 consecutive weeks.* Symptoms of a Major Depressive Episode usually develop over days to weeks. The duration of a Major Depressive Episode is variable, with untreated episodes lasting 6 months or longer. Mania, when it does present, is of the Hypomanic order. In the majority of cases, there is a complete remission of symptoms, and functioning returns to the premorbid level. (pp. 320–327)

6. *Cyclothymic disorder*: Defined as a chronic, fluctuating mood disturbance involving numerous periods of hypomanic symptoms and numerous periods of depressive symptoms. The hypomanic symptoms are insufficient to meet full criteria for a Manic Episode, and the depressive symptoms are insufficient to meet full criteria for a Major Depressive Episode. *During the 2-year period, any symptom-free intervals last no longer than 2 months.* The description is made only if the 2-year period of cyclothymic symptoms is free of Major Depressive, Manic, or Mixed Episodes. (pp. 363–366)

The lifetime prevalence of bipolar I disorder, characterized by one or more manic episodes or mixed episodes, has varied from 0.4 percent to 1.6 percent in community samples (American Psychiatric Association 1994), with the prevalence rate for North America being close to 1 percent (Tillson 1996). The lifetime prevalence of bipolar II disorder, characterized by one or more major depressive episodes and at least one hypomanic episode, is approximately 0.5 percent in community samples (American Psychiatric Association 1994). The lifetime prevalence of cyclothymic disorder, characterized by numerous periods of hypomanic symptoms and numerous periods of depressive symptoms, has varied from 0.4 percent to 1 percent in community samples (American Psychiatric Association 1994).

Considering this variety of mood disorders, even trained clinicians and psychiatrists maintain that the job of diagnosis in clients does not come easily (Winokur, Clayton, & Reich 1969). The diagnostic tool often used for assessing mood disorders is an interview guide developed by Endicott and Spitzer (1978) for trained clinicians. Called the Schedule for Affective Disorders and Schizophrenia (SADS) and employing a face-to-face interview, along with the client's medical history, it comes in three versions: the regular version (SADS), the lifetime version (SADS-L), and the version for measuring change in clients (SADS-C).

WHY NARCISSISM IS THOUGHT TO BE COMMON AMONG CORPORATE AND POLITICAL LEADERS

Narcissism Defined

Various degrees of narcissism, manifested by grandiosity and extreme self-centeredness, appear to be more common in powerful people than in the commonfolk (Dart 1998), say the experts, where the prevalence of significant degrees of this trait appears to be less than 1 percent of the general population. Narcissistic traits may be particularly common in adolescence as compared to other life stages, but its occurrence does not necessarily indicate that the adolescent will go on to have narcissistic personality disorder. During middle life, adults with narcissistic personality disorder seem to have special difficulties adjusting to the onset of physical and occupational limitations inherent in the aging process. Of those diagnosed with narcissistic personality disorder, 50–75 percent are male (American Psychiatric Association 1994, p. 660).

Working adults and corporate leaders (like Langner and G) with high degrees of narcissism not only have a grandiose sense of self-importance but routinely overestimate their abilities, outwardly appearing to be boastful and pretentious (American Psychiatric Association 1994, p. 658). Though they may blithely assume that others attribute the same value to their efforts, narcissists are often surprised when the praise that they expect and feel that they deserve is not forthcoming from others. Moreover, narcissists are often preoccupied with fantasies of unlimited success, power, brilliance, beauty, and ideal love—as was G. Said one of G's organizational members:

Some believe he wants to be Number One because it is good for him, not for the company. They report he buys out competitors, trying to secure 100% of the market share, even though after having 80%, it is too expensive to try to get more. They say, he has a need for something successful. The company is his own baby.

Narcissists require excessive admiration, in large part, because their self-esteem is very fragile (American Psychiatric Association 1994, p. 659). Thus, they are preoccupied with how well they are doing and how favorably they are regarded by others. Like G, they expect to be catered to and are puzzled or furious when this does not happen. For example, they may assume that they do not have to wait in line and that their priorities are so important that others should defer to them. Like G, they get easily irritated when others fail to assist them in their very important work.

Narcissists expect to be given whatever they want or feel they need, no matter what it might mean to others (American Psychiatric Association 1994, p. 659). For example, like G, they may expect great dedication from others and may overwork them without regard for the impact that their own workaholism has on others' lives. Said one organizational member about G: "He categorizes people into tigers and turkeys. His attitude is, 'What did you do for me this week?' Alternatively, 'If you don't like it here, leave. You're lucky to have a job.' "

Narcissists like G generally have a lack of empathy; they have difficulty recognizing the desires, subjective experiences, and feelings of others (American Psychiatric Association 1994, p. 659). Not only are they fixated on their own welfare and well-being, but they are often contemptuous and impatient when others talk about their problems and concerns. Often, they are oblivious to the hurt their remarks or behaviors may inflict on the suffering or the needy. Moreover, like G, when they recognize the needs of others, they often view them disparagingly as signs of weakness or vulnerability. Said one organizational member: "G was nice to me when I was ill, then later he fired me without an explanation."

Narcissists are often envious of others, but outwardly they state that others are envious of them. They may even begrudge others their successes or possessions, feeling that they—not the others—better deserve the desired achievements, admiration, or privileges (American Psychiatric Association 1994, p. 659). Not only do they harshly devalue the accomplishments of others, but narcissists like G are outspokenly rude in their comments about others who have accomplished. Said one organizational member about G:

He decides without facts that the other person is wrong. He publicly excoriated a consultant who had been called in to speak to the group on better communications. He looks for signs of weakness in people, signs of uncertainty and fear. He believes black and white about people: they are good or no good. People are accused of "masturbating in the corner" or "playing with themselves." He is demoralizing and degrading.

Narcissists are extremely sensitive to "injury" from criticism, failure, or rejection. Although they may not show it outwardly, criticism haunts narcissists, leaving them feeling humiliated, degraded, hollow, and empty. Frequently, they are known to react with disdain, rage, or defiant counterattack. Such outward aggressive manifestations may then lead to periods of social withdrawal or appearances of humility—desperate attempts to mask and protect their notions of grandiosity. Narcissists notoriously suffer from impaired interpersonal relations (American Psychiatric Association 1994, p. 659); unless they have their own projected drives for high achievement and fame, other adults having to work or live with narcissists often find the "going" very difficult. Said one organizational member about G:

> They see him as fierce and fearless in turning on the opposition and getting to the heart of a matter. Regardless of how painful it is, he exposes people. They say, he will relentlessly track you down if you are disloyal. He spent hundreds of thousands of dollars trying to sue someone who left the company for another similar type of organization. In his fights with other people and customers, he goes through things from the sewer to the heavens. He is concerned about failure. He wants odds less than zero. For him, failure is not an option.

Sustained periods of grandiosity in narcissists may be associated with hypomania, and narcissistic personality disorder, in particular, has been associated with anorexia nervosa, substance abuse (especially cocaine), and histrionic, borderline, antisocial, and paranoid personality disorders (American Psychiatric Association 1994, p. 660).

The Etiology of Narcissism

Most high-degree narcissists had early childhood problems, punctuated either by excessive affective attention by one parent (typically, the mother) and excessive affective inattention by the other parent (typically, the father) or, like G, by separation from both parents. Thus, mental health investigators, when exploring the pathogenesis of narcissistic disorders, tend to focus on the earliest phases of development in the child, particularly the separation-individuation process (Bleiberg 1988).

"Separation" refers to the child's growing capacity to experience an identity separate and distinct from his or her mother, that is, to develop a mental self-representation that has boundaries and is differentiated from the representation of "the object." The subjective experience of separation in a well-adjusted child would correspond to insights such as, "I am aware that mother and I are separate individuals, not one and the same."

"Individuation" defines the process of progressive structuralization of the child's internal world, encompassing the evolution of increasingly effective stress-coping and adaptive life skills. These capacities include ego functions such as reality testing, cognition, affect modulation, and drive regulation that guarantee autonomy from others in a "self-healing" way. The subjective experience of individuation in a well-adjusted child would correspond to insights such as, "I am aware that I can perform for myself the soothing, protective, equilibrium-maintaining functions my mother used to perform for me" (Bleiberg 1988, pp. 5–6).

Unlike their "self-healing" counterparts, narcissistic children do not reach appropriate degrees of cognitive and emotional autonomy. Instead, the normal resolution of the separation-individuation process is thwarted. In fact, such distortions can be correlated with specific patterns of mother-child codependent interactions in both borderline and narcissistic individuals.

For example, the mothers of future borderline adults tend to take pride in, and find gratification in, their infants' dependencies. In multiple ways, these mothers reward their childrens' passive-dependent, clinging behaviors. As the children display more active, exploratory, autonomous strivings, these mothers emotionally withdraw or punish their children in subtle or overt ways. The central message that they communicate to their infants is that "to grow up is to face the calamitous loss or withdrawal of maternal supplies, coupled with the related injunction that to avoid that calamity, the child must remain dependent, inadequate, symbiotic" (Bleiberg 1988, p. 8). In short, the overall developmental consequence for the future borderline adult is a "disease-prone" inhibition of both separation and individuation. Often, this unhealthy emotional dependency on another individual transfers to other "objects" in adulthood.

Future narcissistic adults face a "modified" maternal injunction. These children receive the consistent message that it is safe to go through the motions of growing up, but only if everything accomplished remains in relation to the maternal object. The overall effect of this form of mother–child interaction is "to inhibit or preclude separation, while allowing a significant degree of individuation to proceed, to desynchronize the two subprocesses, as it were (Bleiberg 1988, p. 8)." This cognitive and emotional "splitting" tends to transfer to other "objects" in adulthood. For example, with G, when organizational members could not tolerate his "overcontrol," he fired them impulsively.

Narcissistic children tend to have particular attributes that make them more likely to be selected for a special role in their families. Like Harry Langner, unusual beauty, precocious development, and uncommon gifts increase these children's odds of being invested with their parents' own narcissistic aspirations. Moreover, certain environmental conditions can exacerbate narcissistic presentations. Particular circumstances surrounding the child's birth, such as a death in the family or older parents' longing for a child, also endow the child with a special meaning to the family. The child's gifts and meaning are glorified by parents who perceive their child as a sort of appendage, a source of pride and gratification, the provider of the goodness and appreciation that they feel entitled to but have been denied. Thus, while inflating their child's omnipotence, the parents have a need to exercise tight control on their child's performance. The child is the so-called "apple" of the parents' eyes but may not fail or disappoint them, because their own self-esteem has become entangled with the child's magnificence. At the same time, these parents tend to ignore, ridicule, or reject the weak, frustrated, sad, or vulnerable aspects of their child. Because they are, in essence, troubled by their own dependency and vulnerability, the parents emotionally withdraw when their child is helpless or in pain. Thus, as a form of conditioning, the child's omnipotence and sense of uniqueness are fostered, and the "exhibitionistic display of competence" is rewarded. At the same time, vulnerability, weakness, pain, and frustration drive the parents away or elicit humiliation. In short, the narcissistic child's "self" soon reflects the shaping power of those injunctions. The child begins to experience as "me" those aspects of self that elicit the parents' delighted response, but he or she cannot integrate the range of more troubled feelings, needs, and self-images into the core sense of self that were linked with the parents' withdrawal (Bleiberg 1988, pp. 9–10).

Other factors lead to narcissism. Adopted children, like G, are often forced to assimilate the "injury" of their adoption. They can never ignore that their first parents gave them up, and future abandonment looms as a realistic possibility. Furthermore, obstacles that adopted children, like G, encounter prevent achieving an early reciprocal relationship with the adoptive mother. For example, the fact that adoptions are rarely finalized during the first months of a child's life can leave both the adoptive parents and the adopted child feeling forever "on probation," thus hampering the formation of a trusting, smoothly reciprocal, and self-healing attachment (Bleiberg 1988, p. 10).

In summary, this early vulnerability determines, initially, in older narcissistic children and, later, in narcissistic working adults and corporate leaders an inability to relinquish "omnipotence." The child's grandiosity becomes even more inflated as it joins forces with life's stressors. In an attempt to tenaciously cling to "omnipotence" as a means of developing self-worth, narcissists—young and old—tend to develop a host of defensive stress-coping cognitions and behaviors, including, but not limited to, protecting their self-boundaries from the intrusion of perceived "controlling" others bent on transforming the individual into their narcissistic extensions. Thus, grandiosity becomes the nucleus around which the narcissistic child and, later, the narcissistic adult or corporate leader establishes a sense of self. In short, the world becomes a stage, and other people at work and at home become an audience from which to extract the admiration that fuels self-esteem and that reinforces a precarious sense of self.

On a final note, experts believe that the greater the narcissistic adult's defensive need for omnipotence, the larger the discrepancy experienced by the individual between his or her inflated sense of self and the real strengths and competences that he or she has developed (Bleiberg 1988, pp. 10–11).

Political and Corporate Leader Narcissists

Besides G and Harry Langner, there have been narcissists of varying degrees of historical fame, including Richard Nixon and John Kennedy, who presented with periods of grandiosity and risk taking during their terms in office. Some investigators would even allege that they were risky in their personal and sexual activities. In the United States in 1998, a similar question arose regarding President Bill Clinton's narcissistic predispositions during and on his way to the top.

Experts recognize that some degree of narcissism, risk taking, and seemingly reckless actions are not uncommon traits among persons in power, from presidents, to star athletes, to corporate leaders. "It's all in the realm of understandable behaviour; undesirable behaviour, perhaps, but understandable behaviour," says Errol Leiffer (Dart 1998), a clinical psychologist and professor in the California Graduate School of Professional Psychology in Fresno, California. "As a male grows in status and power, he starts to feel he is entitled to whatever he wants, whenever he wants it," says Professor Leiffer. "The shame and humility and other things that limit the rest of us dissipate. Many men of power have that attitude. The rules are different when you are powerful."

To varying degrees, almost all politicians display narcissism, affirms Jack Vaeth (Dart 1998), attending psychiatrist at Shepard Pratt Health Systems, Baltimore. Narcissism, he adds, can be a key to ambition and success, but it can also be a personality disorder in the more extreme cases. Narcissism, emphasizes Dr. Vaeth, is a lifelong pattern. From early on, narcissists believe they are entitled to things and have special abilities and talents beyond those of others. They are driven by fantasies of unlimited success. They have a need to be acknowledged as brilliant and often seek academic credentials separating themselves from others. Interested in beauty, they are often attractive people who surround themselves with other attractive people. Because they often want to be popular, they can be charismatically charming when they want to be, glib, and good public speakers. "They often admire other famous people and will emulate them," Dr. Vaeth says (Dart 1998). "George Patton, who was very Narcissistic, thought he was the reincarnation of Alexander the Great." Dr. Vaeth notes that narcissists have two defense mechanisms that make them more resilient than most people to shame. "They are incredible at denying the truth . . . and they can rationalize. Most people get so embarrassed [by their behavior] that they want to run away. They will resign. They can't face what many Narcissists are capable of facing. . . . But the same drives that can put Narcissists on the top can also topple them" (Dart 1998).

After all, say mental health experts, "risk propensity" is relative. There is a clinical sensation-seeking scale that measures people's tolerance of so-called "risky" behavior, affirms Gregory Schutte (Dart 1998), a psychology professor at American International College in Springfield, Massachusetts. "People identified as scoring high on the sensation-seeking scale tend to be extraverted, very outgoing compared to those low on it, and have more sexual partners and affairs," he says. "They like to have a lot of things on their plates." However, cautions Professor Leiffer, "many people who engage in the alleged [sexual] behaviour of [say] Mr. Clinton do not experience it as risk. They just want to do it and could have some kind of arrangement in their marriage."

Politicians and others in power are sometimes "compartmentalized risk takers," adds Betty Glad (Dart 1998), a political psychologist and presidential scholar at the University of South Carolina. "It's not a seamless web. They have various corners of personality. Some are risk takers in private lives and careful in public lives, or vice versa." For example, former president Jimmy Carter was a big risk taker at Camp David, she said, staking his historical reputation on a risky Middle East deal. Nixon sought out crises during his term of office to show his mettle, she added. While taking risks is part of their jobs, politicians and corporate leaders can sometimes get reckless, concludes Glad. "Sometimes they want to get caught." They have an unconscious need to still be human—and not a god. In a sense, their recklessness is a silent cry for help.

The Prognosis

What happens when and if help is sought by narcissists? What is the prognosis for their movement toward greater "self-healing" potential?

First, note mental health experts, narcissists tend not to seek help because they don't perceive that they have a problem. Even in failed marriages—which are not uncommon for narcissists—they often go into counseling sessions alleging that they don't have a problem, but the spouse does. In short, narcissists are difficult to treat. This reality is particularly so because the narcissist exerts intense pressures on any potential helper, viewing the counseling session, even, as a competition and seeing the helper in a disdainful way, note experts Kennedy and Charles (1991). Thus, the first concern for professionals (like G's consultants) involved in counseling narcissists is to avoid being incorporated into their psychological maneuvering.

Moreover, note Kennedy and Charles (1991), narcissists, if challenged beyond their "comfort zones," can become aggressive or even violent.

Counselors should recognize the potential gravity of the Narcissist's reactions to loss or the threat of loss. Their rage can be literally murderous in nature and effect and it may well be the pathology beneath the killing or other physical harming of spouses at the time of a marital breakup. Persons with Narcissistic personality problems may, therefore, be disruptive to the already challenging nature of marriage counseling [as a case in point]. Their sense of grandiosity and entitlement, coupled with their seeming inability to feel empathy for others, make them difficult to work with and, in certain circumstances, dangerous to others. (p. 299)

WHY MOOD DISORDERS ARE THOUGHT TO BE COMMON AMONG EMINENTS AND LEADERS

Review of Studies Investigating "Mood Disorders" and Creativity in Eminents, Scientists, and Leaders

By now the reader has already learned from the 1978 study findings of Goertzel, Goertzel, and Goertzel and from the 1972 study findings of Martindale (see Chapter 1) that "creative eminents," in particular, tend to experience depression and bipolar disorders. But, even if we were to assume that "successful" corporate and political leaders are equally predisposed to mood disorder "pain," is the picture regarding personal outcomes necessarily negative?

The answer to this question appears to be a qualified no. As expert Robert Albert (1992) recently affirmed:

What is important to understand is that creative individuals have the capacity to not deny this pain, but to use it. Very much products of the early years, in which they had little or no say, it is fascinating to see how these confused moments, unexpected losses, loneliness and harsh circumstances can become the framework and tools of their art. Many of us would agree that this holds for artists, but doubt that it holds for scientists. This is merely because it [the mood disorder pain] is so much more evident for artists than for scientists [or for corporate leaders, for that matter]. Artists talk about themselves; scientists often do not have the emotional vocabulary or inner grammar to do so. (p. 326)

Corporate leaders, as Tillson (1996) affirmed, "closet" their affective pain to save the company's and their own reputations.

If we further assume that creative types—artists, scientists, and corporate leaders alike—experience creativity in their periods of mood disorders (DeLong & Aldershof 1983; Jamison et al. 1980), then what "component" is likely responsible for this remarkable link between "creativity" and "madness"?

In her recent study on mood disorders and patterns of creativity in 47 British "eminent" artists and writers, Jamison (1992) attempted to answer this question. She noted that a very high percentage of the total "eminent" study sample—38 percent—had been treated for mood disorders and that 75 percent of those had been given antidepressants or lithium or had been hospitalized. With the exception of the poets, the "eminent" creators reported being treated for depression, not for mania or hypomania. Moreover, the majority (89 percent) reported having "intense, highly productive and creative episodes," lasting for two weeks (35 percent), for one to four weeks (55 percent), or for longer than a month (25 percent). These "creative episodes" were reportedly characterized by increases in enthusiasm, energy, self-confidence, speed of mental association, fluency of thoughts, elevated mood, and a strong sense of well-being—descriptions attributed to hypomania in the DSM-IV (American Psychiatric Association 1994). Given these results, Jamison (1992) concluded that hypomania was the critical component for creativity.

To determine whether hypomania was equally responsible for creative output for "eminents" in other careers—including social, religious, political, and military leaders—Jamison completed a follow-up study in 1991. Her results confirmed that hypomania was the critical "creative" component.

Corporate leaders—could they be similarly hypomanically "creative"? While the response to this question is not clear-cut, as no similar study has been done on this population to date to assess this possibility, the answer appears to be a tentative yes. Experts now say that a startling number of CEOs and other high-achieving businesspeople likely have bipolar disorders (Tillson 1996). Simply put, if one travels in hard-driving business circles, or if one has a boss who does, says Dr. Sam Ozersky, a senior consultant at Toronto Hospital's Mood Disorders clinic, chances are that there is someone in these circles who, like G, has some version of the bipolar disorder. Manic-depression "self-selects" to "any profession that requires stupendous effort, energy, confidence and willingness to take risks" (Tillson 1996, p. 26). What's more, the important characteristics a corporate leader needs to make a company "sing"— intelligence, confidence, clarity of thought, stamina, creativity, and productivity—are the very traits heightened during hypomanic episodes. "When you're in that state," adds Julie, a young professional in the public sector who has bipolar disorder, "things become extremely clear. Seeing the big picture is a real asset. It's what takes you to the top" (Tillson 1996, p. 26).

How Bipolar Mood Disorders Reportedly Affect Corporate Leaders

G, in the previous case, admitted to others in his company and to the consultants that he was a manic-depressive who was once on lithium for mood moderation. Comparing the notes on Harry Langner's behavior with those on G's leads one to believe that both may be bipolar sufferers. But how frequently do corporate leaders, like G, openly admit to others, that they are bipolar in nature?

To Stay "Closeted" or Not. Pierre Peladeau, the late mercurial tycoon responsible for the second-largest commercial printing empire in North America, U.S. media mogul Ted Turner, the late Vancouver stock promoter Murray Pezim, and former real estate magnate Robert Campeau were all manic-depressives who, unlike most of their bipolar corporate leader peers, became "uncloseted." But why did they "come out"?

Tamsen Tillson, in her recent piece in *Canadian Business* (1996), attempts an answer to this intriguing question:

The few businesspeople like Pierre Peladeau who have gone public about being Manic-Depressive tend to be unequivocal, controversial individuals. They've all held the brass ring firmly in hand, and they've all lost it from time to time. Turner's obsession with his own death for many years extended to his keeping on hand the gun his father had used to kill himself, according to one biographer; Pezim has had electroshock treatments; Campeau went on and off his medication to try to channel his moods, all the while dazzling the North American business community with his ill-fated, debt-propelled takeovers of Allied Stores Corp. and Federated Department Stores Inc. in the mid-'80s. That such people are able to say they're Manic-Depressive and the world be damned is, essentially, a luxury few others can afford. For most Manic-Depressives, their illness is more like a blight that would thwart their professional goals if revealed. Manic-Depression may be the reason they are among their companies' top performers, yet it is also their deepest, darkest secret. (p. 28)

For those bipolar corporate leaders who are contemplating becoming "uncloseted," should they? According to Dr. Sam Ozersky, probably not. "Manic depressives only survive [professionally] if they have a lot of power—if they're Ted Turner," he says (Tillson 1996, p. 28). Dr. Ozersky counsels his bipolar patients not to tell employers about their illness unless they absolutely have to. Dr. Sagar Parikh, head of the Bipolar Clinic at the Clarke Institute of Psychiatry in Toronto, agrees. "Would you go to a lawyer, or for that matter, a doctor or a businessman knowing that person has Manic-Depressive illness?" (Tillson 1996, p. 28).

There is still in the late 1990s a real social stigma against mood disorders, particularly manic-depression. There is still such a lack of understanding about the benefits—as well as the costs—of the various mood disorder types. For example, says Dr. Parikh, one of the major benefits of those in the hypomanic phase is increased production: 10 percent of those who have manic-depression actually perform better in their jobs than a "healthy" individual. "[Manic depression] gives them that extra bit of panache to do the big deal," says Parikh (Tillson 1996, p. 27).

But other corporate leaders who have not quite made it to the top position in their companies apparently do have to be careful in sharing "the word." Carol, a vice-president in the financial services industry, is certain that others would use the knowledge of her manic-depressive illness to undermine her authority. She once confided her secret about being a manic-depressive to a colleague. The next thing that Carol knew, he had told his boss, and, later when she disagreed with him during an important meeting, he snapped that maybe she should take a Valium. Being sensitive to rejection, Carol was upset. "What he was doing was threatening me, [implying] that the information was going to come out," she says. "Both of those guys are gone [from the company], but I'm always worried, because others there are no better. I have no reason to trust that they're going to take the information in a sensitive manner" (Tillson 1996, p. 28).

Aimless, Reckless Whims and Heavy Alcohol Consumption. Given that bipolars and hypomanics can be extremely creative and productive, what, besides sensitivity to rejection, is the big problem with being mood-disordered? According to mental health experts, aimless, reckless, and potentially dangerous whims can also accompany bipolars in their upward spirals, particularly if alcohol consumption is involved. For example, one day in 1972, Pierre Peladeau decided he wanted to go to Tokyo. He took the flight, did some "inconsequential" business, and returned home 24 hours later. Another time, Peladeau flew off to make movies in Rome, although he had no prior interest in producing films. A similar impulse to launch a newspaper called the *Philadelphia Journal* in 1977 cost him about $14 million before he closed the failed effort. "It's stupid," said Peladeau in a recent interview. "I didn't know what the hell I was doing. When I was drinking, it was worse" (Tillson 1996, p. 26).

A fact remains that within the family constellations of mood-disordered patients, more alcoholism exists than would be expected from general population figures (Winokur, Clayton, & Reich 1969, pp. 30–31). One of the more impressive studies investigating the relationship between bipolar disorders and alcohol consumption was conducted in 1968 by Mayfield and Coleman (Winokur, Clayton, & Reich 1969). In their study group of 59 clients suffering from manic and depressive episodes, these researchers reported that 20 percent of them had a history of excessive drinking—and mostly when they were in their manic phases (p. 31).

In 1969, Winokur, Clayton, and Reich completed (pp. 75–76) another critical study on 100 manic clients who were admitted to the hospital to determine if there was evidence of increased alcohol consumption prior to their hospital admissions. Of the 100 admissions, a sizable 42 percent of the clients reported an increase in alcohol consumption (from 6 ounces to 37 ounces) prior to admission, and in no clients was a decrease in consumption reported. Men were more likely to increase their alcoholic drinking than women (54 percent vs. 35 percent) during a manic phase. In all cases of heavy drinking, the researchers found the degree of social disruption due to alcohol to be considerable, attested to by the fact that "abuse of alcohol" was the main reason for admission to the hospital in 24 of these 42 cases. While in the hospital, no client exhibited withdrawal symptoms. Though mental health clinicians have generally considered that clients who consume pathologic quantities of alcohol do so initially to obtain relief from anxiety and depression, this research team found that for manics, at least, this theory has little support. The manic patients tend to drink in company rather than alone—and may, in fact, be drinking heavily to keep company with other heavy drinkers rather than for the effect that the alcohol has on them. In contrast, the alcoholic clients frequently claim that "feeling bad" or "being unable to sleep" is the basis of their drinking. In essence, the effect of alcohol on the manic seems—as in Peladeau's case—to dissolve whatever restraints are left. Then, the whims begin.

Loss of, and Lack of, Insight. Another cost associated with bipolar disorder is the so-called loss of insight, which occurs especially during the height of the disorder. According to Dr. Parikh, though bipolar patients have a tendency to avoid reaching insight that they have a mood disorder problem—coupled with the fact that it takes, on average, 10 years from the onset of manic-depressive illness for most clients to receive a correct diagnosis—an even worse problem for clients is their never reaching insight that they have a mood disorder problem (Tillson 1996, p. 27).

In fact, writes Tillson (1996), though ironically, employers and co-workers worry about manic-depressives whose condition has been diagnosed, they should worry more about those who remain "closeted" and have not been diagnosed. She shares this story of a bipolar corporate lawyer who was lacking insight about his condition until tragedy struck—which is, sadly, too often the case:

Former lawyer Philip Upshall did an incredible amount of damage to himself, his family and his clients because no one knew about his illness—not even Upshall. Until 1990 he lived the busy but agreeable life of a prosperous corporate lawyer in the Toronto area. "I was just a person who needed very little sleep, who was very active in the community, highly involved—motoring right along," he says. A father of four, Upshall was a pillar of his town. He was involved in the Salvation Army and several social clubs. He ran federal and municipal political campaigns and did some fund-raising for the local Conservatives. Then he began to lose control. "You're just marching on to your own little tune," Upshall says. "It's not until you have your big fall that you start to look back at what might have been an indication of an illness." Upshall loved golf and, over a two-year period beginning in 1990, sank $100,000 into golf club memberships and equipment. Yet he had time for only eight or nine games each year. His wife found sets of new clubs that he never used scattered around the house.

Far from suspecting something was wrong, Upshall felt happier and more self-confident than at any other time in his life. "When you're flying, you're flying," he says, with vigor (and a bit of longing). "You feel like you're Jesus Christ. There isn't anything you can't do." Upshall invested his clients' money in the stock market—without telling them. "I don't know that you really realize that what you're doing is illegal," he says. "You really, honestly, believe that you are all-powerful and people would want you to do it." Of the approximately $3 million Upshall was alleged to have taken from his clients—most of whom were old friends—almost $1 million was lost. When his mood took a nosedive and the unvarnished realization of what he'd done hit him, Upshall plunged into a suicidal depression. "One of the gals I hurt, she called me up three days before I decided to commit suicide and asked me to officiate at the wedding of her eldest daughter," he says. "I'll never forget that." She would soon discover that Upshall had lost more than $100,000 of her retirement money.

Upshall's almost-successful suicide attempt landed him in hospital, where he was finally diagnosed as being Manic Depressive. Then the local police came to visit, and he was charged with numerous counts of fraud, breach of trust and misappropriation of funds. He was tried and sentenced to two years in jail and subsequently lost his license to practise law. Paroled in June 1993, Upshall found that his marriage was over and he felt few of his old friends wanted anything to do with him: "Generally speaking, all of those people have said, 'Goodby, I don't want to talk to you again because you're dirty.' And I can't say that I blame them." (p. 28)

Suicide Attempts. Upshall's story provides yet another cost of uncontrolled manic-depression: suicide attempts. In 1970, on the basis of available data, mental health experts Guze and Robins estimated that 15 percent of all persons with major affective illness will commit suicide. In a more recent, 1988 study by Black, Winokur, and Nasrallah, the researchers concluded that the percentages of deaths by suicide and the standardized mortality ratios of the bipolar clients in their study were lower than those found in the unipolar (depressed) subjects. Though this research team cautioned that other researchers have reported different outcomes for other client samples, it would appear that for bipolars, the risk for suicide ideation and follow-through is greater during the depressive, rather than during the manic, episodes.

Costs to the Family and to the Organization. There is yet another cost regarding bipolar illness: often the family members of bipolars talk about their lives being disrupted financially, psychologically, or both. Stated simply, unmedicated bipolars are difficult to live with and, say coworkers, difficult to work with. The picture of the difficulty becomes quite clear after hearing about the case of G.

As Kennedy and Charles (1991) so aptly put it:

Manic people are always on the go, they seem difficult to contain or to keep on one subject, and after some exposure to them, one suspects that the roots of their enthusiasm are not as simple as they at first seem. Such individuals do not seek counseling because they do not find their agitation and increased activity uncomfortable. If Manic Depressive patients experience, or their families observe, symptoms necessitating professional attention, they should be referred to a psychiatrist for evaluation and appropriate treatment, such as with the drug lithium carbonate. (p. 206)

But by all means, caution Kennedy and Charles, don't ignore the problem.

Too often, family members and coworkers contribute to the bipolar's problem by ignoring it or rationalizing it away. Sometimes, as in G's case, coworkers have a lot to gain by accepting the high-return status quo of the mood-disordered CEO, despite its difficulties. "Sometimes people collude inadvertently," says Dr. Ozersky. "They don't want Hypomanics to settle down." (Tillson 1996, p. 34)

Carol's story tells it like it is:

Like many others who have Manic Depression, Carol doesn't sleep well, and has often [like G] ended up at the office in the middle of the night. She found out she was Manic Depressive nine years ago, after an extended period of insomnia wore her down to such a point that she began making mistakes at work—big ones. Her colleagues, who could see something was wrong, covered for her. Alarmed at her haggard appearance, her family convinced her to see a doctor, who referred her to a specialist who made the diagnosis. "I never did anything like walking into a room naked, but frequently I did have inappropriate use of the old mouth," she says. "People found me highly entertaining, great at a party, but a royal pain in the ass." Carol remains gregarious and painfully forthright. Her words sprint along and she punctuates her speech with startling, wide-flung gesticulations. She pauses, well aware of how it must look, and points out that she is not Hypomanic—she's medicated. (Tillson 1996, p. 33)

The Prognosis. Despite the fact that theirs is one of the most treatable mental ill-health disorders, health clinicians estimate that up to 70 percent of bipolars resist taking their medication. There are several reasons for their noncompliance, among them being that bipolars see lithium medication schedules as an indication that they are somehow "flawed"; like G, bipolars often quit their lithium medication when they think that they are feeling better and are, therefore, "cured"; bipolars dislike the weight gain, shaky hands, and stomach upset associated with the medication; and bipolars say that lithium "interferes" with their concentration and makes them "less creative" (Tillson 1996, p. 34).

But are these complaints regarding lithium treatment justified? In 1989, experts Prien and Gelenberg investigated such complaints by reviewing the research literature on drug treatment for bipolar disorder. At the completion of their study, this research team concluded "that lithium is not a panacea for Bipolar Disorder" (p. 840). While lithium treatment resulted in 50 percent fewer episode recurrences than the placebos in the studies reviewed, the average failure rate for lithium in preventive treatment studies was a significant 33 percent. Moreover, even among the lithium "responders," only about 20 percent were expected to achieve complete prevention of episodes, with the remaining 80 percent showing varying frequencies and severities of recurrences. Also, lithium seemed to be a particularly poor treatment for clients with a history of rapid cycling (i.e., four or more episodes per year). The long-term side effects of weight gain, plyuria, and fine hand tremor did often lead to lithium noncompliance. Finally, since lithium appears to have a teratogenic (i.e., birth defect) effect, its use during pregnancy is not advised.

Prien and Gelenberg concluded that the anticonvulsant carbamazepine (having a molecular structure resembling that of imipramine and synthesized for its potential antidepressant effect) seems to be a likely alternative to, or complement to, lithium treatment, especially for those getting little relief from lithium alone. However, cautioned these researchers, before concluding that lithium is not working for clients, clinicians should consider a number of other points to optimize compliance:

1. A search for nonpharmacologic factors, such as psychosocial stressors, should be undertaken to uncover other causes of poor client response. If found, psychotherapy or stress management for clients should be advised.

2. The dosage of lithium prescribed should be reviewed, for although some patients respond well with serum levels as low as 0.5 to 0.6 meq/liter, other clients require levels as high as 0.8 to 1.2 meq/liter.

3. A questioning of clients about whether they are taking the full dosage prescribed—or if they are "cutting back" to avoid the undesirable side effects—needs to be completed. A word or two about the importance of full compliance should then be forthcoming.

4. The possibility of lithium-induced hypothyroidism for clients developing depression during lithium treatment needs to be considered, especially if the depression is characterized by apathy, fatigue, psychomotor retardation, and other hypothyroid-like symptoms. In the latter case, a dosage of L-thyroxine could be prescribed.

THE MEANING AND PREVALENCE OF ANTISOCIAL PERSONALITY DISORDER AND PSYCHOPATHY IN WORKING ADULTS AND CORPORATE LEADERS

Would G simply be a naricissistic, mood-disordered CEO, or is he more dangerous than that? Though the consultants "smoothed over" the fact that G had some antisocial traits, he did seem to have a lot of pent-up rage. What's more, bipolar disorder experts Winokur, Clayton, and Reich (1969, p. 62) report that over 80 percent of manic episodes are characterized by hostility, generally verbal but at times physical, and that, on average, about 15 percent of the hospitalized admissions are due to assaultive or destructive behaviors. So, what is the distinction between "anger outbursts" and antisocial personality disorder?

As noted earlier, antisocial personality disorder is *an enduring pattern of disregard for, and violation of, the rights of others*, and the estimated prevalence rate of this disorder in community samples is about 3 percent in males and 1 percent in females. Psychopaths, as a special set, will kill if they have to in order to meet their selfish needs. While psychopaths are typically antisocially disordered personalities, antisocially disordered personalities are often not psychopaths. Psychopaths are remorseless predators who often use charm, intimidation, manipulation, and even cold-blooded violence to attain their ends. . . . When G "acts out" his rage, he seems more likely (like a lot of angry corporate leaders) to yell, to throw things, or to fire people rather than to kill them. Thus, he would not qualify as a psychopath. As the consultants for G noted, G's disregard for, and violation of, the rights of others is not enduring. Rather, it is sporadic and typically stressor-induced. Moreover, it is highly likely that G's "anger fire" is quite controlled, falling just below a critical "5" level on Grossarth-Maticek's and Eysenck's Type 3 and Type 6 antisocial trait scales. That is not to say that one day G's "fuse" could not be ignited and, thus, exceed the critical "5" level.

As noted in Chapter 1, the popular press has alleged that many more corporate leaders than we would expect are antisocially disordered. Dr. Babiak (McFarland, 1996) offers a clinical case:

Dave is a successful senior manager in a large U.S. company who has achieved promotions and regular salary increases. He has been also been identified as a destructive psychopath by New York-based industrial and organizational psychologist Paul Babiak. "This person was very different from any other problem employee," says Dr. Babiak, who discovered Dave during a consulting job for the company about 10 years ago and continues to chart his career.

Dave, who holds a degree from a U.S. state college, was known by colleagues for his disruptive behaviour, verbal tirades, and selfish, unreliable and irresponsible actions. He plagiarized work and brushed aside concerns when caught. He fabricated some credentials, then argued he did nothing wrong. He appeared unconcerned with how others perceived him and described himself as "a model" employee.

He was also a master of office politics, courting favour with senior managers and creating divisions within the workplace to advance his causes and harm his perceived enemies. Among senior managers, he was believed to have management talent and potential. His aggression was seen as ambitious. Dave is still with the organization, rising near its highest ranks following a merger with another company. He has had detractors fired; others have seen their careers ruined. . . . And he is far from unique.

Assessing the Outward Signs of Psychopathy. If psychopaths are walking the corporate hallways, what are their "outward signs"? First, note mental health experts, the image of the drooling serial killer does not always fit. Robert Hare, a professor at the University of British Columbia and Canada's leading researcher in psychopathy, has coined the term "subcriminal psychopath" to identify so-called psychopaths working among us—including our corporate leaders. Though on the outside they may look like the "guy next door," Dr. Hare estimates that thousand of psychopaths like Clifford Olson or Ted Bundy could be walking the streets of North America.

Says Dr. Hare (*The National Magazine* 1995):

For every Bernardo, Clifford Olson or Hanibal Lector, there could be thousands, maybe ten thousand other psychopaths out there, and they're plying their trade, they're walking around the streets. They're doing what they do naturally, which is to use and abuse other people. . . . What's a psychopath? Well, all sorts of different definitions. I suppose one could say that these are more or less natural born predators. They're careless, remorseless, impulsive, eccentric individuals. They have a stunning lack of empathy, a complete lack of concern for you as an individual. They are individuals without conscience, as a matter of fact. These are people who operate according to their own rules. They don't internalize the rules of society. They operate according to what they feel is right for themselves. (p. 2)

But are psychopathic personalities "sane"? "Sane. Absolutely," says Dr. Hare. "They know the difference between right and wrong. They know what they're doing is wrong by somebody else's standard. They don't agree with those standards, but they know it. Yes, intellectually they know that there is a difference between right and wrong" (p. 3).

Dr. Hare (1991) has developed a 20-item checklist, shown in Table 5.1, to help clinicians assess the outward signs of psychopathology in criminal populations. Most of the traits shown in Table 5.1 are treated as open concepts, says Dr. Hare, meaning that the rater is provided with a description of a trait and with some behavioral exemplars and is asked to make a judgment about the extent to which a person has the trait, using a 0–2 scale (where 0 means that the trait does not apply and where 2 means that the trait definitely does apply). Thus, the maximum score a person could be given is 40. In most forensic samples, the distribution of scores is approximately normal, with a slight negative skewness. A cutoff score of 30 has proven useful to differentiate the "purer" psychopaths (Hare, Hart, & Harper 1991). The mean score for prison inmates, notes Dr. Hare, is about 23.

There is strong evidence, says Dr. Hare, that the inventory is assessing two stable, oblique factors of psychopathic personality. The items defin-

Table 5.1
Items in Hare's Psychopathy Checklist

ITEMS and Factors
1. Glibness/superficial charm: Factor 1
2. Grandiose sense of self-worth: Factor 1
3. Need for stimulation/proneness to boredom: Factor 2
4. Pathological lying: Factor 1
5. Conning/manipulative: Factor 1
6. Lack of remorse or guilt: Factor 1
7. Shallow affect: Factor 1
8. Callous/lack of empathy: Factor 1
9. Parasitic lifestyle: Factor 2
10. Poor behavioral controls: Factor 2
11. Promiscuous sexual behavior: ?
12. Early behavior problems: Factor 2
13. Lack of realistic, long-term goals: Factor 2
14. Impulsivity: Factor 2
15. Irresponsibility: Factor 2
16. Failure to accept responsibility for actions: Factor 1
17. Many short-term marital relationships: ?
18. Juvenile delinquency: Factor 2
19. Revocation of conditional release: Factor 2
20. Criminal versatility: ?

Source: Hare & Harper (1991).

ing these factors were identified in Table 5.1. Factor 1, says Dr. Hare, reflects a set of interpersonal and affective characteristics, such as egocentricity, lack of remorse, callousness, and so forth—the type of behavior that one typically finds in narcissists (such as that measured by Grossarth-Maticek's and Eysenck's Type 3 scale). Factor 2, he notes, reflects those aspects of psychopathy related to an impulsive, antisocial, and unstable lifestyle (and measured by Grossarth-Maticek's and Eysenck's Type 6 scale). So which factor is the more critical to the psychopathic disorder and its negative consequences? Very recent evidence seems to show that Factor 1, specified by the core personality traits, including superficiality, habitual lying, manipulativeness, and callousness, is more discriminating (Cooke & Michie 1997).

Psychopathy and Leadership: When to Expect Them. Many successful businesspeople have large egos, cool demeanors, and an uncanny knack for office politics. But psychopaths have much deeper problems, say the experts. They feel no true allegiances, even in their personal lives—no loyalty, no guilt for dirty deeds done, no remorse. They lie easily and frequently but can be charming when they want to be. So how many psychopaths are roaming the halls of large industry today? Though no study has been completed thus far to give us an accurate reading on this one, if Hare's assertions are right, the prevalence rate in the population could be as high as 3 percent, depending on the degree of "psychopath purity."

Dr. Babiak, who says he has identified at least six psychopaths in various companies in the course of his organizational work, describes a common workplace trait when a psychopath is present that he calls "discrepant views." Says Dr. Babiak (McFarland 1996): "It occurs when a large portion of an organization really likes this individual and thinks he [or she] has high potential and they even feel they're really close buddies; while there's another half of the organization that thinks [he's/she's] the devil or evil. A 'snake' is a word that is commonly used." These "snakes" get hired because they do well in interviews, where they can turn on the charm. Often their credentials are exaggerated or fabricated, but no one checks carefully.

Dr. Babiak further notes that this psychopathic personality does not typically succeed well in traditional, bureaucratic organizations with well-established controls, rules, and operating systems. Instead, psychopaths more often exploit organizations that are going through restructuring or downsizing or mergering. "There is chaos, or breakdowns of norms and values in the culture, and in that chaotic milieu, the psychopath can move in and do very well," says Dr. Babiak (McFarland 1996).

Dr. Hare affirms that psychopaths are really good at knowing when to come into people's lives and into organizations. On a daily basis, notes Dr. Hare, psychopaths are good at reading "empathy" and "weakness" in others. "They can construct an emotional facsimile of someone and act on it, but they're not emotionally 'connected' to other people," he says (McFarland 1996). So, are there certain individuals who are enticing "marks" for psychopaths? "Absolutely," posits Dr. Hare. "I mean, sort of like 'natural targets'? Oh, yes. People who believe in the inherent goodness of humanity, people who want to go out and help. There are all sorts of groups that are trying to help other people. They're genuine, they're honest in their intentions, and so on. They're ideal 'marks' for the psychopath" (*The National Magazine* 1995, p. 14).

While psychopathic individuals on the street can "con" one or two individuals, a psychopathic manager can pull off a much larger charade.

"What a psychopath is good at doing," says Dr. Babiak, "is not only manipulating people as individuals, but manipulating an entire group of people and managing these discrepant views between the two camps. That's a skill that's much more scary" (McFarland 1996).

Besides business, would psychopaths "self-select" to other professions? Dr. Hare posits that professions such as psychiatry and law tend to attract a greater number of psychopaths than we would expect because they offer access to power over people, an irresistible lure. Dr. Hare also believes an assessment of people working on the Vancouver Stock Exchange, which has been plagued by scams, would also find a disproportionate number of psychopaths. Dr. Hare concludes, "The very bright ones aren't going to become labourers or go work in a factory. They're going to get into a field where they can make a lot of money and have power and prestige" (McFarland 1996).

Protection for Companies. So how does a company protect itself from psychopaths? Since psychopaths are notorious for doing well on standardized personality tests, Dr. Hare recommends that companies protect themselves by using the screening version of his 20-item test. Other organizations, such as the national police force in Portugal, he says, use it because the screening system formerly used recruited too many "Rambos" to the force (McFarland 1996).

Protection for Individuals. So how do individuals protect themselves? Dr. Hare (*The National Magazine* 1995) advises:

You've got to be vigilant, obviously. You've got to find out as much as you can about the disorder. In fact, you've got to come to the realization that this is not a myth; I'm not making this up. These people actually do exist, and there are predators out there, and . . . if you don't want to be eaten by one of these people—sort of psychologically, emotionally, or sexually, you've got to be aware of the problem. You've got to understand that everybody out there is not a warm, loving individual. There are predators out there.

Prognosis for Psychopaths. Can psychopaths be cured? Says Dr. Hare, (*The National Magazine* 1995): "There's no evidence that we can [cure], but on the other hand, we haven't developed the appropriate techniques. It's possible in the future we'll find out that there's some way of changing their behaviour. Now think about it from their perspective. What is it you cure?"

THE BOTTOM LINE

This chapter opened with the case of narcissistic, manic-depressive, rage-controlled G. After hearing about how a high-powered group of consultants was hired by G's firm to turn the organization (and G) around, we went on a journey to better understand what it was that G was suffering from, what could be done for G and for others like him, and what responsibility other people within the organization had to also help turn things around for the better.

By the time we finished understanding about personality types at the chapter's end, I think that many of us would admit that G was not as "disease-prone" as he, at first, appeared to be. If placed on his lithium (or some alternative), we discovered, G might even be more tolerable. Compared to other psychopaths perhaps roaming the halls of corporations, G was likely a much more rage-controlled, more creative guy than we (and likely the consultants) originally gave him credit for. Plus, G had adequate ego strength to offset, to some degree, his mood liabilities. But, let's not kid ourselves or G; he really should give medication and, perhaps, even psychotherapy another try.

The theme that exists, we also discovered, between narcissists, bipolars, and psychopathic types is that all three tend to avoid reaching insight that *they* have a problem. Of these three groups, we saw that there is the most hope for the bipolars.

Another point that emerged very strongly from Chapter 5 is that we have no real indicator of the prevalence in present-day corporate leaders of these three disorders, since no studies to date have been completed in this regard.

Finally, for those who are interested and are wanting closure, G never really "bought" the recommendations of the consultants hired to help him. G told them bluntly, "Well, I didn't do what you told me. It was like putting a condom on a stud bull" (Levinson, Sabbath, & Connor 1992). G also told L that he was going to sell his company, net $4 million to $5 million out of the sale, and perhaps buy back one of the smaller parts of the company. G bragged that he would turn the latter into a $50 million business in ten years.... Some six months after he completed the sale, G sent L a videotape of his departing ceremonies from the company. In the videotape, said the consultants, G projected his conscious good image of omnipotence, perfection, and honesty onto his followers. He used human metaphors along with analogies, likening business to war. His humor was biting. While seemingly complimenting people, his underlying sarcasm came through. He quoted from classical literature and used street language. The eulogies continued to reflect his striving for omnipotence. (So, in G's mind, is he human, or is he a god?)

REFERENCES

Achebe, C. (1987). *Ant hills of the savanna*. London: Heinemann.
Albert, R. S. (1992). Personal dynamics and creative problems in exceptional

achievement. In R. S. Albert (Ed.), *Genius and eminence*. Oxford: Pergamon Press, pp. 325–328.

American Psychiatric Association. (1994). *Diagnostic and statistical manual of mental disorders. Fourth edition. DSM-IV*. Washington, DC: American Psychiatric Association.

Black, D. W., Winokur, G., & Nasrallah, A. (1988). Effect of psychosis on suicide risk in 1,593 patients with unipolar and bipolar affective disorders. *American Journal of Psychiatry*, 145, 849–852.

Bleiberg, E. (1988). Developmental pathogenesis of narcissistic disorders in children. *Bulletin of the Menninger Clinic*, 52, 3–15.

Cooke, D. J., & Michie, C. (1997). An item response theory analysis of the Hare Psychopathy Checklist—Revised. *Psychological Assessment*, 9, 3–14.

Dart, B. (1998). Power leads men to risky business, psychologists say. *The Globe and Mail*, January 31, p. A18.

DeLong, G. R., & Aldershof, A. (1983). Associations of special abilities with juvenile manic-depressive illness. *Annals of Neurology*, 14, 362.

Endicott, J., & Spitzer, R. L. (1978). A diagnostic interview: The Schedule for Affective Disorders and Schizophrenia. *Archives of General Psychiatry*, 35, 837–844.

Guze, S. B., & Robins, E. (1970). Suicide and primary affective disorders. *British Journal of Psychiatry*, 117, 437–438.

Hare, R. D. (1991). *The Hare Psychopathy Checklist—Revised*. Toronto: Multi-Health Systems.

Hare, R. D., Hart, S. D., & Harper, T. J. (1991). Psychopathy and the DSM-IV criteria for antisocial personality disorder. *Journal of Abnormal Psychology*, 100, 391–398.

Jamison, K. R. (1991). Manic-depressive illness, creativity and leadership. In F. K. Goodwin and K. R. Jamison (Eds.), *Manic-depressive illness*. Oxford: Oxford University Press, Chapter 16.

Jamison, K. R. (1992). Mood disorders and patterns of creativity in British writers and artists. In R. S. Albert (Ed.), *Genius and eminence*. Oxford: Pergamon Press, pp. 351–356.

Jamison, K. R., Gerner, R. H., Hammer, C., & Padesky, C. (1980). Clouds and silver linings: Positive experiences associated with primary affective disorders. *American Journal of Psychiatry*, 137, 198–202.

Kennedy, E., & Charles, S. C. (1991). Borderline and narcissistic personality disorders. In *On becoming a counsellor*. New York: Continuum, pp. 206, 295–304.

Leigh, D., Pare, C. M. B., & Marks, J. (1977). *A concise encyclopedia of psychiatry*. Lancaster, U.K.: M.T.P. Press.

Levinson, H., Sabbath, J., & Connor, J. (1992). Bearding the lion that roared. *Consulting Psychology Journal*, 44, 2–16.

McFarland, J. (1996). Managing: Is your boss a psychopath? *The Globe and Mail*, January 9, p. B11. Based on these two sources: Babiak, P. (1995). When psychopaths go to work: A case study of an industrial psychopath. *Applied Psychology: An International Review*, 44, 171–188; Hare R. D. (1993). *Without conscience: The disturbing world of the psychopaths among us*. New York: Pocket Books.

The National Magazine. (1995). What is a psychopath? Reference 89830–1, December 5, CBC-TV, time 22:25, length 29 minutes, pp. 1–16.

Prien, R. F., & Gelenberg, A. J. (1989). Alternatives to lithium for preventive treatment of bipolar disorder. *American Journal of Psychiatry*, 146, 840–848.

Tillson, T. (1996). The CEO's disease. *Canadian Business*, 69, 26–28, 33–34.

Winokur, G., Clayton, P. J., & Reich, T. (1969). *Manic depressive illness.* Saint Louis: C. V. Mosby.

CHAPTER 6

The Path to Corporate Success: How Status, Income, Perks, and Accoutrements Motivate Those to Reach for the Top

There is nothing more difficult to take in hand, more perilous to conduct, or more uncertain in its success than to take the lead in the introduction of a new order of things.
—Niccolò Machiavelli, *The Prince*, 1532

A CASE IN POINT (JANG 1998)

Texas oilman J. P. Bryan has stunned the oil patch by relinquishing the reins of Gulf Canada Resources Ltd., spurring debate about the legacy of his three-year mission to revive Gulf and raising questions about whether he was "pushed out."

Mr. Bryan, who created waves in Canada's oil patch with his tough-talking management style and penchant for acquisitions, announced February 9, 1998, that he has "stepped down" as Gulf's president, chief executive officer, and as a company director. Richard Auchinleck, Gulf's chief operating officer, is the new president and CEO.

A self-described "outsider," Mr. Bryan said he met recently with Gulf's Board of directors, and they came to a "mutual decision" that the company's future would be better guided by Mr. Auchinleck because of its need to focus on internal growth. "The Board really wants somebody to lead it from here on who has more of an operational and internal focus, who can harvest the things that I brought to the company. I don't disagree with that," Mr. Bryan said in an interview in Calgary.

"I've always said that I think there are certain people who have talents for certain occasions." He also complained that too much attention has been paid to his personality.

Mr. Bryan, whose pay packet totalled $1.76 million in 1996, had exercisable stock options valued at $12.8 million at the end of 1996, according to Gulf's latest management information circular.

Industry analysts say Mr. Bryan would have preferred to stay on for another year, but with commodity prices in the doldrums, the flamboyant Texan's talents as a deal maker didn't fit with the pressing need to "nurture" Gulf's existing assets.

While opinions differ on whether Mr. Bryan was a breath of fresh air or a loud-mouthed American, he received general praise for rescuing Gulf from the brink of bankruptcy and turning it into a global energy player.

Gulf still faces tough times ahead, in part because of a $2.7 billion debt load. Within six months or so, to help pay down debt, Gulf plans to sell $400 million in non-core assets, including a corporate jet and a ranch in Nevada, Mr. Auchinleck said.

Formerly part of the Reichmann family's energy empire, Gulf racked up losses totalling $645 million from 1990 to 1995, but posted a $37 million profit in 1996 and earned $204 million in the first nine months of last year.

Although Mr. Bryan is proud of the turnaround, he said he realizes that some Calgarians will be happy to see him fly away for good to the United States, where he spent most of his career as an investment banker. He slashed 40% of Gulf's staff after taking over the top job in January, 1995, and offended Calgary's business community by deciding in the autumn of 1996 to move Gulf's executive offices to Denver, Colorado. Although Mr. Bryan spearheaded the move, there are no plans to relocate the executive offices back to Canada now that he has resigned—it would just be too expensive.

After a series of acquisitions, Gulf's payroll has steadily crept back to almost 1,200 jobs, where the staffing level stood before Mr. Bryan arrived on the scene.

Mr. Bryan said that he hopes his criticisms about the close-knit nature of Canada's oil patch and observations about Quebec separatists won't overshadow his legacy at Gulf. "I enjoyed being here in Calgary, in spite of what some people may be led to believe. I have a lot of affection for Canadians and this community," Mr. Bryan said. "Frankly, I was always in the role of 'the outsider.' It's sad that I was taken somehow as arrogant or whatever and that's not the way I meant it."

Mr. Bryan, 58, said he disagrees with those who portrayed him as an unsophisticated American after he suggested in June, 1996, that Quebec separatists should either start their own country with a bit of land or "if a small, isolated group of you want to go back to France, we'll get you a boat."

He acknowledged that "in retrospect, I probably could have phrased it differently, for sure in a more elegant way. But I just think this secession idea is horrible. If these Quebec guys go, why shouldn't others? It seems to me that the next separation entity would be Alberta. It could be a freestanding unit. Alberta has got great natural resources and people with a lot of vigour and entrepreneurial spirit. It seems like Alberta would be a logical candidate, but I'm totally opposed to separation."

Mr. Bryan said he's "looking forward to getting some rest" after a gruelling three years at Gulf. His plans include spending more time at the family ranch in West Texas and at houses in Colorado Springs and his hometown of Houston. "Maybe after six months or a year, maybe I'll find another challenge that I'm up for. But right now, I'm looking forward to doing as little as possible."

Mr. Bryan said Mr. Auchinleck "is an engineer and an outstanding talent. He's better suited to go into the bowels of the company and get the value out of it. I think my talents have been used to their very best on behalf of Gulf."

Under Mr. Bryan, Gulf went on a shopping spree and its stock market value soared to more than $2.5 billion from $600 million. Last year's acquisitions included the $1.11-billion hostile takeover of British-based Clyde Petroleum PLC and the $688-million friendly purchase of Calgary-based Stampeder Exploration Ltd.

"J. P. made an impact both inside the oil industry and also outside," said Ian Doig, publisher of Calgary-based energy newsletter "Doig's Digest."

Neil Leeson, a Calgary-based industry analyst who follows the U.S. oil and gas sector, said the departure of Mr. Bryan leaves Gulf vulnerable to being taken over, possibly by a large U.S. producer. Gulf has already been viewed as a possible takeover target in recent weeks, and "you're going to see Gulf on the block before the year is out," Mr. Leeson predicted.

Gulf shares fell 60 cents to $7.60 on February 9, 1998, on the Toronto Stock Exchange as investors got rattled about Gulf's future without controversial Mr. Bryan. Industry analysts say Gulf needs to cut its $2.7 billion debt load and also examine what to do with the heavy oil assets acquired in the Stampeder deal, which is hurting Gulf because heavy oil prices have dropped even further than light crude prices.

Oil and natural gas prices have been slumping for more than four months, forcing many producers to reassess their priorities, industry analysts say. And while some investors have bailed out in the short term, it makes sense in the longer term to have Mr. Auchinleck strengthen existing assets rather than go on the acquisition trail, analysts say.

Gulf's international assets, including its North Sea holdings and joint ventures in Indonesia, were part of the portfolio overseen by Mr. Auchinleck, who is also CEO of a publicly traded subsidiary, Gulf Indonesia Resources Ltd. Mr. Auchinleck, 46, has worked at Gulf for more than 22 years. Gulf chairman Earl Joudrie described Mr. Auchinleck as the ideal new CEO because he has served as Gulf's chief operating officer since last July and head of international operations since 1995.

Mr. Bryan said he's pleased that he hired oil patch veteran Edythe (Dee) Parkinson-Marcoux last October to head Gulf's new heavy oil division. However, he said previous plans to launch an initial public offering this summer [1998] of the heavy oil division will be delayed until heavy oil prices recover. "Longer term, I think the future of the oil business in Canada is still in heavy oil," Mr. Bryan said.

In terms of growth strategies, there is no doubt that Mr. Bryan and Mr. Auchinleck approach things differently. Despite the deep debt-cutting facing Gulf [Partridge 1998a], Mr. Auchinleck said that Gulf still plans to grow aggressively, just not through the sort of major acquisitions with which Mr. Bryan made his mark. "We've got terrific assets . . . and our focus over the next three years is going to be to extract value from those assets and to continue to improve the balance sheet and our financial capability," Mr. Auchinleck told analysts during a recent conference call conducted from Gulf's Denver executive offices. "We are going to remain alert to opportunities, but I don't think you'll see us making any major acquisitions over the next one to two years."

INTRODUCTION

If you were a power-oriented, achievement-motivated, need-to-help-society kind of person, what kind of career would you choose? One that has "major" status and compensation rewards, right? Well, according to a recent clipping ("Feeling Poorer?" 1998), despite the fact that in Canada "successful" CEOs can earn millions, the highest-paying "top three" jobs that professionals seem to be turning to, instead, are in this order: judge (where men earn, on average, $129,000 and women earn, on average, $118,000), specialist physician (where men earn, on average, $137,000 and women earn, on average, $86,000), and family physician (where men earn, on average, $117,000 and women earn, on average, $82,000). Why isn't corporate leader at the top of this professional "wanna-be" list?

Experts feel that with the increasing "turmoil at the top" of organizations and with the personal costs associated with staying in and "doing battle," increasingly, even those corporate leaders who have enjoyed the "corporate game" are finding its pain and personal torture a bit too much to justify, especially over the longer haul. Brenda Barnes from Pepsi is just one case in point of a leader who recently decided to turn in the corporate towel (Wente, 1997). J. P. Bryan is another case, even though he might choose to come back and play "the game" in six months' time.

Without question, every time a top corporate leader leaves "the game," even for a little while, the adrenaline in the corporate and media pipelines flows. For example, the news of J. P. Bryan's departure from Gulf Canada in the early weeks of 1998 caused a major "dismissal adrenaline flow" among organizational theorists and stock market analysts. Why? Because, until recently, "the dismissal" of a CEO has been a unique and infrequent event, requiring the strongest exercise of power (Boeker 1992). Estimates are, for example, that during the years 1965 through 1974, there were only about 20 such "dismissals" in the 200 largest nonfinancial firms in the United States. For decades now, organizational academics have generally thought that for CEOs to be dismissed, they must lack sufficient power. Even during periods of poor financial performance, if the CEOs are powerful, the academics have reasoned, it is unlikely that they will acquiesce to dismissal efforts (Boeker 1992).

Surprise! Over the past couple of years, the waters have gotten quite "rough" at the top. The reality is that in 1997 and in 1998, top executives' exits in U.S. and Canadian firms—sometimes voluntary and sometimes not—have put considerable "heat" on their corporate boards of directors. Bryan's exit from Gulf Canada Resources Ltd. is just one recent Canadian example, and in 1997, the United States saw its fair share of CEO succession debacles.

Recently, turmoil "at the top" has been destabilizing some of the best-known U.S. and Canadian companies. At times, the stories in the press have gotten embarrassingly "ugly." For example, during the week of July 18 1997, AT&T Corp.'s president, John Walter, abruptly "quit" after just nine months on the job, following mounting strain with the chairman whom he was supposed to replace. On his way out, the board that hired Walter publicly declared that he lacked the "intellectual leadership" to run AT&T (Lublin 1997). Just a week before Walter's departure, Apple Computer Inc.'s CEO, Gilbert Amelio, resigned after failing to turn around the wounded personal-computer legend. He was the third "unsuccessful" CEO whom Apple's board hired in four years. A truly diligent board might have seen a "red flag" in Amelio's track record as chairman and CEO of National Semiconductor Corp., where "half of the Board was hot on his heels for lack of tangible performance," National Semiconductor Corp's board member Gary Arnold said following Amelio's departure (Lublin 1997).

Boards of directors are supposed to make sure that these sorts of snafus don't happen, and now they're starting to feel the corporate heat. So who is to blame for all of this corporate upset—the CEOs who've allegedly "failed" in their missions, or the boards of directors who hired them? That is the question that we attempt to answer in Chapter 6.

"Heightened shareholder activism has politicized Boards so they think in good guy-bad guy terms," says Jeffrey Sonnenfeld of the CEO College at Emory University's business school. "They abdicate and give everything to the good guy, but if they think the guy is a villain, they go to the public and vilify him" (Lublin 1997). John Walter serves as just one recent case in point of a CEO who was, in essence, victimized and vilified by his own board members. Not only did the AT&T board give chairman and CEO Robert Allen relatively free rein in the search for Walter—and agree to a gradual transfer of power for the top job—but the AT&T directors didn't interfere when Allen thwarted Walter's efforts to assert himself once in the "top gun's" job. Then, after losing a president twice in one year, the AT&T board somehow reached insight that "they" had a problem. The AT&T board finally dropped Allen from their search committee of independent directors (Lublin 1997).

Frequent turnover at the top "is 100 percent the Board's problem," affirms Harry Edelson, managing partner of Edelson Technology Partners, a venture-capital fund in Woodcliff Lake, New Jersey, that manages money for AT&T and other big companies. "The buck stops there" (Lublin 1997). But does it? Organizational academics would argue, on the contrary, that "strong" CEOs actually carry the trump cards.

The objective of Chapter 6 is to look at the "political game" that seems to exist between corporate boards and their CEOs. Like J. P. Bryan and the other CEOs who "lost out" at one stage of "the game," we try to understand why. We also try to understand why women seem to be given little opportunity to partake as equal members in "the game." We begin where Brenda Barnes and J. P. Bryan seem to have left "the game," having played it for a considerable period: at one phase or another of burnout.

TO BURN OUT OR NOT TO BURN OUT: THAT IS THE CEO'S QUESTION

Why is it that only 6 percent of affluent Canadian baby boomers surveyed in 1998 for Royal Trust said that their measure of "success" was having an executive position in their company, while a significant 39 percent said that "success" was being able to stop working? (Clements 1998). In the last few minutes, did you wonder why, after 22 years of "doing battle" at the top of Pepsi's corporate ladder, Brenda Barnes would call it "quits" just when the company said that they were grooming her for even bigger things in the corporate pipeline? Did you wonder why—after agreeing to his "voluntary" dismissal from Gulf Canada—J. P. Bryan would want to take off at least six months and "do as little as possible"?

Would you find it odd that in recent months Canada's historically "civil" CEOs would seem to be taking public speaking lessons from Rambo? (McNish 1998). For example, John Cleghorn and Matthew Barrett have pitched their recently announced and controversial merger of the Royal Bank of Canada and the Bank of Montreal with some very "unbankerly" language. The chairmen recently said that they want to stop "dicking around on the beach" and "bulk up" with a merger to "kick ass" in the global market. Furthermore, Tom Stephens, CEO of struggling MacMillan Bloedel Ltd., told employees in a November 1997 newsletter to stop thinking like "losers" and "get off their butts" to turn around the troubled forest products manufacturer (McNish 1998).

The answer to all of these questions, it seems, is short and to the point: yes, these behaviors are "odd," but they are understandable and symptomatic of a condition called "burnout." Put simply, burnout is the result of too much energy going out and not enough social-emotional refueling coming in.

To be sure, getting involved in, and staying in, the corporate leader political game is "taxing." But because of their motivations to get to the top or to stay there, corporate leaders often do not perceive their burnout "red flags" when they do present, or they consciously choose to ignore them so that they can continue on with their climbs and challenges. However, even corporate leaders have a breaking point; after running on energy fumes for too long, their "moment of awakening" eventually descends like a lead balloon. Sometimes it manifests as emotional exhaustion, and sometimes it manifests as boredom with the job. Sometimes it comes out as "Rambo talk." Sometimes it just feels like a dull hum.

"[Chronic] [s]tress is probably the biggest factor behind the tough talk [recently heard in CEOs]," says McNish, author of the interesting piece "Rambo Talk Reflects Brutish Business World" (1998). "With the rise of shareholder activism," notes McNish, "CEOs are under siege from impatient stakeholders to boost profits at a time when global competitors are eroding their markets."

Sandy Cotton, a leadership expert at Queen's University in Ontario, agrees. "The world of the CEO has become nasty, brutish and short-term oriented. [CEOs] are under intense pressure to produce short-term results and they are choosing strong impact words [and strong impact behaviors] to convey their determination to achieve those results" (McNish 1988). Senior executives also want to convey to employees and to governments a sense of urgency to win support for painful cuts or unpopular transactions such as mergers.

But are there positive returns on these seemingly uncivil Rambo outbursts? "In some circles," emphasizes McNish, (1998), "the hairy-chested talk is winning public relations points, if only because it gives a more human face to CEOs." It is, in essence, a "cry for help" from those who are trying to sustain their rise to the top. But, from a gender perspective, cautions Cotton, tough talk is also very masculine talk, and that may not play well with the women who make up a big share of these companies' workforces and clientele. "This is very male language. How do you think females are supposed to interpret this [cry]?" (McNish 1998).

Other present-day organizational onlookers concur with Cotton. "It's up-front and refreshing," CBC radio host Avril Benoit commented to Royal Bank's Cleghorn during an interview in February 1998, after his Rambo talk outbursts, but few onlookers would admit that this tough talk is good for business over the longer term (McNish 1998). Academic critics of "Rambo talk" say that it might rally the troops in the short term, but it runs the risk of eroding employee morale and customer loyalty over time. It's one thing to cultivate a survival-of-the-fittest atmosphere for a struggling company, but profitable organizations such as banks and automakers do not need generals barking commands. The best leaders even in tough times, notes McNish, are charismatic ones—choosing the right words that inspire, rather than intimidate, workers.

Maybe "Chainsaw" Al Dunlap, business' modern-day version of Rambo, is the guy who is acting as mentor for these Canadian Rambo equivalents, posits McNish (1998). The former U.S. paratrooper, corporate turnaround artist, and author of *Mean Business* is the "ultimate Rambo" in pinstripes. Ever since he slashed 35 percent of the workforce at money-losing Scott Paper Co. and delivered billions of dollars of gains through a merger with Kimberly-Clark Corporation in 1995, investors have lionized his brutal business style. Basically, Dunlap wields a "take-no-prisoners" approach to business. When he walked into a crowded room of managers at troubled disposable cup maker Lily-Tulip Inc. in 1983, he pointed to a pair of men and said: "You two stay—the rest of you are fired. Goodbye." Dunlap himself has said, "You're not in business to be liked. If you want a friend, get a dog" (McNish 1998).

Mark Kingwell, a University of Toronto professor and author of *A Civil Tongue*, regards the arrival of "mean" CEO language as part of a continuing decline of that unique Canadian trait—CEO civility. "Unfortunately," says Kingwell, "civility is seen to be synonymous with weakness. Civility is the first thing that dies when 'the heat' is on" (McNish 1998).

A Closer Look at How Burnout Manifests in Corporate Leaders

In the economically challenged 1990s, both male and female corporate leaders have increasingly fallen victim to burnout, a condition discovered in the 1980s for people in the health services. That is, as a result of sudden resignations or firings, "premature" or "overextended" retirements, and blocked promotions, increasing numbers of corporate leaders are seeking professional assistance for what in their minds is a real problem: a decreased motivation to perform the challenging work that used to turn them on (Davidson & Cooper 1983). Moreover, note mental health experts, burnout is recognized as symptomatic of all managerial activity, regardless of organizational type or level (Davidson & Cooper 1983).

Burnout has been variously defined by mental health experts as emotional exhaustion resulting from chronic tension and stress, a state of energy depletion produced by continuing frustration of personal needs on and off the job, and the accumulation of stressors great enough to push individuals beyond their comfortable, "elastic" coping limits to strain (Davidson & Cooper 1983). In any or all of these cases, the result is the usage of considerable amounts of finite life energy—with low or negative returns on these energy investments.

While burnout manifests itself in corporate leaders in varying ways, "progressive burnout" has been associated with a broad range of negative presentations, ranging from Rambo talk and exaggerated irritability, to excessive CEO absenteeism and "risky" corporate decision making. One common burnout "red flag" cited by CEOs is a feeling of "all-encompassing fatigue"—which they find odd, given their hypomanic tendencies. Other reported burnout "red flags" include blaming others for work-related problems, complaining about work aspects that were not previously areas of concern, arriving late and leaving early from work, bickering with one's coworkers or spouse, feeling relatively unproductive or unimportant in one's job, craving to be alone, needing sleep but not feeling refueled by it, and suffering from various physical ailments and illnesses (Davidson & Cooper 1983).

Left unattended, note the burnout experts (Davidson & Cooper 1983; Maslach & Jackson 1985), these "red flags" can continue on an increasingly energy-exhausting cyclical process that is difficult to break without a mental health professional's interventions. Sometimes, both personal and organizational interventions are required to bring the affected corporate leader's system back to health.

In 1985, Maslach and Jackson, the researchers who popularized the concept with their development of the Maslach Burnout Inventory (MBI), said that high-end burnout is characterized, in various degrees, by three major presentations:

- *Emotional exhaustion*, whereby a corporate leader's emotional resources are depleted, and the feeling that he or she has nothing left to give others at a psychological level prevails;
- *Depersonalization*, whereby a corporate leader develops cold and callous attitudes about his or her coworkers or clients and increasingly uses "Rambo talk" (or the old line, "Here's a quarter; go call someone who cares"); and
- *Personal accomplishment decreases*, whereby a corporate leader develops a negative evaluation of his or her task accomplishments, whereas formerly these would have been perceived positively.

While researchers are still debating whether there are consistent phases to the burnout phenomenon, there is, as yet, no conclusive finding in this regard (Schell 1997). There is increasing evidence, however, that female corporate leaders may often verbalize emotional exhaustion as the primary complaint, and male corporate leaders may often verbalize depersonalization as the primary burnout complaint (Davidson & Cooper 1983; Greenglass 1991).

Why Corporate Leaders Are "At Risk" for Burnout

But, aside from this minor difference in initial verbalization, note the experts, "workaholic" male and female corporate leaders who are at the top of their corporations are "at risk" for eventual burnout. In 1985, for example, Nelson and Quick noted that male corporate leaders may become "workaholics" and, thus, be at increased risk for burnout because of (1) role overloads brought on to promote and maintain their image as "successful" achievers and providers, (2) excessive pressure and "power-play" conflicts from attempts to exercise leadership, and (3) career goal discrepancies. Moreover, noted this research team, women corporate leaders display similar "workaholic" tendencies for all of the same reasons; plus, like Brenda Barnes, their burnout levels can be further exacerbated by their gender struggles in trying to meet both work and family obligations.

Moreover, note present-day burnout experts, even if corporate leaders—male and female alike—have strong "self-healing" predispositions existing within them, these traits can become chronically "challenged" by pathological energy demands placed on them in present-day "Type A" workplaces. Left in the Type A battle zone for too long, even the predominantly "self-healing" corporate leader can become burned out by an overly demanding and unforgiving work situation.

In their 1984 Canadian study on 244 male and female supervisors and corporate leaders in nine types of organizations, Cahoon and Rowney found that "pathologically strained" middle managers had almost twice as many scorers in the "high-burnout zone" as their entry-level and senior-level counterparts. However, emphasized these researchers, consistent with Cooper's 1984 research on global leaders, almost 20 percent of the top corporate leaders in 1984 reported "high-end" burnout scores. Whether these percentage findings would hold for corporate leaders in "taxing" 1998 remains a void not yet reported on.

Measuring Burnout Potential

To assess "burnout potential" in working adults and in corporate leaders, clinicians typically give clients the 22-item self-report inventory called the MBI, developed by Maslach and Jackson in 1981.

DETAILS ON THE CEO-BOARD "GAME"

The question then arises, if the CEO-board "game" is so risky that present-day corporate leaders are, increasingly, falling prey to burnout, where is the risk?

Before we get into the details of the risk involved in the CEO-board "game," we need to make it clear that this "game" runs concurrently with the stress-personality-mood "game" discussed at length for the first five chapters. Some players, like Brenda Barnes, eventually give up on the CEO-board "game" to win at the mind-body health "game." Other players, like J. P. Bryan, just take a break from the CEO-board "game" for a while until their energy returns. Then, there are the corporate leaders who decide to stay in the CEO-board "game," despite their potential losses on the mind-body health "game." Because of the risk involved, over the past 30 years, academics have been trying to figure out what sorts of strategies are required to get in, to stay in, and to win the CEO-board "game."

Objective of the CEO-Board "Game"

Though some academics might argue against this point, the objective of the CEO-board "game" is "to win" in the power struggle. "Winning," in very basic terms, means being able to get in and to stay in "the game." Inevitably, when players enter such a political "game," somebody stays, and somebody goes—so say experts Harrison, Torres, and Kukalis (1988). Here, then, lies the risk.

The Player Position

The Ultimate: CEO/Board Chair Position. Players, it seems, can choose to become "a board member only" or "a CEO and a board member, combined." Obviously, the more "power titles" that players accumulate, the greater the likelihood that they can stay in "the game" longer (i.e., have a long tenure) and accrue a major compensation package (including salary, bonus, and stock options). While Harrison, Torres, and Kukalis (1988) firmly believe that the best position to play for is the "CEO/board chair combined," other experts like Belliveau, O'Reilly, and Wade (1996) have recently argued that the compensation committee chair on the board is a worthwhile position because large sums of money are involved and because it is status-rewarding, too.

Though, like most games, there is eventually an end to all of the "good times," Harrison, Torres, and Kukalis (1988) have said that you know you are really winning when you attain the CEO position and then move up to the coveted "combined CEO/chair position."

You are still doing fine as a player in the CEO-board "game" when you move upstairs to the less important "chair only" position, but this move should be seen by you as a "red flag" that says you better start looking for another board game to play in.

Always remember: once you hit the "top position," below you there are a lot of seasoned and often ambitious executives who are ready to see you topple! Those below you live for unexpected departures from the "CEO/chair" position, for the transition of the "CEO/chair" position to the "chair only" position, and for the final "transition" position—your retirement, forced or voluntary.

Board Member-Only Positions. For the game players choosing to opt for the board member-only position at any time in the CEO-board "game," having a bachelor's or a master's degree in engineering or in business helps players to get placed on one of the following important board and status-embellished subcommittees (Kesner 1988):

- *Audit Committee,* which sets the scope of corporate audits, reviews completed audits with external auditors, determines the adequacy of internal controls, selects internal auditors, reviews completed audits with internal auditors, reviews company accounting policies and procedures, reviews the completed audits with management, and sets the auditor's fees.

- *Compensation Committee,* which reviews and makes recommendations on compensation for senior management, administers stock option programs, and sets compensation for senior management.

- *Nominating Committee,* which considers stockholder recommendations, selects nominees for directors, and evaluates incumbents.

- *Executive Committee,* which serves as a stand-in to act in lieu of a full board when immediate actions are needed, counsels the CEO on ideas and proposals prior to disclosure to the full board, and oversees the activities of other board committees.

These four committees, besides providing status, play a major role in the protection of stockholders' interests (Kesner 1988). Also, the Securities and Exchange Commission (SEC) considers these committees to be an important tool for monitoring corporate activities and for keeping them "aboveboard." Consequently, the SEC requires companies to report the types of committees used and the particulars on their memberships. The major stock exchanges also have recommendations and regulations regarding the use and the composition of such committees.

Players seeking board-only positions must realize that the opportunities are relatively limited. Until recently, most boards have averaged only 13 directors (Kesner 1988); and with present-day cutbacks, most boards' sizes are shrinking to, on average, about 11 members (Jackson 1997). Also, if one wants to capitalize on the "status" variable, board-only players should consider joining (or, even better, being asked to join), on average, three boards. Also, whenever possible, players would do well to vie for a subcommittee "chair" position.

Once a player gets onto the board, he or she will be called all kinds of position names. Some of these names have more status, depending on where and when you are sitting. For example, as we heard from J. P. Bryan, players will be called either "an insider" or "an outsider." Insiders, like Auchinleck, are current or former employees of a company; they typically hold or have held high-level executive positions and thus offer their boards an in-depth working knowledge of their organizations. Outsiders, like Bryan, come from other companies; they are valued because of their breadth of experience and knowledge, their contacts outside a firm, and their relative independence from previous and present company CEOs (Kesner 1988).

Academics agree that "insiders" and "outsiders" both perform important functions on the board, but if there were a contest in terms of "higher status," probably most academics would say that "outsiders" would have "the edge" because of their so-called valued objectivity. In fact, because of the power struggles that gain life inside boards, organizational critics have raised questions about whether "inside" directors and CEOs, in particular, can properly perform their function of monitoring top management performance, given that they, in essence, are monitoring themselves.

Moreover, say the critics, too many "insiders" on an audit, compensation, or nominating committee might cause problems of "independence" in terms of internal monitoring, setting top executive compensation, or nominating new board members. Because of these very real concerns, various regulatory agencies—including the New York Stock Exchange (NYSE), the American Stock Exchange (ASE), and the National Association of Securities Dealers (NASD)—offer specific guidelines concerning the composition of these key committees. Besides the NASD's suggesting that all four key groups maintain a majority of "outside," unaffiliated members to ensure "independent" judgment and fairness, the NYSE requires that all companies listed on the exchange have an audit committee composed entirely of "independent outsiders." The ASE maintains a similar position (Kesner 1988).

To give potential "game" players an inside look at the kinds of players you will likely meet on these board committees, here are some insights provided by Kesner (1988). During the late 1980s, "outsiders" constituted 63 percent of the board directorships, while "insiders" constituted only 37 percent. Occupationally, business executives represented about 65 percent of the directorships, followed by consultants (6 percent), followed by educational institution representatives (5 percent) or attorneys (5 percent). On a final note, said Kesner (1988), once they got "into the game," board directors in the 1980s liked to stay; their service, on average, was 11 years. Most board directors were males in their 50s, who partook in at least two other boards.

Hints by Academics for Winning the CEO-Board "Game"

First, it needs to be emphasized that for players looking for a very rational and economically driven "game," academics generally advise you to stay out of the CEO-board "game." Using compensation package value as the ultimate dependent measure for "success" at this "game," experts Belliveau, O'Reilly, and Wade (1996) say that many cross-sectional economic studies have explained only 20 percent to 30 percent of the variance in CEO compensation, and in some recent studies, economic variables have explained less than 10 percent of CEOs' compensation.

Experts Baker, Jensen, and Murphy (1988) add that although there is an "enormous amount of research in the economics of contracting . . . [it] offers little guidance in actual compensation arrangements in large organizations. . . . The empirical relation between the pay of top-level executives and firm performance, while positive and statistically significant, is tiny. On average, each $1,000 change in shareholder wealth corresponds to an increase in this year's and next year's salary of only two cents." Ultimately, these researchers add, "it may be that psychologists, behaviorists, human resource consultants and personnel executives understand something about human behavior that is not yet captured in our economic models" (pp. 593, 611, 615).

Until such time as more concrete answers are found by social science experts for explaining the amount of variance in CEOs' compensation package values, many academics have posited that the strategy that seems to pay off is the "likes attract" rather than the "opposites attract" strategy. It has been called by many names, including "the old boys' network," "self-cloning," and "homosocial reproduction" (Zajac & Westphal 1996b).

Now, then, here are some pointers "on winning" from the academic experts:

(1) According to Zajac and Westphal (1996b), the "powerful" boards (i.e., those separating the CEO and the board chair positions, having longer board tenure relative to the CEO's tenure, having lots of "independent outside" directors, and having a higher degree of "outsider" stock ownership) are likely to change the CEO characteristics in the direction of their own demographic profiles. Moreover, the "outside" CEO successors are also typically demographically different from their CEO predecessors but demographically similar to the boards doing the hiring. Zajac and Westphal share the logic behind the "self-cloning":

The underlying logic for why both parties would tend to favor similar successors was explained by the integrated social psychological and sociopolitical perspective. . . . First, by taking a social psychological approach, we established that to the extent that demographic similarity provides a salient basis for in-group membership, deep-seated psychological tendencies toward in-group favoritism can lead both CEOs and board members to favor demographically similar CEOs. . . .

Second, by taking a sociopolitical approach, we established that outgoing CEOs and boards may both favor personally compatible (similar) successor candidates in an attempt to establish greater interpersonal influence over new CEOs and subsequent influence over organizational affairs. In effect, outgoing CEOs favor similar successors in order to preserve their legacies or visions for their organizations . . . and boards prefer demographically similar new CEOs in order to facilitate socialization.

Interestingly, . . . we also find that although outside successors are typically demographically different from their CEO predecessors, they are demographically more similar to members of the firms' boards of directors. . . . The fact that this tendency is greater for outsider than for insider CEO successors is consistent with the notion that boards face greater performance ambiguity and social uncertainty in evaluating outsiders and thus are more likely to rely on demographic similarity as a way to reduce ambiguity and uncertainty. (pp. 83–86)

(2) Zajac and Westphal (1996a) add that contests for "intraorganizational power" can affect "interorganizational ties." Specifically, powerful CEOs seek to maintain their control by selecting and retaining board members with experience on other "passive boards"—whereby the majority of members protect or bolster their CEO's control. Also, powerful CEOs seek to maintain their control by excluding members with experience on more "active boards"—whereby the majority of members opt for increased board monitoring of, and control over, CEOs.

Moreover, powerful CEOs seek older directors for their board members. That is, directors' age is positively associated with subsequent appointments to low-control boards and negatively associated with appointments to high-control boards. Older directors are often perceived by powerful CEOs as more accepting of board "passivity" in controlling management and less likely to embrace newer perspectives reflecting more "active" board involvement and control in management decision making. This important finding suggests that highly paid CEOs may be perceived as individuals accustomed to weak board control, which would increase their attractiveness at low board-control companies and decrease their attractiveness to high board-control companies.

(3) Belliveau, O'Reilly, and Wade (1996) believe that the "social status" of CEOs, relative to that of their compensation committee chairperson, is particularly important in setting robust compensation packages for CEOs—and thus winning at the CEO financial "game." Specifically, when a compensation chair's "social status" is low relative to that of other compensation chairs, or when a CEO possesses more "social status" than his or her compensation chair, the CEO receives more compensation (given controls for firm size, industry, firm performance, and human capital). For instance, although many CEOs have M.B.A.s and, therefore, have high human capital, their educational experience may, more importantly, serve as "social capital"; that is, it increases their "social resources" by providing an affiliation with a prestigious educational institution and opportunities to build influential personal networks. In short, among "successful" and well-compensated CEOs, the "social capital" associated with their educational degrees appears to be much more valuable than the gains in human capital that the degree represents.

Looking at this finding from the board's point of view, one implication is that a board may be able to limit CEO influence over compensation decisions by selecting a compensation chair of very high "social status." Research suggests that doing so may be especially important if a CEO has a long tenure on a board. This finding is also consistent with previous research suggesting that high-status "outsiders" may be better able to monitor CEOs by curbing their "opportunism" (or, shall we say, narcissism?). It is possible that high-status compensation chairs who serve on many boards and participate in many "clubs" know more about the performance and compensation of other CEOs and, therefore, can construct a compensation scheme more appropriately aligned with firm performance.

(4) If there is any rationality in the compensation-scheme-of-things for CEOs, it is in the finding that, as would be expected, as one progresses in the CEO "game" position from the "plant manager," to the "divisional CEO," to the "group CEO," to the "corporate CEO," there is a statistically significant, monotonic increase in compensation (salary, bonuses, and stock options). For example, researchers Lambert, Larcker, and Weigelt (1993), using 1990 dollar expressions, say that the median cash compensation for the plant manager position was $86,311; that for

the divisional CEO position was $174,894; that for the group CEO position was $274,000; and that for the corporate CEO position was $976,410. (The differential size of units across organizational levels and the median sales also exhibited this expected monotonic increase from the plant manager to the corporate CEO.)

Lambert, Larcker, and Weigelt said in closing: "[S]hareholders allow the CEO to have long tenure or appoint Board members because they are convinced that there are few 'agency' problems with this manager. Thus, shareholders are willing to pay this manager a compensation premium for this trust, and managerial power need not have the types of undesirable consequences typically assumed by sociologists" (p. 459).

(5) As insurance against hostile takeovers, boards often consider "golden parachutes" or "GPs" for incumbent management teams—and CEOs are glad when they do. By definition, a GP is any contractual agreement that will potentially provide the CEO with a payment contingent upon a change in control of the company. The magnitude of these payouts can be significant. For instance, a decade ago, 10 executives from Primerica received $98.2 million as a result of a takeover, and present-day estimates are that about 30 percent of the top 250 industrial companies have GPs for their corporate leaders. With the economic uncertainties of the 1990s, the number of GPs continues to grow (Wade, O'Reilly, & Chandratat 1990).

Though the payment is generally made only if the CEO is fired following a change in control, note Wade, O'Reilly, and Chadratat (pp. 600–602), payment has been awarded even if the CEO does not leave or leaves voluntarily. Powerful CEOs with a higher tenure relative to the board are more likely to receive a GP. From a social influence perspective, say these researchers, CEOs with a higher relative tenure are more likely to have appointed other board members, who may then feel a "reciprocal obligation." This supposition was strengthened by their finding that the percentage of the board composed of "outsiders" appointed after the CEO, appointment was even more important than relative tenure. These study results suggest that it is more important that a CEO simply be appointed before "outside" board members than it is for him or her to be appointed a long time before members of the board. This reality enables the CEO to influence the selection process.

There is some "power" logic behind GPs. The general argument in favor of GPs is one of aligning incentives between shareholders and management (Wade, O'Reilly, & Chandratat 1990). The logic is that an entrenched management, faced with a takeover bid that may lead to job loss, is likely to resist the offer to protect management's jobs, even though such an offer might be in the shareholders' interest. Evidence also shows that GPs are associated with a positive security market reaction; from this angle, GPs provide incentives to management to pay attention to the stockholders' interests and not to the top managers' potential job loss.

But aren't GPs a bit of "overkill"? Apparently not. Though labor disputes and white-collar crimes were the most common forms of business "crises" in 1997, says a study (Church 1998) by the Institute of Crisis Management (ICM), hostile takeovers were the fastest growing reason companies experienced "crisis." In all, the ICM found a 19 percent increase in the number of crisis events reported in the news in 1997 compared to the previous year. As takeover crises mount, so do GP considerations.

(6) Finally, if you are a CEO in a firm whose profits have been declining *four or more years in a row*, warns Columbia University organizational expert Warren Boeker (1992), recognize that this is a major "red flag" for you. Studies have also shown that the presence of a large number of "outsiders" on a board *and* a significant concentration of stock ownership in the hands of institutions or groups other than management are additional "red flags" for CEOs, an indicator leading to their dismissal. Under the latter conditions, a CEO's power vis-à-vis the board is low, increasing the likelihood of board-initiated "succession."

Now for the good news, CEO game players. Even during sustained periods of low firm performance, CEOs can stay in "the game" longer if (1) their ownership position is great, (2) the firm ownership by other individuals is more dispersed, and (3) a greater proportion of the board members appointed by the CEO are "insiders" (Boeker 1992).

If all else fails fatewise, confirms Boeker, CEOs whose firm performance is poor can stay in "the game" longer *if they can convince the board that they are valuable and that "the problem" lies with other top managers.* (Imagine that!) Thus, powerful CEOs can displace the blame for poor performance onto their subordinates, particularly their second-tier managers of the organization, who will subsequently be replaced.

A Summary Profile of Those Who Have Played "the Game" Well

We come now to the interesting question of who has played the CEO-board "game" well in recent years. Using compensation package value as the criterion for "winning," the boom in technology shares is churning out U.S. billionaire winners of "the game" by the scores, as the technology industry continues to grant CEOs more stock options than any other industry (Associated Press 1997). At the end of 1996, for example, Microsoft chair Bill Gates took home a compensation package worth at least $38.7 billion U.S.—and Bill Gates was not alone. Paul Allen and Steve Ballmer, also of Microsoft, received $14.8 billion U.S. and $8.2 billion U.S., respectively. Other billionaire "high-tech" CEOs included Larry Ellison of Oracle, bringing in $8.2 billion U.S., Gordon Moore of Intel, bringing in $8 billion U.S., and Michael Dell of Dell, bringing in $4.7 billion U.S. (Associated Press 1997).

North of the border, pockets of Canadian CEOs are also "winning" at the CEO-board "game," but their compensation packages are not as munificent as those south of the border. Not quite four months into 1998, Richard Currie, president of supermarket giant Loblaw Cos. Ltd., already stands a strong chance of emerging as Canada's best-paid and most successful "game" player. Since early January, Currie has cashed in options and share appreciation rights (SARs) on more than 1 million shares, netting him a whopping $29.5 million Cdn in pretax gains (Partridge 1998b). To put this in perspective, Currie's is the biggest haul from this variety of executive "win" since Magna International Inc. founder and chairman Frank Stronach set the Canadian record of $32.2 million in 1995.

In terms of winning at the board membership "game," within recent years, about 90 percent of the North American directorships have been held by white males in their 50s with a university degree and with a CEO position in some other corporation (Burke 1996).

In short, female corporate leaders seem not to be faring too well at "the game." They are way behind in North America in terms of both board directorships and CEO positioning. In the United States, the number of Fortune 500 companies with female board directors rose less than 3 percent in 1997 and less than 3 percent in 1996, following jumps of 9 percent from 1993 to 1994 and 7 percent from 1994 to 1995. As of 1997, women constituted just under 11 percent of Fortune 500's 6,081 directors seats, a gain of about 7 percent since the early 1980s (Jackson 1997).

The major factor keeping women off boards is CEO status; the job description for board membership has often demanded that the individual be a CEO—and women just have not been there yet. As of 1995, just 57 women held positions of executive vice president or higher in Fortune 500 companies. Moreover, of the top five earners in each of the Fortune 500 companies, just 47, or 2 percent, were women. Of these, 16 were chief financial officers (CFOs) and one was CEO. By October 1997, there were two U.S. female CEOs (Jackson 1997).

In Canada, as of 1997, while 34 percent of Canadian corporate managers and administrators were women, only 9 percent of the corporate directors were women, and only 2 percent of the CEOs among Canada's top 500 companies were women. Joy Calkin, whose case appeared in Chapter 4, was one of them. Maureen Kempston Darkes, CEO of General Motors of Canada Ltd., was another, as was Bobby Gaunt, president of Ford Motor Company of Canada Ltd. (Wells 1997). Given this poor showing of women in the North American corporate leader positions, say the experts at Catalyst, a nonprofit U.S. research group that works to advance women in business, "we must retire the myth that women have already 'made it' [i.e., at winning in the CEO-board game]" (Wells 1997, p. 60).

THE BOTTOM LINE

This chapter opened with the case of J. P. Bryan, a CEO who surprised everyone in the Canadian oil patch a few months ago with his announcement that he was giving up the helm of the company he had turned from a moribund wreck into a multibillion-dollar powerhouse. The questions immediately raised by the business community were: Did J. P. "jump," or was he "pushed," and is Gulf better or worse off with him gone? (Ingram 1998a).

Before attending to these two questions, I'd like to turn to an observation raised at the start of this chapter: regardless of whether J. P. Bryan jumped or was pushed, he appeared to show signs of "burning out." In reviewing the literature on burnout, we came to the conclusion that with all the "turmoil at the top" of organizations in recent years, at least 20 percent of today's corporate leaders are at risk for high-level burnout. These burnout symptoms, we noted, range from "Rambo talk" utterings to the more severe kinds of emotional exhaustion, depersonalization, and job accomplishment dissatisfaction.

We then looked more closely at the CEO-board power "game" to better understand it and to hear from the experts on how corporate leaders and board directors might better their "odds" for winning at "the game." At the end of this chapter, we noted that in North America, men in their 50s, with a university education and with a CEO title in some other corporation were particularly good at "winning" the so-called self-cloning game, both status-wise and financially. Women, on the other hand, were especially poor at it. They didn't have two basic game-entry criteria: a CEO title elsewhere and the established "social network."

Rumor has it that increasingly more women in North America are starting up their own firms and "self-cloning" via the female gender. For example, once again there were recent rattlings in the Canadian oil patch that 34-year-old Jackie Rafter has started her own business called Roxy Capital Corporation and that her board is all female (Ingram 1998b). If starting one's own business just isn't "in the cards" for women, experts say that some frustrated and burning-out North American female corporate leaders are finding the "odds" of winning the CEO-board "game" somewhat healthier in transnational corporations (Adler 1997).

Now it's time to revisit the two questions posed at the start of this section. Was J. P. Bryan pushed out, or did he quit? Is Gulf better or worse off with him gone?

"On the first question," says Ingram (1998a), "opinion is leaning toward the pushed theory. Until now there has been no hint from anyone at Gulf of any departure plans, which tend to be widely telegraphed by CEOs looking to ease their way out of a company. Analysts say Gulf met with them [just before J. P.'s departure] to brief them on plans, and there was no inkling that this [departure] announcement was coming."

As for the question of whether Bryan's presence has been good or bad for Gulf, there is no easy answer, affirms Ingram (1998a):

On one hand, many observers—and even some critics—say he produced tremendous value at Gulf, through innovative deals and a clear grasp of financial leverage, and that shareholders benefited as a result. Gulf's market value has more than quadrupled since he took over in early 1995, and that's hard to argue with. On the other hand, some say J. P. was also a loose cannon, both in terms of Gulf's corporate strategy and in his personal dealings with other players in the oil patch. He not only loaded the company up with debt—$2.7 billion or so— *but he also seemed to take great delight in stressing that he wasn't part of the cozy old-boys' network. He even moved his head office to Denver, a further snub.*

Not a good game move, J. P. Enter from stage left: "insider" Auchinleck.

REFERENCES

Adler, N. J. (1997). *International dimensions of organizational behavior*. Cincinnati: South-Western College Publishing, p. 309.

Associated Press. (1997). Rich list ranks top tech types. *The Globe and Mail*, September 23, p. B15.

Baker, G., Jensen, M., & Murphy, K. (1988). Compensation and incentives: Practice vs. theory. *Journal of Finance*, 18, 593–616.

Belliveau, M. A., O'Reilly, C. A., III, & Wade, J. B. (1996). Social capital at the top: Effects of social similarity and status on CEO compensation. *Academy of Management Journal*, 39, 1568–1593.

Boeker, W. (1992). Power and managerial dismissal: Scapegoating at the top. *Administrative Science Quarterly*, 37, 400–421.

Burke, R. J. (1996). Why aren't more women on corporate boards? Views of women directors. *Psychological Reports*, 79, 840–842.

Cahoon, A. R., & Rowney, J. A. (1984). Managerial burnout: A comparison by sex and level of responsibility. *Journal of Health and Human Resources Administration*, 7, 249–264.

Church, E. (1998). Management briefs: Crisis time. *The Globe and Mail*, March 3, p. B13.

Clements, W. (1998). Spectrum. *The Globe and Mail Report on Business Magazine*, 14, p. 124.

Davidson, M. J., & Cooper, C. L. (1983). *Stress and the woman manager*. Oxford: Martin Robertson.

Feeling poorer? You're right. (1998). *The Globe and Mail*, May 31, p. A4.

Greenglass, E. R. (1991). Burnout and gender: Theoretical and organizational implications. *Canadian Psychology*, 32, 562–579.

Harrison, J. R., Torres, D. L., & Kukalis, S. (1988). The changing of the guard: Turnover and structural change in the top management positions. *Administrative Science Quarterly*, 33, 211–232.

Ingram, M. (1998a). J. P. Bryan: Hero and/or villain? *The Globe and Mail*, February 10, p. B2.

Ingram, M. (1998b). They're not Charlie's angels. *The Globe and Mail*, February 24, p. B2.

Jackson, M. (1997). Companies slow to appoint female directors: Survey. *The Globe and Mail*, October 2, p. B16.

Jang, B. (1998). Bryan leaves Gulf Canada. *The Globe and Mail*, February 10, pp. B1, B10.

Kesner, I. F. (1988). Directors' characteristics and committee membership: An investigation of type, occupation, tenure, and gender. *Academy of Management Journal*, 31, 66–84.

Lambert, R. A., Larcker, D. F., & Weigelt, K. (1993). The structure of organizational incentives. *Administrative Science Quarterly*, 38, 438–461.

Lublin, J. S. (1997). The Wall Street Journal: Top executives' exits put heat on boards. *The Globe and Mail*, July 18, p. B8.

Maslach, C., & Jackson, S. E. (1981). The measurement of experienced burnout. *Journal of Occupational Behaviour*, 2, 99–113.

Maslach, C., & Jackson, S. E. (1985). The role of sex and family variables in burnout. *Sex Roles*, 12, 837–851.

McNish, J. (1998). Rambo talk reflects brutish business world. *The Globe and Mail*, February 10, p. B18.

Nelson, D. L., & Quick, J. C. (1985). Professional women: Are distress and disease inevitable? *Academy of Management Review*, 10, 206–218.

Partridge, J. (1998a). Gulf Canada to slash debt. *The Globe and Mail*, February 21, p. B1.

Partridge, J. (1998b). Options spell pay dirt. *The Globe and Mail*, April 18, pp. B1, B6–B7.

Schell, B. H. (1997). *A self-diagnostic approach to understanding organizational and personal stressors: The C-O-P-E Model for Stress Reduction.* Westport, CT: Quorum Books, pp. 267–286.

Wade, J. B., O'Reilly, C. A., III, & Chandratat, I. (1990). Golden parachutes: CEOs and the exercise of social influence. *Administrative Science Quarterly*, 35, 587–603.

Wells, J. (1997). Stuck on the ladder. *Maclean's*, 110, pp. 60–64.

Wente, M. (1997). Why I'll never be CEO. *The Globe and Mail*, October 25, p. D7.

Zajac, E. J., & Westphal, J. D. (1996a). Director reputation, CEO-board power, and the dynamics of board interlocks. *Administrative Science Quarterly*, 41, 507–529.

Zajac, E. J., & Westphal, J. D. (1996b). Who shall succeed? How CEO/board preferences and power affect the choice of new CEOs. *Academy of Management Journal*, 39, 64–90.

PART II

An Empirical Look at How Successful Corporate Leaders See Themselves

Corporate Leaders: A Descriptive Profile of Their Stress Levels, Influence Strategies, and Earnings

During the past two decades there has been a dramatic increase in the number of women who are pursuing managerial and professional careers. Many of these women have prepared themselves for careers by undertaking university education where they now comprise almost half of the graduates of professional schools such as accounting, business, and law. Research suggests that these graduates enter the workforce at levels comparable to their male colleagues and with similar credentials and expectations, but it seems that women's and men's corporate experience and career paths begin to diverge soon after that point.

—R. J. Burke & G. MacDermid (1996)

A CASE IN POINT (KEENAN & McFARLAND 1997)

Bobbie Gaunt has heard all the talk and now she wants some action. "Someone asked me not too long ago if I was proud of the fact I'd broken through the glass ceiling," says the president of Ford Motor Co. of Canada Ltd. "I said I would be proud if I believed I had."

The number of women selling cars, trucks and minivans in showrooms is growing, and women buy 50% of the vehicles sold in North America and influence 80% of the purchase decisions. Yet Ms. Gaunt is one of two female CEOs of Canadian car makers.

Moreover, women still make up only a small proportion of senior executives or board members of Chrysler Corp., Ford Motor Co., General Motors Corp., and their largest parts suppliers. Both the auto makers and parts companies can't seem to shake the persistent image that their industry is still "an old boys' club."

"The [auto parts] industry is a bunch of middle-aged, mid-50s, white men from Michigan and Indiana," says one Wall Street observer who insisted on anonymity. "They're all frat boys. They all have class rings and one of these big fat Mont Blanc pens and they wear gold bracelets and Rolex watches they won in a sales competition. It's a really good-old-boy kind of industry. They care about nothing but University of Michigan football and dirty jokes."

That view may be harsh, but there is no disputing that complaints of discrimination and harassment keep cropping up at both the parts companies and the auto makers. Most recently, auto parts giant Magna International Inc. of Markham, Ontario, Canada, was hit by a sexual discrimination lawsuit from a female sales representative in one of its offices in suburban Detroit. Among the negative gender issues arising from the suit are admissions by Magna salesmen that they regularly entertained potential car company customers at strip clubs in the Motor City. The allegations in the suit . . . became public just days after Mitsubishi Motor Corp. of America settled out of court with 27 women who accused the company of sexual harassment. The Japan-based auto maker still faces a U.S. government lawsuit involving several hundred women at its assembly plant in Normal, Illinois. "It's the macho industry," says the CEO of one Canadian auto parts company, who ackowledges that the industry is still in the 1980s when it comes to gender relations.

Ms. Gaunt says change in the auto industry is happening, but it hasn't come far enough or fast enough yet. "When I look back at 25 years I've certainly seen significant changes," she says. "But as with anything that I think is as huge as this industry, and as old as this industry is, we're really talking about cultural change. And changing cultures and changing behaviours takes a very long time."

One of the reasons for the macho tradition, says Norman Solomon, dean of business at the University of Windsor in Ontario, Canada, is that many parts manufacturers still have traditional, entrepreneurial cultures created and maintained by strong-willed company founders. Most are non-unionized. Many of the entrepreneurs were skilled tradesmen and the executive ranks within those companies are often filled with people who are promoted by company founders and share their views, Prof. Solomon says. "You have to look at how many of these companies get started up," he says. "They're entrepreneurial companies started by people with a technical background, and Magna is a good example of that."

Magna was founded in 1957 by Austrian tool-and-die maker Frank Stronach, who remains chairman and controlling shareholder of the company. The CEO, Donald Walker, is Mr. Stronach's son-in-law. The sole woman among the 13 executives in the senior ranks of the company and on its board is Belinda Stronach, daughter of the founder and wife of Mr. Walker.

The attitudes of senior executives—even in companies as large as Magna with its $7.7-billion in sales last year—are pivotal in creating a corporate culture, says David Cole, director of the University of Michigan's Office for the Study of Automotive Transportation (OSAT). Mr. Stronach has a reputation as a strong-willed traditionalist, Prof. Cole says. "A leader, particularly when it's somebody with a very strong personality, is going to be reflected down through an organization."

Mr. Stronach is famous for initiating the Magna Employees Charter, which includes a guarantee of fair treatment free from discrimination, an employee profit-sharing program, and a hotline to register complaints anonymously. Considering the aforementioned harassment allegation against Magna, the program has not, however, fully prevented problems from spilling outside the company into the courts or fully protected women's comfort levels within the organization. Accepting and approving business activity costs involving strip bars, according to one industry veteran, "certainly puts a female account manager in a difficult situation."

It's worse if the strip-club atmosphere is brought back into the workplace. Women working in Magna's sales division in Detroit testified [among other things, that] they were referred to as "cupcake" or "kumquat" and faced unwelcome touching and advances from male colleagues. . . . Magna has said that it will defend itself against the suit and does not condone the type of customer-wooing activities that were outlined in the depositions. . . .

Sales executives for several parts companies in Detroit say their companies don't condone client entertainment at strip bars and, in some cases, forbid it. But entertaining customers is essential in building a relationship, they say. "You can't develop a relationship with someone by sitting across the desk from them for 10 minutes once a month," one executive says. Adds another industry source: "You may be able to get an audience instead of a voice mail, but does it get you the deal? No."

The auto makers have tried to address the issue with strong codes of conduct that—in GM's case, at least—prevent their employees from accepting gifts, free lunches, golf games or other entertainment from suppliers. Ms. Gaunt, who began her career in sales at Ford in 1972, says that part of the business represents "probably the finest example of the good-old-boy's club." But she says she succeeded without indulging in macho pursuits such as taking clients to strip clubs or football games. "I had to find other ways to get the amount of time I needed with my customers—at that time Ford and Lincoln Mercury dealers—in order to get the job done and perform in a way I wanted to perform." Her most common strategy was long visits to dealers and invitations for them to teach her about their companies. "I discovered early on that dealers love teaching about the business. I took clear advantage of it, I made no bones about it and they were happy to do it."

The automotive industry is conscious of its macho reputation and officials say it is trying to change—although the fact that tire maker Pirelli SpA of Italy still prints a calendar of nude women every year is evidence that some still aren't getting the message.

Margaret McGrath, president of parts manufacturer PPG Canada Inc., laughs about the time earlier in her automotive career when she was posted to work in Brazil. She was initially told that she wouldn't be able to go on any business trips, but was later told that the rule was changed. The reason? Her boss got permission from his wife to travel with a woman executive. But Ms. McGrath points to her own career as evidence that the industry has changed. She has risen steadily through the ranks at PPG Industries Inc. of Pittsburgh, a glass and paint supplier to auto makers around the world. Her most recent promotion was to head the company's Canadian operations, which have 2,000 employees at five plants. "They offered me my present position as president of PPG Canada when I was eight months pregnant," she notes. "I think that alone says a fair amount about the company." But she knows of no other female CEO in the Canadian parts sector and is the only woman on the Board of the industry's Automotive Parts Manufacturers Association.

The industry is not nearly as traditional and male-dominated as it appears from the outside and is changing, says Maureen Kempston Darkes, president of General Motors of Canada Ltd. Part of the reason is that executives are paying attention to the issue and trying to create a culture that values diversity. "Will I say our job is done?" she says in an interview at the company's head office in Oshawa, Ontario. "Absolutely not. We have a long way to go."

At GM Canada, a women's advisory council that Ms. Kempston Darkes was instrumental in creating plays a key role, she says, in advising the company's strategy board and in identifying issues. The council has helped create job-sharing and telecommuting programs for GM Canada workers and formalized mentoring programs.

At Ford, a women's marketing committee formed in the 1970s now has more than 200 members drawn from the engineering, manufacturing, sales and marketing ranks. It offers advice on many aspects of the business—such as advertising, product development or sales techniques—and provides mentoring to women in the organization.

Many observers think the next generation of executives coming along will have even more women in its ranks. For example, the number of women engineers enrolled in educational programs in Canada has climbed steadily, reaching 19% of classes in 1996, up from 11.3% in 1986, according to the Canadian Council of Professional Engineers. Undergraduate business classes, too, are routinely about 40% women today, and many of these women go to work for the Big Three [automakers] on co-op terms, says Prof. Solomon at the University of Windsor.

Prof. Cole at the University of Michigan adds that auto companies could operate successfully in the past with predominantly male work forces, but they cannot continue that way in the future. "You could have a very traditional chauvinistic view of the role of women and you're going to go out of business," he says. "It's very difficult to find competent people and if you're operating from a smaller pool than your competition, then you're in a whole lot of trouble."

Ms. Kempston Darkes points out that bringing more women into business, and especially into higher ranks, is a simple matter of understanding your customers. "It makes very good business sense; the more the inside of your company can mirror your outside customer base, the more you'll understand that customer base."

Change—at least in terms of progress for women in the work-force—appears to be happening more quickly at the auto makers, while the auto parts companies lag behind. Prof. Cole says part of the reason is that the car manufacturers have far higher public profiles than the parts makers have, in large part, because their products are sold at the retail level—and often to women. "For auto manufacturers, the visbility of them in terms of social issues is pretty high, so they're very sensitive to this [issue of gender equality] at the Board level. Poor practices can hurt you very directly in the pocketbook." Parts companies, by comparison, are more invisible to consumers, says Cole.

Prof. Solomon further credits the influence of unions in car manufacturing for helping advance the cause of women in the work force. In contrast, parts manufacturers, he notes, are less often unionized, thus impeding their progress in the gender balance issue.

Margaret McGrath of PPG Canada says her gender isn't an issue for her to deal with, but for men to adjust to, and she made that point clear when she was being interviewed for a job at Ford early in her career. "If [men] haven't had the experience of working with women, well, that's something they're just going to have to learn."

Ms. Gaunt says that although she's impatient with the pace of change (relating to women's advancement), she is optimistic about the future, in part, because there are more women waiting in the wings for executive positions than she has ever seen. The question, she says, is whether they will get the top jobs. If they do, she says, "I will personally look at it as the return on much of the investment I've made in this business over the past 25 years."

INTRODUCTION

The preceding case describing women's struggles for equality and upward mobility in the auto industry appears to be generalizable to other male-dominated professions, such as law. For example, an attention-grabbing piece on the front page of *The Globe and Mail* recently read: "Missing in court: Women on the bench" (Makin 1998). This article said that many concerned legal observers are stumped by the present-day tepid interest that Canadian women lawyers have shown toward being a judge—a job that (as noted in Chapter 6) combines prestige, job satisfaction, and job security and is the #1 choice among professionals.

The main criteria for potential judges, continued Makin, are relatively straightforward—10 years at the bar and "a level of professional distinction." It is rumored in legal circles that where qualified male and female candidates are available for the judge job, the women generally "get the nod." But is this myth or reality?

As in the automobile manufacturing industry, the law profession is highly visible to the public. Thus, the legal profession needs to have its fair share of women judges to keep up with the representation of women in the general population. "It is important that the bench reflect the community," says Chief Justice Patrick LeSage of the Ontario Court of Justice (General Division). "[But] [w]ith 10 or 20 per cent of judges being women, it is not reflective" (Makin 1998, p. A1). While no year-to-year gender breakdown is available, Judge LeSage adds that he has the distinct impression that the number of women applying for the job of judge has fallen in recent years. Considering all of the efforts put forth by the provincial and federal governments for bringing more women into higher legal positions, one has to question whether this investment has paid off.

If, as the rumors suggest, women candidates do, indeed, "get the nod" for judge vacancies when they apply, then the success rate for female candidates should be such that, over time, more and more females are motivated to apply for the bench. But have women lawyers been all that successful in the judge appointment race, thus raising their motivations over time? If the judge gender trend is best quantified in terms of both interest in, and appointments to, the Ontario Court's Provincial Division, posits Makin, then the picture for Canadian women lawyers is dismal, as LeSage posits. While the number of female candidates for the Ontario court peaked at 137 in 1990, only 22 female candidates applied in 1995, and just 30 female candidates applied in 1997. Furthermore, in terms of the overall percentage of women who have been successful in making it to the provincial bench since 1989, only 49 of the 134 female appointees, or 36 percent, made it (Makin 1998). Such figures call into question the rumors suggesting that women candidates "clearly get the nod" when it comes to the bench vacancies.

So, what are the likely "turnoffs" for women regarding the position of judge? Money may be a big factor, posits Makin. It may very well be that female lawyers who have made it to the top in their law firms are reluctant to take a drop in pay to become a judge. But, counters a woman judge recently appointed to the bench in Ontario, the pay disadvantage of being a judge is easily offset by the predictable hours and more "even stresses" of judging, as compared to practicing law (Makin 1998).

Besides money, plain old discrimination by "the old boys" in the selection process is another factor that is commonly cited by women as a turnoff, says Makin. As in business corporations, a perception that men are favored for the new judge appointments, especially if there are a token number of women judges already, is a key factor. Why apply, the critics say, if you have no realistic chance of being selected? "One hears anecdotally that women feel a concerted effort was not being made to appoint women for the sake of being women," says Michelle Fuerst, a prominent Toronto criminal lawyer. "It is human nature that if you think you are not going to succeed at something, sometimes you don't even take the step," she said. "No one wants to feel that they failed or were found inadequate" (Makin 1998, p. A2).

An Ontario female judge who wants to remain anonymous says that up until the past few years, some women may have been put off by a group of stereotypically crusty "old boys" who populated the bench. Many of them had been appointed decades earlier, she notes, largely for political reasons. She recalls, too, that shortly after being appointed as judge herself, she was confronted by a veteran male judge who said, in surprise: "What are you doing here? We already have some girls here." Those days are virtually over, this female judge affirms. "There are a lot fewer of those guys. The nature of the bench has changed so much. It is much younger" (Makin 1998, p. A2).

But has the nature of the bench really changed toward gender equality in recent years—to the same degree or any more than the corporate pipeline has changed? Does "younger," as the Ontario female judge posited, necessarily equate to being more open and flexible in terms of workforce diversity? Though I am not equipped to answer these law profession questions at this point, these are the kinds of questions that prompted Mr. Larose and me to look more closely at how present-day corporate leaders—male and female—see themselves and their present-day work environments.

We also got into an interesting discussion about whether men and women are equally motivated to pursue a corporate leader position in the late 1990s, given the almost-heroic criteria sought by boards to fill the top spots when vacancies do arrive (witness the report of Hart and Quinn [1993; see Chapter 2])—or when they are forced to arrive, which seems to be occurring more frequently. The rampant suggestions of old-boy cronyism still existing in the corporate pipeline—how could this reality be empirically validated? Moreover, given the ever-increasing "turmoil at the top," we began to question if, besides Type As, other disease-prone personality types—such as the Type Cs and the narcissists—have begun to filter into the corporate leader positions. Finally, given the present-day corporate challenges and economic instabilities that present to those at the top, we questioned if the stress levels reported, the influence strategies used, the compensation packages received, and the mood profiles experienced by those trying to stay at the top (or those seeking to make it there) have changed significantly from measures taken for corporate leaders during the 1980s.

To help us answer some of our questions and to fill some voids in the literature, in 1997 Mr. Larose and I sent a comprehensive, 14-page questionnaire on stress, personality, mood, and compensation to 1,000 Canadian corporate leaders. Expecting some adjustments for cultural differences, we thought that our questionnaire findings should be generalizable to corporate leaders in other developed countries around the globe. Part II details our study hypotheses and our findings. Chapter 7 presents our initial data analyses regarding Canadian corporate leaders' stress levels, influence strategies, and compensation received.

THE PROCEDURE FOLLOWED IN THE CORPORATE LEADER STUDY

Details on the Procedure

The names of 1,000 corporations were randomly selected from 1,782 Canadian corporations listed in the 1997 issue of *The Financial Post Directory of Directors* (Financial Post Data Group 1997). The highest-ranking corporate officers in each of the randomly selected corporations were contacted by telephone and were asked either directly or indirectly (i.e., through their executive assistants) to participate in the study. They were told that the study's purpose was to investigate personality factors, influence strategies, stress levels, moods, and incomes (defined as salary plus bonuses) of today's corporate leaders.

Once interest was shown, a questionnaire was mailed to the corporate officers within 48 hours. If they were later unable to complete the form, we requested that another corporate officer do so. We requested that the questionnaire be completed within 72 hours of reception and that the completed form be returned in the self-addressed, postage-paid envelope provided.

The Questionnaire

Covering Letter. As an incentive, the corporate officers were told in the covering letter not only that the results of the survey would be used to build a unique profile of the corporate world's "movers and shakers" but that those participants wanting a personalized summary of their questionnaire results could get this by completing the return address sheet. They were also told that the questionnaire was reviewed and met university ethical standards.

Questionnaire Parts. The questionnaire had these parts:

- Part I included the 14-item Perceived Stress Scale (PSS), developed by Cohen, Kamarck, and Mermelstein in 1983.
- Part II included an adaptation of the 11 POIS influence strategy scales (27 items in total), available from University Associates, San Diego, California (1982).
- Part III included (1) the 70-item Personality, Stress, and Disease Inventory of Grossarth-Maticek and Eysenck (1990) and (2) the 31-item Manic and Depressive Behavior Self-Report Inventory (MDBSI) developed by us with the consulting assistance of Dr. Jean Endicott; and
- Part IV included six demographic items relating to the corporate leaders: age, sex typing, formal schooling, annual personal income (salary plus bonuses), employing company type, and job title.

Response Rate and Sample Characteristics

Response Rate. Although 521 questionnaires were received by the deadline, not all of the forms were complete enough for analysis. In total, 400 usable forms were analyzed, representing a corrected response rate of 40 percent. Considering the difficulty in obtaining survey compliance with this corporate officer population, and given the generally low response rates previously reported (i.e., in the 25–30 percent range), we felt that the obtained response rate was very good.

Sample Characteristics. Several indicators suggested a good cross-section of corporate leader response. Consistent with recent reports on gender representation, the majority of the corporate leader sample was male (85 percent, $n = 329$), while the minority was female (15 percent, $n = 57$). Given that most corporate leaders are age 50 and over by the time that they make it to the top, the results showed the average age of the corporate leader respondents to be 51.29 ($N = 386$, SD: 8.53) and the median to be 52. Consistent with other recent study findings, the women corporate leaders were, on average, younger (M: 46.51, $n = 57$, SD: 9.64) than their male counterparts (M: 52.11, $n = 329$, SD: 8.05).

Also consistent with previous reports on educational levels, the corporate leader respondents tended to be university-educated, with 38 percent having completed an undergraduate degree and with 38 percent having completed a graduate degree. Moreover, the corporate leader respondents were well represented across 35 company types, with the largest numbers placing in financial services (14.4 percent, $n = 55$); metals and minerals (6.8 percent, $n = 26$); consumer products (5.5 percent, $n = 21$); business services (5.2 percent, $n = 20$); computer services (5 percent, $n = 19$); and oil and gas or industrial products (4.7 percent, $n = 18$).

The corporate leaders' titles were predominantly vice president (23.9 percent, $n = 77$), president (21 percent, $n = 67$), CEO (15 percent, $n = 47$), president/CEO (13.4 percent, $n = 43$), and CFO (9.6 percent, $n = 31$). Using Forbes and Piercy's (1991) definitions to differentiate between "top management" and "second-tier management," we coded as "1" the top management corporate leader positions (i.e., those having the positions of chairman, vice-chairman, president, CEO, chief operating officer, chief administrative officer, or any combination of these) and as "2" the second-tier corporate leader positions (i.e., the vice presidents, the CFOs, the human resource management directors, and others of like status). Given this coding scheme, 57 percent ($n = 183$) of the respondents were top management, and 43 percent ($n = 139$) were second-tier management. The majority of the male respondents placed in top management (69 percent, $n = 182$) rather than in second-tier positions (31 percent, $n = 83$), while the majority of the female respondents placed in the second-tier positions (69 percent, $n = 31$) rather than in top management (31 percent, $n = 14$).

Reliability of Indexes for Questionnaire Parts I and II

With the exception of the "Coalition" POIS scales (each having only two items), the obtained Cronbach alpha reliability coefficients for the 14-item PSS scale and for the other POIS scales ranged from 0.68 to 0.93, thus being adequate and consistent with previous reports (Cohen, Kamarck, & Mermelstein 1983; Kipnis & Schmidt 1988).

HYPOTHESES REGARDING CORPORATE LEADERS' STRESS LEVELS REPORTED, INFLUENCE STRATEGIES USED, AND COMPENSATION RECEIVED

The Gender Stress Issue

The PSS scale was chosen for use in this study because it measures the degree to which adults find their lives to be unpredictable, uncontrollable, and overloading—issues that have been consistently reported to be central components in pathological distress (Averill 1973; Lazarus 1977; Cohen 1978). While women in community samples have obtained a slightly higher PSS mean score than their male counterparts (25.6 and 24.0, respectively), this difference has not been found to be statistically significant (Cohen, Kamarck, & Mermelstein 1983). Also, though male and female corporate leaders may verbalize different initial outward signs of distress and burnout (Jick & Mitz 1985; Greenglass 1991), no consistent, significant difference in mean stress score has been found for these two gender groups (Nelson & Quick 1985).

• *Hypothesis 7.1*: It was hypothesized that the mean PSS scores for both the male and the female corporate leaders will place in the normative 24.0–25.6 range and that there will be no significant, statistical difference in mean PSS score for the male and female corporate leaders.

The Control and Job Position Stress Issue

Since the 1970s, organizational researchers have found a relationship between "perceived control" in organizational members at all levels of the hierarchy and reduced job stress. For example, as a result of the 1978 Swedish sawmill study of Johansson, Aronnson, and Lindstrom, the activation theory of job stress was generated. This theory posits that organizational members' psychological, behavioral, and physiological well-being should be maximized at intermediate or moderated levels of intrinsic job arousal or stimulation. Beyond such moderated levels of arousal, however, pathological job distress and disease-proneness generally occur. Research empirically investigating the activation theory has led to such outcomes as the person-environment (P-E) "fit" theory and the job demands/job control theory.

The P-E "fit" theory, developed in the late 1970s and popularized in the United States by researchers Hackman and Oldham (1980), suggests that the degree of "fit" existing between organizational members' needs and their jobs—regardless of their placement in the organizational hierarchy—largely determines the degree of personal control, psychological well-being, and job satisfaction experienced by them.

The job demands/job control theory, also developed in the late 1970s and popularized by Karasek (1979) in the United States and by Warr, Cook, and Wall (1979) in the United Kingdom, suggests that open, empowering work environments are particularly effective in aiding organizational members at all levels of the organizational hierarchy to daily appraise their varying job demands and, when necessary, to moderate them to remain "in control." The latter assumes that intrinsic job demands and job latitude largely determine whether organizational members will become "eustressed" by their jobs over the longer term and remain healthy, or if they will become "distressed" by their jobs over the longer term.

In short, proponents of both the P-R "fit" theory and the job demands/job control theory maintain that the autonomy and the P-E "fit" conditions are such that as one ascends the corporate ladder, one is better able to remain "in control." Thus, CEOs are in the best position for being "in control." Present-day researchers caution that the organizational factors essential to such eustressful work conditions for top managers vary within companies and between cultures (Ganster & Schaubroeck 1991), some of which are more open and empowering than others.

Moreover, affirm present-day researchers, in the economically challenging 1990s, "strained" CEOs are increasingly "downloading" or "scapegoating" their distress onto the second-tier corporate leaders (Boeker 1992), placing them at risk for feeling "out of control" and for experiencing higher levels of distress and burnout.

- *Hypothesis 7.2*: It was hypothesized that the mean PSS score for the second-level corporate leaders will be significantly higher than that for the top management corporate leaders.

The Distress-Burnout "Risk" Estimate Issue

Mental health researchers in the 1980s began to focus on the role that organizational control or perceived lack of it plays in the progression of burnout symptomology in corporate leaders. For example, in their 1984 study on 244 male and female corporate leaders in nine types of organizations, Cahoon and Rowney found that middle managers, having reduced organizational control and relatively high organizational responsibilities, had almost twice as many scorers in the "high-burnout" zone as their entry-level or their senior-level counterparts. However, Cahoon and Rowney also found that almost 20 percent of the top-ranking corporate leaders reported "high-end" burnout scores, an estimate consistent with Cooper's (1984) findings for top managers in the United States, Sweden, and Germany.

Researchers have recently suggested that with the increasing turmoil at the top of organizations (Boeker 1992), the percentage of corporate leaders at risk for mental ill health and burnout may be higher.

- *Hypothesis 7.3*: It was hypothesized that though the overall PSS mean score for the corporate leader sample will place in the normative 24.0–25.6 range, the percentage having PSS scores 20 percent higher than the "normative" score of 24 (i.e., a PSS score meeting or exceeding 30) will exceed the previously reported estimates of about 20 percent.

The Influence Strategies Used by Corporate Leaders and Their Relationship to Distress

Since the appearance of the term "burnout" in the 1980s, mental health experts have been trying to understand the relationship between corporate leaders' styles of thinking and behaving and their distress and burnout propensities. For example, in 1983, Meier posited that deep information processors, those who can remember both their positive affective (PA) and negative affective (NA) life experiences, would be less at risk for burnout because of their more flexible information-processing capabilities. In contrast, shallow information processors, those who tend to remember primarily their NA life experiences, would be more at risk for burnout because of their psychoneurotic traits.

In 1991, Leiter further posited that, besides PA- and NA-balanced information processing, balanced behavioral repertoires are important for long-term stress reduction and burnout prevention. Leiter said that adults who rely on "control" stress-coping behavioral strategies—searching for the root cause of their problems and constructively working toward resolution of them—are less at risk for burnout than are adults who rely on "escapist" stress-coping behavioral strategies—avoiding the search for the cause and displacing their problems onto others.

As a result of two major studies completed by Kipnis and his colleagues (Kipnis & Schmidt 1988; Kipnis et al. 1994), we now know that managers tend to "take control" by influencing upwardly using reasoning, first, followed by coalitions, and by influencing downwardly using reasoning, first, followed by assertiveness. CEOs, in particular, are the least stressed and best paid if they utilize a tactician style of upward influence and are the most stressed and the least paid if they utilize a shotgun style of upward influence, placing a high priority on aggressiveness. Kipnis' findings on managers regarding the selective and limited use of aggression to influence others support other study findings on moderately stressed adults (Gambrill & Richey 1975; Friedman & Rosenman 1974).

- *Hypothesis 7.4*: It was hypothesized that present-day male and female Canadian corporate leaders would tend to influence upwardly for general purposes using reasoning, first, followed by coalitions; moreover, they would tend to influence downwardly for general purposes using reasoning, first, followed by assertiveness.

- *Hypothesis 7.5*: It was hypothesized that the "highly distressed" present-day male and female Canadian corporate leaders would be those utilizing a "shotgun" influence style, characterized by high scores on assertiveness, both upwardly and downwardly.

The Compensation Received by Corporate Leaders

Finding some logical way of projecting Canadian corporate leaders' compensation package values (salary plus bonuses) was a difficult chore for a number of reasons. As noted in Chapter 6, compensation package values for corporate leaders appear not to be largely economically based but are social status-based. Also, compared to their U.S. male counterparts, Canadian male corporate leaders appear to fare considerably more poorly on the compensation yardstick. In both the United States and Canada, female corporate leaders tend to fare significantly more poorly than their male counterparts.

Three key studies reported in 1990 and 1991 helped us to understand more clearly the "social status" phenomenon regarding compensation and the specific outcomes reported in the literature. Three questions relating to compensation for present-day corporate leaders were addressed.

Why are U.S. CEOs (males, in particular) so well paid relative to their CEO counterparts elsewhere around the world? In their comprehensive review of the recent scholarly literature on compensation packages for North American CEOs, Delacroix and Saudagaran (1991) concluded that there exists no convincing link between CEO compensation in the 1990s, on one hand, and either CEO performance or company performance, on the other. From a cultural point of view, North Americans are very generous in their compensation package awards to CEOs as compared to other industrialized nations around the world. As a case in point, in 1988, at least 20 American male corporate executives earned more than $1 million in salary and bonuses—not including perks, stock options, and other forms of deferred compensation. If other forms of compensation were included in the package for 1987 alone, at least 300 U.S. CEOs earned more than $1 million. If stock options were included in the package, by 1989 total U.S. CEO compensation packages in excess of $10 million were common for male CEOs.

Elsewhere around the world, noted Delacroix and Saudagaran, the CEO compensation packages were much more modest. For example, the mean salary and bonuses for male Japanese CEOs in 1987 was 57 million yen or about $400,000 U.S. The highest annual Japanese CEO pay recorded for 1987 was $7.8 million U.S., which compared unfavorably with the U.S. winner for 1987—Jim Manzi of Lotus, who took in $26.3 million U.S. Moreover, in 1987 in large companies with annual sales of over $1 billion, the mean value of salaries and bonuses of American CEOs was more than twice that of West German CEOs and nearly three times that of British CEOs. This compensation package profiling for CEOs remained even in 1989.

Delacroix and Saudagaran further suggested that if industrialized nations' CEOs' relative purchasing power were graphed, and if the U.S. CEOs' compensation value were set at "100," then the adjusted compensation values for CEOs in other industrial nations would place at or below "60." Having followed this procedure, Delacroix and Saudagaran found that Canada placed at 60, Switzerland placed at about 50, Spain placed at about 47, the United Kingdom placed at about 45, France placed at about 44, and Germany placed at about 42. The researchers then bluntly asked, Why are U.S. CEOs so well paid relative to their CEO counterparts elsewhere around the world?

Delacroix and Saudagaran argued that an established and still-growing body of scholarly literature suggests that U.S. CEOs are not rewarded according to their work performance or their company's performance per se but according to some other factor. Certainly, there is no shortage of CEO talent in the United States, they affirmed, that would make U.S. CEOs' munificent compensation packages supply- and demand-driven. Moreover, according to statistics, neither market processes nor a lottery-like process seems to be able to account for the systematic difference in remuneration paid to U.S. CEOs and that paid to CEOs in other industrialized countries. Delacroix and Saudagaran, therefore, speculated that U.S. CEOs' rather munificent compensation packages must serve merely as "a mythical social function." Simply put, Americans, in particular, and other developed countries, to a lesser degree, use high CEO compensation packages primarily as evidence that someone is "in charge of the complex and befuddling spectacle of a modern economy" (p. 673).

Finally, Delacroix and Saudagaran suggested that a likely problem behind the high compensation packages doled out to CEOs for their social worth is that the latter may reach a level where the conventional relationship between amount of reward doled out and quality of performance manifested actually reverses itself. "We are suggesting," concluded these authors, "that high CEO salaries may, in and of themselves, constitute golden parachutes" (p. 674).

If corporate leaders are paid handsomely for the social function that they serve to society, are women, on average, paid less by their firms for serving similar social and "visibly in-charge" functions? According to the 1991 study of Cannings, investigating the sources of female–male earning differences in 685 middle managers (62 percent male, 38 percent female) in a large Canadian company, the answer appears to be an unequivocal yes.

Though the male managers in Cannings' study were, on average, about two years older than the female managers and had been with the company, on average, over one year longer, the performance scores of the female managers were higher than those of the males. Both the male and the female managers, however, showed the same level of attachment to the company. Also, while the male managers had built, on average, more extensive informal networks than their female counterparts, their span of control was less than that of the females. From an educational perspective, the females had, on average, more professional degrees than their male counterparts, but the males got significantly higher returns on their professional degree investments. *In short, the male middle managers earned, on average, 18 percent more than their female middle manager counterparts.*

Cannings said that her statistical analysis indicated that the earnings of female middle managers were penalized not by their lack of commitment to the organization or by their lack of performance or by their lack of formal education but by their disproportionate responsibilities for work in their family homes. The index of division of labor in the household was over twice as high for the female middle managers as compared to the male middle managers.

Though Cannings' 1991 work was clearly Canadian and middle management-oriented, Morrison and Von Glinow's 1990 review of the extant literature on women's earnings in management levels at the lower, middle, and upper ranks revealed a consistently bleak compensation yardstick picture. Attempting to put a percentage difference on compensation packages for male and female corporate leaders, Morrison and Von Glinow summarized their literature review findings as follows:

Those women and minorities who have advanced into management often find reward differentials. There is evidence that at higher occupational levels, women are less satisfied with their pay than are men. One study of 2,600 employees found substantial wage differences between men and women in managerial levels; *another reported that "women at the vice presidential levels and above earn 42% less than their male peers."* Earnings of Black men in management come closer to those of White men. (p. 201; emphasis mine)

Morrison and Von Glinow attributed lower compensation packages paid to women corporate leaders not to their responsibilities in the home (as did Cannings) or to their personalities, behaviors, or motivations, or to their age but to some other "critical" factor. These researchers expounded:

Data disputing both sex and race deficiencies come from the AT & T Assessment Center reports, which showed that female and male managers were more similar than different on personality and motivation factors as well as abilities. . . . There is considerable other evidence that women and men in management roles have similar aspirations, values, and other personality traits as well as job-related skills and behaviors. . . . Donnell and Hall's unusually large field study of nearly 2,000 matched pairs of female and male managers led them to conclude that the disproportionately low numbers of women in management can no longer be explained away by the contention that women practice a different brand of management from that practiced by men. (p. 201)

The "critical" factor contributing to women managers' lower reward packages seems to be founded in "relative social capital," concluded Morrison and Von Glinow. Whether it be called "the old boys' network" or "tokenism" or "self-cloning" or "homosocial reproduction," women corporate leaders seem to be paid less than their male counterparts largely on the grounds that socially, if for no other reason, they are worth less (Morrison & Van Glinow 1990).

This research team further concluded that women's lack of opportunity and power in organizations and the sex ratio of male-to-female groups within organizations both help to explain women's ongoing lack of top managerial success and poor compensation:

For example, Kanter's classic research pointed out that if a management cadre is at least 85% men, then the women in the group are "tokens" who very visibly represent women as a category whether they want to or not. These tokens' performances are hindered because of the pressure to which their visibility subjects them and because members of the dominant group exaggerate differences according to stereotypes they believe about women. [As was further suggested in the automobile case at the start of this chapter,] women . . . also face sexual harassment, which may be a result of skewed sex ratios favoring men. (p. 203)

Thus, women having corporate leader potential but wanting to leave the politicking in organizations to others have increasingly found that starting their own companies is one feasible and more palatable option. Leaving for other careers is another option. Noted Morrison and Von Glinow: "Women started their own businesses at six times the rate that men did between 1974 and 1984. Of the 100 leading corporate women identified by a *Business Week* survey in 1976, nearly one third had left their corporate jobs for other pursuits 10 years later" (p. 201).

What, on average, are present-day Canadian male and female corporate leader compensation packages (i.e., salary plus bonuses) worth? In 1997 and in 1998, male CEOs in the United States, in particular, were remunerated quite munificently for their functions served to society—to the tune, as noted in Chapter 6, of billions of U.S. dollars. What, relatively, should present-day Canadian male and female corporate leader compensation packages (i.e., salary plus bonuses) be worth? Moreover, what strategies would we expect the high earners to rely upon for getting their "just rewards"?

Let us consider that Lambert, Larcker, and Weigelt (1993) reported that in the early 1990s, U.S. CEO mean salaries ranged from $80,072 to $537,865—depending on the CEO's status within the organizational hierarchy. Based on these figures, it seems reasonable to expect, therefore, that in 1997, after using Delacroix's and Saudagaran's 60 percent "adjustment compensation factor" for Canadian corporate leaders, the 1997 mean compensation value (salary plus bonuses) for Canadian corporate leaders should place in the $48,043–$322,719 range, and the mean for the less socially valued second-tier corporate leaders (Lambert, Larcker, & Weigelt 1993) and the female corporate leaders should place closer to the recently reported $200,000 mark (Richard Ivey School of Business 1998). Moreover, the mean for the "socially valued" top management group should exceed the $300,000 mark, as earlier reported by Lambert, Larcker, and Weigelt (1993).

Finally, regarding influence styles and compensation package rewards, consistent with the "self-cloning" literature described at length in Chapter 6 and consistent with Kipnis et al.'s (1994) findings regarding the use of "friendly" upward influence strategies for personal gains, we could probably safely surmise that the "high earners" would likely profile as male, in the top management ranks, in their 50s, and committed to using "friendly" and "coalition" strategies rather than "reasoning" to influence upwardly for a better financial package.

- *Hypothesis 7.6*: It was hypothesized that present-day male Canadian corporate leaders would receive significantly higher compensation package (i.e., salary plus bonuses) mean scores than their female counterparts, with the male mean score meeting or exceeding the $300,000 mark and with the female mean score placing closer to the $200,000 mark.

- *Hypothesis 7.7*: It was hypothesized that the present-day top management corporate leaders would receive significantly higher compensation package (i.e., salary plus bonuses) mean scores than their second-tier counterparts, with the former having a mean score exceeding the $300,000 mark and with the latter having a mean score placing closer to the $200,000 mark.

- *Hypothesis 7.8*: It was hypothesized that the "high earners" in the 1997 Canadian corporate leader sample (i.e., those having a mean score meeting or exceeding the sample mean score) would profile as "the old boys' network."

Specifically, the high-earner profile would include males in the top management ranks, in their 50s, and committed to using "friendliness" and "coalition" influence strategies rather than using "reasoning" to influence upwardly for higher compensation.

STUDY FINDINGS

The questionnaire responses of 400 Canadian corporate leaders served as the database for the testing of the present set of hypotheses. Except for the finding that about 40 percent of the present-day corporate leaders—not 20 percent—are at high risk for distress and burnout, this first phase of analysis regarding our 1997 Canadian corporate leader study brought few other surprises. In fact, in the first grouping of eight hypotheses, seven were found to be fully supported. Our findings regarding this first phase can be summarized as follows:

• Consistent with Hypothesis 7.1, there was no significant difference found in mean PSS score for male and female corporate leaders. Both groups reported PSS mean scores in the normative range (with the male and the female mean scores being 24.68 and 24.32, respectively), indicating that both sexes seem to be able to cope, within reason, with the stressors associated with their corporate leader positions.

• Consistent with Hypothesis 7.2, there was a significant difference found in PSS mean score for the top management and the second-tier corporate leaders. As conjectured, the second-tier group of corporate leaders reported higher stress levels (M: 25.09, SD: 8.66, $n = 139$) than their more in-control top-management counterparts (M: 22.06, SD: 8.28, $n = 182$).

• Consistent with recent media reports about increasing turmoil at the top of organizations and with Hypothesis 7.3, the percentage of corporate leaders at risk for mental ill health and burnout—36.8 percent—was almost double that found for corporate leaders in the 1980s (i.e., about 20 percent).

• Consistent with Hypothesis 7.4, the present-day corporate leaders tend to influence upwardly for general purposes using, first, reasoning, and second, coalitions. Moreover, they tend to influence downwardly using, first, reasoning. However, contrary to Hypothesis 7.4, the present-day corporate leaders tend to influence downwardly using, second, coalitions rather than assertiveness. No significant gender differences were found regarding influence styles of corporate leaders.

• Consistent with Hypothesis 7.5, the present-day, highly stressed corporate leaders tend to practice a "shotgun" style of influencing others, relying heavily on assertiveness and deal-making to influence upwardly and relying heavily on assertiveness to influence downwardly.

• Consistent with the recent compensation literature on social worth and with Hypothesis 7.6, the male corporate leaders were compensated significantly more by their boards (*M*: $322,488, *SD*: $224,576) than their female corporate leader counterparts (*M*: $219,050, *SD*: $173,280).

- Consistent with the recent compensation literature on social worth and with Hypothesis 7.7, the top management corporate leaders were compensated significantly more by their boards (*M*: $364,151, *SD*: $261,711) than their second-tier counterparts (*M*: $249,812, *SD*: $180,085).

- Consistent with the recent literature on women's alleged lack of progress made during the 1990s in terms of gender equality in the corporate world and consistent with Hypothesis 7.8, the high-income earners meeting or exceeding the sample mean of $307,000 were "old boys' network" in character. They were male, in the top management positions, in their early 50s, and committed to using "friendly" or "coalition" strategies rather than using "reasoning" to influence upwardly for a better compensation package.

THE BOTTOM LINE

Part II, Chapter 7 opened with one case and one article summary, the former describing the present-day struggles of women in the automobile industry in North America, and the latter describing the struggles of Canadian female lawyers contemplating becoming a judge. The theme behind both of these pieces was similar to that raised in Chapter 6: women's progress in terms of gender equality in the upper ranks of the workplace and in the professions has been slow or even regressive in recent years.

Without opening a sizable "can of worms," let it suffice to say that on this issue there have been two schools of thought among the experts. One school believes that women continue to move ahead in terms of gender equality, and the other school believes that there has been not only a slowing of progress but a regression in recent years. One objective of Chapter 7 was to explore empirically which of these two schools appears to be closer to the reality existing in today's corporate pipelines—at least the way that present-day Canadian corporate leaders see it.

Another objective of Chapter 7 was to explore more fully the present-day stress levels, influence styles, and compensation package values of Canadian corporate leaders, with special attention paid to the female and second-tier subgroups.

The hypotheses surrounding the topic area on gender equality were that while both male and female corporate leaders would perceive their stress levels to be similar once nearing the top or reaching the top of organizations, when it came to compensation package worth, females, in particular, would report significantly lower compensation package values. This reality, it was conjectured, would be caused not by women's lack of formal education or by their lack of broad-based behavioral skills or by inferior influence strategies but by their inability to "counterforce" the old boys' network and to be perceived by their boards as "socially worthy."

The hypotheses surrounding the second-tier corporate leader group suggested that, relative to their top management counterparts, they would be perceived by their boards not only as being "less worthy socially" but as less "in control." Therefore, the second-tier corporate leaders would report as significantly more distressed and as more poorly compensated. Moreover, it was conjectured that, if the organizational waters became troubled, likely the second-tier corporate leaders would receive the blame and the distress, if not "the ax"—not their top management counterparts.

All in all, this first set of findings relating to stress, influence strategies, and compensation indicates that not much has changed toward greater gender equality for female corporate leaders since the 1980s. While appearing to hold their own in terms of distress management and influence strategy usage, women corporate leaders are paid significantly less than their male counterparts. The analysis further revealed that, as in earlier decades, the old boys' network of high earners seems to remain alive and well in the corporate environment in the late 1990s.

Two recent articles on the appearance—and/or disappearance—of women in leadership positions were printed in March 1998. The first article to appear, entitled, "Women Snap Up Prime Jobs," was written by John Kettle and posited that from 1975 to 1996, Statistics Canada's figures indicated that Canadian women—not Canadian men—snapped up 57 percent of the new managerial positions and 65 percent of the professional jobs. Though admittedly he was not able to detail the share of jobs held by women at each level of management or in the professions to confirm whether women actually made their way to the "very top," Kettle did affirm that such a finding "may shatter a few notions of the glass ceiling that is said to prevent them [women] from getting their fair share of top jobs." He goes on to say, "What the numbers do suggest is that something like a socio-economic revolution took place in the past two decades, making women closer [to] equal partners in management and the professions. Some of the numbers might even be used to suggest that men are now being discriminated against—or perhaps they prove that on an even playing field, women really are smarter."

Kettle's is one interpretation of the present-day corporate and professional reality confronting men and women. The second article to appear, entitled, "Where Women Work, and Why" (Editor 1998), had a totally different "take" on the male-female gender equality issue in the late 1990s. The thesis of this second piece can be summarized by the words appearing in the opening paragraph: "It wasn't too long ago that women were being told: 'You've come a long way, baby.' Amend that slogan. Women, it seems, came a long way into the traditional working world sometime in the 1970s and 1980s and then headed out again for other pastures. And no one seems to have a clear explanation for this."

The writer of the second article goes on to say that the evidence of the nonprogressive or even regressive workingwomen's odyssey is everywhere in Canada and in the United States, with the example of the reduced number of applicants going for judges' positions in Canada in recent years being just one case in point cited.

Looking at these two articles and considering the two schools of thought regarding women's progress in the corporate pipelines and in the professions over the last decade, it would appear that, given this first phase of study findings, the second article and the school positing little or no progress are closer to the reality picture drawn by the corporate leaders themselves.

REFERENCES

Averill, J. R. (1973). Personal control over aversive stimuli and its relationship to stress. *Psychological Bulletin*, 80, 286–303.

Boeker, W. (1992). Power and managerial dismissal: Scapegoating at the top. *Administrative Science Quarterly*, 37, 400–421.

Burke, R. J., & MacDermid, G. (1996). Gender awareness education in organizations. *Psychological Reports*, 79, 1070.

Cahoon, A. R., & Rowney, J. A. (1984). Managerial burnout: A comparison by sex and level of responsibility. *Journal of Health & Human Resource Administration*, 7, 249–264.

Cannings, K. (1991). An interdisciplinary approach to analyzing the managerial gender gap. *Human Relations*, 44, 679–694.

Cohen, S. (1978). Environmental load and the allocation of attention. In A. Baum, J. E. Singer, & S. Valins (Eds.), *Advances in environmental psychology*, Vol. 1. Hillsdale, NJ: Erlbaum, pp. 1–29.

Cohen, S., Kamarck, T., & Mermelstein, R. (1983). A global measure of perceived stress. *Journal of Applied Social Psychology*, 24, 385–396.

Cooper, C. L. (1984). Executive stress: A ten-country comparison. *Human Resource Management*, 23, 400.

Delacroix, J., & Saudagaran, S. M. (1991). Munificent compensations as disincentives: The case of American CEOs. *Human Relations*, 44, 665–678.

Editor (1998). Editorial: Where women work, and why. *The Globe and Mail*, March 28, p. D6.

Financial Post Data Group. (1997). *The Financial Post directory of directors*. Toronto: Financial Post.

Forbes, J. B., & Piercy, J. E. (1991). *Corporate mobility and paths to the top: Studies for human resource and management development specialists*. Westport, CT: Quorum Books, pp. 58–59.

Friedman, M., & Rosenman, R. H. (1974). *Type A behavior and your heart*. New York: Fawcett Crest.

Gambrill, E. D., & Richey, C. A. (1975). An assertion inventory for use in assessment and research. *Behavior Therapy*, 6, 550–561.

Ganster, D. C., & Schaubroeck, J. (1991). Work stress and employee health. *Journal of Management*, 17, 235–271.

Greenglass, E. R. (1991). Burnout and gender: Theoretical and organizational implications. *Canadian Psychology*, 32, 562–579.

Grossarth-Maticek, R., & Eysenck, H. J. (1990). Personality, stress, and disease: Description and validation of a new inventory. *Psychological Reports*, 66, 355–373.

Hackman, J. R., & Oldham, G. R. (1980). *Work redesign*. Reading, MA: Addison-Wesley.

Jick, T. D., & Mitz, L. F. (1985). Sex differences in work stress. *Academy of Management Review*, 10, 408–420.

Johansson, G., Aronnson, G., & Lindstrom, B. O. (1978). Social psychological and neuroendocrine reactions in highly mechanized work. *Ergonomics*, 21, 583–589.

Karasek, R. (1979). Job demands, job decision latitude, and mental strain: Implications for job redesign. *Administrative Science Quarterly*, 24, 285–306.

Keenan, G., & McFarland, J. (1997). The boy's club. *The Globe and Mail*, September 27, pp. B1, B5.

Kettle, J. (1998). Women snap up prime jobs. *The Globe and Mail*, March 19, p. B13.

Kipnis, D., & Schmidt, S. M. (1988). Upward-influence styles: Relationship with performance evaluations, salary, and stress. *Administrative Science Quarterly*, 33, 528–542.

Kipnis, D., Schmidt, S. M., Swaffin-Smith, C., & Wilkinson, I. (1994). Patterns of managerial influence: Shotgun managers, tactitians, and bystanders. In L. A. Mainiero & C. L. Tromley (Eds.), *Developing managerial skills in organizational behavior*. Englewood Cliffs, NJ: Prentice-Hall, pp. 184–187.

Lambert, R. A., Larcker, D. F., & Weigelt, K. (1993). The structure of organizational incentives. *Administrative Science Quarterly*, 38, 438–461.

Lazarus, R. S. (1977). Psychological stress and coping in adaptation and illness. In Z. J. Lipowski, R. Lipsi, & P. C. Whybrow (Eds.), *Psychosomatic medicine: Current trends*. New York: Oxford University Press, pp. 14–26.

Leiter, M. P. (1991). Coping patterns as predictors of burnout: The function of control and escapist coping patterns. *Journal of Organizational Behavior*, 12, 123–144.

Makin, K. (1998). Missing in court: Women on the bench. *The Globe and Mail*, March 11, pp. A1–A2.

Meier, S. T. (1983). Toward a theory of burnout. *Human Relations*, 36, 899–910.

Morrison, A. M., & Von Glinow, M. A. (1990). Women and minorities in management. *American Psychologist*, 45, 200–208.

Nelson, D. L., & Quick, J. C. (1985). Professional women: Are distress and disease inevitable? *Academy of Management Review*, 10, 206–218.

Richard Ivey School of Business. (1998). Study shows CEOs consider women's advancement key factor. *Women in Management*, 8, 1–2.

University Associates. (1982). *POIS, Form M*. San Diego: University Associates.

Warr, P., Cook, J., & Wall, T. (1979). Scales for the measurement of some work attitudes and aspects of psychological well-being. *Journal of Occupational Psychology*, 52, 129–148.

CHAPTER 8

Corporate Leaders: An In-Depth Analysis of Their Personality and Behavior Patterns

Your article on stressed-out CEOs should be read by all business executives. Many will recognize themselves. But for any young person contemplating a business career, a totally false impression is given. No one needs to work 75 to 120 hours a week to manage a large corporation effectively. The real question is: are all the hours worked necessary, or even useful, in the effective management of the enterprise?

Personally, I am very wary of any of my executives who work excessive hours. That usually means they are micromanaging their team. Any company's prime asset is the creativity of its management. But nothing sucks creativity out of a management group faster than being micromanaged by their leader.

The workaholic manager struggles to fill every waking hour. The productive manager is focused on molding the best creative work force and pointing them in the most effective strategic direction.

—M. Harris (1997)

A CASE IN POINT (TILSON 1997)

What follows are excerpts from the piece to which CEO Milton Harris is referring.

When he is in Vancouver, Les Hammond works about 75 hours a week. But the 51-year-old accountant, investment banker and entrepreneur says his four international mining and technology companies, including ASEAN Holdings Inc. and Global Explorations Corp. (both based in Vancouver), take him abroad more often than not. Then, Hammond says, he works a *lot* of hours. "Let's see," he says, thinking aloud, "six hours times seven days, subtract that from the total hours . . . about 120 hours." Per week. That's more than 17 hours a day—say from 7:00 A.M. through until after midnight. Hammond calls it "running flat out," and he claims to have kept up this pace for 10 years.

His stamina may be unique, but Hammond's work habits are not. His wife has long complained that he's too focused on work; Hammond admits his life lacks balance, but he says he has no choice. "Business is extremely competitive, and you've got to be prepared to be at it 24 hours a day," he says. "I'm not saying it's right. I'm not saying it's healthy. I'm saying that's just the way it is."

As a successful executive, Hammond is part of an influential group that keeps the wheels of business in Canada turning. As a poster boy for Overworkers Anonymous, his example confirms the widely held stereotype that the price of admission to the club is high. But beyond anecdotes and conventional wisom, experts say not much is really known about the psychological state of Canadian executives and the stress they shoulder. What kind of people make it to the top? And what price do they—along with their families, coworkers and shareholders—pay for their success? No one has ever attempted such a profile. Until now.

This spring, Hammond was one of 400 randomly selected executives from large Canadian companies who agreed to describe how they think and behave—to reveal their feelings and their strategies—in a questionnaire designed by researchers at Ontario's Laurentian University of Sudbury. The results of that study, presented here in a *Canadian Business* exclusive, paint a startling portrait. Rather than revealing a mental profile that is a blueprint of surety and strength, the study suggests that the fight to get ahead—or even to keep pace—has become a life-or-death proposition for far too many executives.

Take Hammond. His high-energy, career-oriented personality may allow him to keep up a grueling work schedule, but according to the Laurentian study, he has made a trade-off of Faustian proportions. The personality that enables him to succeed also predisposes him to cardiovascular disease. And Hammond is not alone. . . .

Other executives in the Laurentian study blame their high-stress scores on a business culture that has begun feeding on itself. Terry Cooke, an entrepreneur and inventor based in Markham, Ont., who recently left an executive vice-president's job with Sony of Canada Ltd. to market a new utility knife, says he saw a proliferation of "dysfunctional behavior" during the 14 years he spent as an executive in Toronto with Calgary-based Shell Canada Ltd. and the nine years he spent with Sony Canada. Then, as now, Cooke started work at dawn so that he could be home in time for dinner. He recalls how he was told in one performance evaluation at Shell Canada that because he starts his day so early, nobody sees him working long hours. His work was excellent, yet Cooke's boss implied that he should stay later for appearances' sake. "People want to get up the corporate ladder, so they'll do what it takes," Cooke says. "Your ability to manage, to be visible and to give your boss what he wants—not what he needs—is more important than doing the actual job." Cooke swears that at 4 P.M. every day at Shell, "people grab folders and walk up and down the halls so they can be seen."

Other executives attribute their high stress levels to a shake-up at the management level. Marten A. Mol is a Toronto-based executive who serves on six boards and also took part in the study. Mol, an executive coach, says, "There's tremendous conflict for executives right now." Not only are executives taking the fall for economic downturns and outmoded management trends, but they're also being called upon to transform themselves. Mol recounts a visit to the office of one company president who was having problems with sales, marketing and morale: "Within two minutes, he went out and started to give one of the managers a good licking." Asking around, Mol found out that the only time the boss appeared among the employees was when there was a problem, and if he did so five times, the workers knew they were in deep trouble. "There are hundreds [of executives] like that," he said. "This is not unique."

When Jim Estill thinks of balance, he thinks of finding the razor's edge of maximum productivity. "I think of business as running a marathon," he says. "You set a pace that you can maintain forever." In order to stay in shape for his 60-to-80-hour weeks, Estill— who is president and CEO of both EMJ Data Systems Ltd. of Guelph, Ontario, and Hookup Communications Inc. of Oakville, Ontario—sticks to a vegetarian diet, gets lots of exercise and "wills" himself into needing less sleep and maintaining a positive mental attitude. ("I choose to be high-energy," he says.) He doesn't even allow himself to think in terms of stress. "I deliberately have to design systems to cope with what I call 'volume,' " he says. "That's what I'm dealing with. Five hundred e-mails a day. A hundred telephone calls. There's never enough time."

Estill's systems have worked out just fine, he says. Except for one thing: his marriage. "You can't just say, 'OK, we're going to have quality time from 7:00 to 7:30.' " He has been separated for three years now. "Yes, I think that's a price I paid," he admits. "That was a miscalculation I made in my life."

With all the work Estill puts into keeping a healthy balance, he takes issue with the fact that the Laurentian study placed him in the anti-emotional and cancer-prone Type 5 category. But if the researchers are right, Estill's efforts at self-control could, over time, exact their price, just as they do for many of his peers.

Corporate psychologist Dr. Richard Allon says that executives often don't realize that they're suffering from too much stress, sometimes ending up in his office after landing in hospital with what feels like a heart attack. He says that many of them begin by saying: "I'm productive, my career is going like gangbusters and you're here talking about changing lifestyles. Is this going to make me less productive?" The answer to that, Allon says, is no. Whether they realize it or not, stressed people are less productive.

The perception that it is counterproductive to slow down won't change until society starts to see stress vulnerabilities in the same light as ailments such as diabetes or a weak heart, says Nesea Martin, executive director of the Mood Disorders Association of Metropolitan Toronto. Businesspeople can get treatment and stay healthy by taking care of themselves, making sure they get enough sleep, eating properly and exercising. "Unfortunately," says Martin, "some of the things that make for good psychological health don't make for good business."

And, for now at least, that means more and more company for people such as Hammond. "I don't know how I handle it," he says. "I don't eat right. I don't sleep. I don't exercise. My doctor says I'm a miracle." Naturally, a study telling Hammond that he is at risk of having a stroke isn't about to stop him from trying to be the first person in the office every morning and the last to leave at night. Even though he admits that those evening hours aren't as productive as those in the mornings, he isn't about to change. He is setting an example. And besides, he says, "There's always something to do."

INTRODUCTION

Let's face it, every career has its job stressors, but at what point do individuals decide that the costs of doing the job far outweigh the benefits? That's an interesting question, and looking at the preceding case on corporate leaders, one gets the distinct impression that for this group, the personal costs allowed are considerable. So on which yardstick might these corporate leaders be assessing the benefits of staying in, and keeping up, the hectic pace?

One obvious yardstick that they might be processing is compensation. In Chapter 6, we reviewed some of the munificent salary-bonus-stock option compensation packages given to U.S. CEOs in the last year, noting that some earned billionaire status. We also noted that Canada had its fair share of millionaire CEOs. Thus, many members of North American society might surmise that such munificent financial packages could feasibly offset a considerable number of job stressors for these CEOs. Or they might surmise that the stock options, more than the salaries and bonuses, keep CEOs "plugging away."

Following a U.S. trend, stock options have in the past decade become "the president's choice" for Canadian public companies, large and small, when it, theoretically at least, comes to spurring on CEOs to greater profits (Partridge 1998). For example, option gains of $23.5 million propelled Robert Gratton, president and CEO of the Desmarais-controlled Power Financial Corp. (with a 1997 profit of $603 million) to a total compensation package of $27.4 million, including a base salary of $1,758,000 and $2 million in bonus pay. The latter made Gratton No. 1 on the list of 100 of Canada's best-paid CEOs for 1997. No. 2 on the list was Gerald Schwartz, chairman and president of Onex Corp., who packed in a hefty total of $18,775,640, including a base salary of $899,990 and $6,437,250 in bonus pay.

In fact, during 1997, 50 CEOS reportedly made between $27.4 million and $2.0 million (Partridge 1998), including base salary, bonuses, and stock options. Bryan, former CEO of Gulf Canada Resources Ltd., made the list at total compensation of $3,030,725, including one of the highest Canadian CEO base salaries of $1,056,021 and $1,426,700 in bonus pay. Although, in theory, corporate boards pay big awards to their CEOs to yield high profits, such expected returns are not always realized. For example, just behind Bryan in the compensation payout race was INCO Ltd. CEO Mike Sopko, whose total package totaled $2,829,576, including a base salary of $861,097 and $549,607 in bonus pay. In 1997 INCO Ltd. posted a profit loss of 57 percent, caused by a combination of "crises"— including a strike, restructuring of the company and layoffs in the face of low nickel prices, and a $4.3 billion investment in Voisey's Bay, Newfoundland. Nine other CEOs joined Sopko with hefty compensation packages in 1997, despite plummeting company profits.

Fifty more Canadian CEOs made between $1.9 million and $909,467 in 1997, including base pay, bonuses, and options. One of "the eminents" in the latter compensation group included the late Quebecor Inc. former chairman and president Pierre Peladeau, who earned $1,537,500, including a base salary of $900,000 and $500,000+ in bonus pay.

But what if we were to leave the "compensation success yardstick" for corporate leaders and turn, instead, to an entirely different yardstick—say, one based on stress-coping and personality predispositions. Now, how would our outstanding corporate leaders do? That was one of the major questions that Mr. Larose and I asked ourselves and our corporate leaders over a year ago.

Chapter 8 develops more fully this theme of "the stress-coping and personality yardstick" for corporate leaders and presents our hypotheses and findings in this regard.

THE PROCEDURE FOLLOWED IN THE CORPORATE LEADER STUDY

The Inventory Selected for Assessing Personality Predispositions

Because we were interested in assessing a fuller range of "self-healing" and "disease-prone" personality traits for corporate leaders besides Type A and Type B, we selected the 70-item inventory developed by Grossarth-Maticek and Eysenck (1990). This inventory provides readings for each individual on the following six type patterns:

- *Type 1*: a *cancer-prone* thinking and behaving pattern, whereby the adult tends to keep "psychological noise" inside. Much "noise" is generated by a fear of losing relationships. Consequently, this type has been found to be emotionally dependent, overly cooperative, unassertive, conflict-avoidant, and depression-prone.

- *Type 2*: a *cardiovascular-prone* thinking and behaving pattern, whereby the adult tends to vent some "psychological noise" outwardly by yelling and (if need be) throwing things. Much "noise" is generated by a fear of losing self-esteem; thus, self- and other-given rewards for this type are linked heavily to social status, finances, and property ownership. While depression likely occurs in this type, it is rarely talked about. Known in the psychosocial literature as the patterned Type A personality, this adult tends to be perfection-fixated, highly job-involved, impatient, and hard-driving and competitive.

- *Type 3*: a *narcissistic and possibly criminal* thinking and behaving pattern, whereby the adult tends to vent much "psychological noise" outwardly by yelling and (if need be) through aggressive behaviors. This type—which is labeled "psychopathic" personality in the extreme—often suffers from poor anger management and an inability to monitor or control anger provocations.

- *Type 4*: a *self-healing and well-balanced* thinking and behaving pattern, whereby the adult is said to be a good energy manager and stress-coper. In the psychosocial literature, this type is said to be autonomous, assertive, task-and-emotion balanced, and a patterned Type B.

- *Type 5*: a *noise-denying, cancer-prone* thinking and behaving pattern, whereby the adult is said to be antiemotional and overrational about stressors causing "psychological noise." Consequently, the "noise factors" tend not to be constructively dealt with and, thus, have a tendency to resurface. While this Type C strain is thought to suffer from depressive episodes, cancer onset is said to manifest in the longer term, particularly after a high-stress period.

- *Type 6*: a still undiagnosed type at this stage of research results, the adult is said to be *withdrawn, antisocial, possibly criminal, and likely a substance abuser*. A tendency toward obsession of some kind has lately been added to the list. In the extreme form, characters like "the Unibomber" might be classified as having this type.

The maximum score that any adult can receive on each of these six type traits is 10. Thus, considering the set of six scores, each respondent's highest score represents his or her strongest thinking and behaving predisposition, the second highest score represents his or her next strongest thinking and behaving predisposition, and so on. Any score meeting or exceeding a critical level of 5 is considered to be a significant personality predisposition for the respondent, consuming sizable quantities of finite life energy. Ideally, a "strong" self-healing adult has a high score on Type 4 and a score below 5 on the five remaining disease-prone types.

Validity Outcomes of the Grossarth-Maticek and Eysenck 70-Item Inventory

Initial Validity Outcome Findings. The initial validity outcome findings of the 70-item inventory were of interest to us, primarily because they seemed to have direct applicability to our study population. In their longitudinal study undertaken in Heidelberg, West Germany, Grossarth-Maticek and Eysenck (1990) distributed the 70-item inventory to almost 16,000 men and 3,000 women of an average age of 50 (similar to that of corporate leaders) and constituting a fairly random sample of the community population. Besides answering these 70 items, the respondents answered questions about their smoking and drinking habits and about their health. Cholesterol level, blood pressure, blood sugar, and other medical details were also measured at this time.

From this large study sample, Grossarth-Maticek and Eysenck selected 216 probands (half were men, and half were women, equated for age) on the basis of their scores on the inventory. Their aim was to find equal numbers of men and women for "prototypes" of each of the six types, such that an adult given "a pure type" label was characterized as having a perfect score of "10" for that type and no score higher than "2" on any other type. Since not many "pure types" were conjectured to exist, the researchers chose the first probands in their lists who fulfilled this stringent requirement.

The probands were followed over a 13-year period, with mortality and incidence of a variety of disorders being the dependent variables of interest. With the agreement of the respondents, diagnoses were obtained from the physicians in charge if any respondent suffered from any kind of diagnosed illness. Addiction to alcohol or drugs was diagnosed according to interviews with relatives of the probands. In the case of death, physicians were consulted, death certificates were examined, and the findings were recorded in the researchers' computer files.

As predicted by Grossarth-Maticek and Eysenck, cancer was frequently diagnosed in the type 1s; in fact, it was as frequent in persons of Type 1 as in those of all other types taken together. Coronary heart disease, as expected, was most frequently diagnosed in the Type 2s, being about three times as frequent as in all other types. The Type 2s also showed significantly higher incidences of ulcer, hypertonia, and diabetes. The Type 3s and Type 4s were relatively healthy physiologically, with few medical diagnoses for the Type 4s, in particular. However, noted the researchers, the scores on substance abuse for the Type 3s were elevated and were worthy of follow-up. The "noise-denying" Type 5s showed clearly elevated scores for endogenous depression and for rheumatoid arthritis. The Type 6s had a high score for addiction to substances, in particular, there being as many addicts of this one type as for all other types combined.

It is clear, concluded Grossarth-Maticek and Eysenck, that the 70-item version possesses a certain amount of validity, as shown by this first empirical validation attempt.

The Predictive Accuracy of the 70-Item Inventory. The predictive accuracy of the dynamic procedure—considering death from cancer, coronary heart disease (CHD), and other causes over time—was established in a group of 868 probands, assigned to a type according to the respondents' scores on the first study occasion and reassessed on their scores 13 years later (Grossarth-Maticek & Eysenck 1990, pp. 360–361). Probands were allocated to a given "type" at the 13-year follow-up if their scores for that type exceeded their scores for any other type, but, unlike on the first occasion, they did not have to be a "pure 10." At follow-up, there were no significant age differences between types.

Respondents were labeled by the researchers as being Stagnant (S) or Developmental (D). The Stagnants showed no change in typing or showed a "worsening" in score and in stress-coping on the second administration of the inventory. The Developmentals showed a change in score indicating an "improvement" in stress-coping the second time around.

Of the 868 probands initially studied, 536 were still alive at the 13-

year follow-up; of those not still alive, 95 had died of cancer, 107 had died of CHD, and 130 had died of other causes. Of those who died of cancer, 6 were in the Developmental category, and 89 were in the Stagnation category. Of those who died of CHD, 18 were in the Developmental category, and 89 were in the Stagnation category. Of those who died of other causes, 16 were in the Developmental category, and 114 were in the Stagnation category.

"It is clear," concluded Grossarth-Maticek and Eysenck, "that this new dynamic way of prediction is highly successful, primarily no doubt because it charts the progress of the way the individual deals with stress. Clearly, if stress is an important cause of death, then a 'D' score indicates that the individual is coping well with his stress and shows psychological improvement, while an 'S' score shows the opposite" (p. 361).

The Reliability of Scales

Though Grossarth-Maticek and Eysenck reported that the test-retest reliability correlations for the 70-item inventory are "all in excess of 0.80 and so quite satisfactory," (p. 359), no Cronbach alpha reliability coefficients for the six type scales were reported for the German group. For the Canadian corporate leader respondents, the Cronbach alpha reliability coefficients for the six type scales ranged from 0.40 to 0.72. Considering that the responses to the 70 items were either yes or no, that the items were translated from German into "literal" English, and that the inventory was lengthy and embedded on pages 7–10 of the 14-page questionnaire, these coefficients seem to be adequate.

HYPOTHESES REGARDING TYPE PREDISPOSITIONS IN CORPORATE LEADERS

Determining relative percentages of the Type A, the Type B, the Type C, and the antisocial types in the corporate leader population was a difficult task for us, given that just about all of the corporate leader personality studies completed to date have focused almost exclusively on Type A patterning (Cooper & Melhuish 1980; Robinson & Inkson 1994; Cooper & Davidson 1982). Having said this, however, the organizational literature has increasingly projected, as highlighted by Hart and Quinn (1993), Hambrick and Fukutomi (1991), Borgeois and Eisenhardt (1988), Jacques (1986), and Kegan (1982) that effective corporate leadership in the challenging 1990s requires a "balancing" and "simultaneous mastery" of seemingly contradictory or paradoxical mind-behavior capabilities—the kind of complexity that would require a fair amount of the flexible Type B/Type 4 patterning.

Now comes the million-dollar question not yet answered in the organizational literature: What percentage of today's corporate leaders would self-report as having large enough quantities of these self-healing, Type B/Type 4 capabilities? We posited that the answer is, That depends on the degree of self-healing "purity" one is projecting. Referring once more to Hart and Quinn's 1993 study findings on 916 U.S. corporate leaders, these researchers deduced that, at most, 10 percent of their sample could be classified as highly or moderately balanced *and* multidimensional—thus, being "purely" self-healing in nature. The remaining 90 percent, they said, were either "low on complexity" or "unbalanced." Applying these deductions to present-day Canadian corporate leaders, we could feasibly expect about 10 percent of them to self-report as "purely" self-healing in patterning (i.e., having their highest score on Type 4 and their remaining Type scores below 5).

If only about 10 percent of the Canadian corporate leaders self-report as "purely" self-healing, then how would the remaining 90 percent likely rate themselves on this personality predisposition yardstick? It is likely, we posited, that, consistent with the just-cited arguments, present-day corporate leaders would need an abundant supply of Type B/Type 4 existing within them to perform satisfactorily but would likely also have some disease-prone conditioning existing within them—such as the workaholism described by Hammond and others in the opening case—that would exacerbate the strain experienced by them. Given this reality, we posited that Canadian corporate leaders would have their highest score on the Type B/Type 4 patterning but have, as well, other disease-prone type scores of 5 or higher.

But is Type A the only disease-prone patterning likely to manifest in these corporate leaders? Likely not, at least if the findings of Grossarth-Maticek and Eysenck (1990) on male and female working adults are considered. The more likely finding would be that, besides Type A/Type 2 traits, other segments of the corporate leader population would likely have Type 1, Type 3, Type 5, and Type 6 traits. While many earlier studies, as noted, found that pathological stress levels were highly correlated with Type A patterning in managers (Cooper & Melhuish 1980; Robinson & Inkson 1994; Cooper & Davidson 1982), it must be emphasized that only the Type A trait was being assessed. Unlike in the Grossarth-Maticek and Eysenck study (1990), cancer-proneness or antisocial traits were simply not assessed. Also, other reported studies on corporate leaders have found either reduced Type A-proneness in the senior leader ranks (Kegan 1982) or a lack of consistency between top leadership positions and Type A-proneness (Pell & D'Alonzo 1958; Stamler, Kjelsberg, & Hall 1960; Bainton & Peterson 1963; Piotrowski & Armstrong 1989).

On a broader basis, other researchers have argued that, besides Type A-proneness, other psychoneurotic traits can manifest in the approximately 20 percent mentally "at risk" segment of the corporate leader population (Cahoon & Rowney 1984; Meier 1983). That such traits would include anxiety, depression, and Type C-proneness seems reasonable, given that corporate leaders have been conditioned to "closet" or to rationalize away (Hambrick & Fukutomi 1991) (like Estill?) their emotional pain.

• *Hypothesis 8.1*: It was hypothesized that about 10 percent of the present-day Canadian corporate leaders would report as "purely" self-healing (i.e., having their highest score on Type 4 and having their remaining five type scores lower than 5). The remaining 90 percent, it was hypothesized, would report as having strong self-healing Type 4 tendencies (i.e., having their highest score on Type 4) *and* some disease-prone tendencies (i.e., having a score of 5 or higher on Type 1, Type 2, Type 3, Type 5, and/or Type 6) or report as "purely" disease-prone (having a score of 5 or higher on a disease-prone type without a Type 4 counterbalance).

Projected Type Differences in Second-Tier and Top Management Leaders

As noted in Chapter 7, to reduce some of their experienced anxiety, top managers likely project the blame for the firm's problems onto the second-tier corporate leaders, thus exacerbating the second tier managers' disease-prone type traits and raising their disease-prone scores.

• *Hypothesis 8.2*: It was hypothesized that, compared to their top-management counterparts, the strained second-tier corporate leader group would report significantly higher mean scores on the various disease-prone type varieties (i.e., Type 1, Type 2, Type 3, Type 5, and Type 6). No significant difference in mean Type 4 score, however, was hypothesized.

Type Predispositions and the Gender and Stress Issues in Corporate Leaders

Type Predispositions and the Gender Issue. There are no indications in the organizational literature suggesting that the type predispositions of female corporate leaders should be any different from those of their male counterparts. Though the stereotype exists that women corporate leaders are more interpersonally skilled and sensitive than their male counterparts, a number of recent studies suggest that this is myth more than reality (Nelson & Quick 1985; Powell 1990). Moreover, both male and female corporate leaders reportedly tend to exhibit the workaholic tendency described by Hammond (Nelson & Quick 1985). Further, in his extensive 1990 review of the current organizational literature regarding male-female managerial similarities and differences, Powell said:

In summary, sex differences are absent in [managerial] task-oriented behavior, people-oriented behavior, effectiveness ratings of actual managers, and subordinates' responses to actual managers. . . . There is not much difference between the needs, values, and leadership styles of male and female managers. The sex differences that have been found are few, found in laboratory studies more than field studies, and tend to cancel each other out. . . . This review supports the "no differences" view of sex differences in management. (p. 71)

There are further indications in the organizational literature suggesting that male and female leaders could be similarly "disease-prone." A number of researchers in the 1980s (Davidson & Cooper 1980; Cooper & Melhuish 1980; Cooper & Davidson 1982) reported that workaholic male and female corporate leaders tend to suffer from the somatic disorders of ulcers, migraine headaches, arthritic pain; from high blood pressure and elevated cholesterol; and from the emotional disorders of fatigue, irritation, depression, and anxiety. Recall that Grossarth-Maticek and Eysenck (1990) found that cancer-prone Type 5s tend to report the disorders of arthritis and depression, while the cardiovascular-prone Type 2s tend to report the disorders of ulcers, elevated cholesterol, and high blood pressure. Thus, to expect that the Type 2 and the Type 5 predispositions would fail to present in present-day male and female corporate leaders would be naive.

Moreover, posited Leiter (1991), adults at all levels of the organizational hierarchy relying on "escapist" stress-coping patterns instead of "control" stress-coping patterns place themselves at risk for burnout and for other health problems. Researchers Jick and Mitz (1985) reported that such escapist stress-coping tendencies often include substance abuse, which was found by Grossarth-Maticek and Eysenck (1990) to typify the Type 3s and the Type 6s. To think that such Type 3 and Type 6 disease-prone tendencies would fail to manifest in "escapist-coping" male and female corporate leaders would be naive.

- *Hypothesis 8.3*: It was hypothesized that the male and female corporate leaders' mean scores on the Type 1 through Type 6 predispositions would not be significantly different.

Projected Correlations between Type Score and PSS Score. It seems reasonable to conclude that the corporate leaders' PSS scores would be positively correlated with their "disease-prone" Type 1, Type 2, Type 3, Type 5, and Type 6 scores and would be negatively correlated with their "self-healing" Type 4 scores.

- *Hypothesis 8.4*: It was hypothesized that the corporate leaders' PSS scores would be positively correlated with their disease-prone Type 1, Type 2, Type 3, Type

5, and Type 6 scores and would be negatively correlated with their self-healing Type 4 scores.

Expected Mean Type Scores for the Corporate Leaders. Finally, it would seem reasonable to expect that the corporate leaders' mean type scores would be highest on the self-healing Type 4 trait and that their mean scores for the disease-prone Type 5/Type C and Type 2/Type A predispositions would be equal to, or greater than, 5. Moreover, given corporate leaders' need to "closet" or "suppress" their distress and discomfort for their own survival and for the image of the firm, it would seem reasonable to expect that the corporate leaders' mean scores for the narcissistic and antisocial Type 3 and Type 6 traits would exceed 2 but be less than 5.

- *Hypothesis 8.5*: It was hypothesized that the corporate leaders' mean scores would be highest on the self-healing Type 4 trait and that their mean scores for the disease-prone Type 5 and Type 2 traits would be equal to, or greater than, 5. It was further hypothesized that the corporate leaders' mean scores for the narcissistic and antisocial Type 3 and Type 6 traits would exceed 2 but be less than 5.

Further Projections Regarding Corporate Leaders' Type Scores

Type Scores and the Influence Style Issue. Consistent with the 1988 study findings of Kipnis and Schmidt, pathologically stressed corporate leaders reportedly seem to use a "shotgun" style of influencing within their organizations—preferring to assert themselves, first, and if this does not bring the expected results, to nonjudiciously use a variety of other influence strategies. Translating this finding into type terminology, compared to their low-to-moderately stressed counterparts, it would be reasonable to conclude that the shotgun corporate leaders would report significantly lower self-healing Type 4 scores and significantly elevated scores on the disease-prone types. Moreover, consistent with the Chapter 7 arguments regarding stress levels and positioning for corporate leaders, it would seem reasonable to conclude that the highly strained and less "in-control" second-tier corporate leaders would be more likely to report as shotguns than their more "in-control" top-management counterparts.

- *Hypothesis 8.6*: It was hypothesized that, relative to their less-stressed counterparts, the highly stressed corporate leaders would report using "shotgun" influence strategies, with a lower Type 4 mean score and with higher mean scores on a variety of disease-prone types (i.e., Type 1, Type 2, Type 3, Type 5, Type 6).

Type Scores and High Compensation. Consistent with the "self-cloning" study findings described in Chapter 6, the "old boys' network" delineated by Morrison and Von Glinow (1990) and the "escapist" study findings of Jick and Mitz (1985), it would be reasonable to conclude that compared to their less well compensated counterparts, the highly compensated corporate leaders would report higher mean scores on the Type A/Type 2 traits and on the narcissistic and possibly substance-abusive Type 3 and Type 6 traits. Moreover, as noted in Chapter 7, the highly compensated leaders would rely heavily on "friendly" and "coalition" upward influence strategies to negotiate a good compensation package, would be males in their 50s, and would tend to be in top management.

- *Hypothesis 8.7*: It was hypothesized that, compared to their less well compensated counterparts, the highly compensated corporate leaders would report higher mean scores on the hard-driving and competitive Type A/Type 2 traits and on the narcissistic and possibly substance-abusive Type 3 and Type 6 traits. Moreover, they would rely heavily on "friendly" and "coalition" upward influence strategies and would be older, in a top-management position, and male rather than female.

STUDY FINDINGS

The results of the study of 400 corporate leaders who completed the 14-page questionnaire on stress, influence strategies, type, and compensation brought a few surprises when the type variable was added to our previous data analysis. The findings regarding this second phase of analysis can be summarized as follows:

- Only 50 of 395 present-day Canadian corporate leaders, or 13 percent, self-reported as being "purely" self-healing. Moreover, 329 of 395 corporate leaders, or 83 percent, reported having strong self-healing tendencies and some disease-prone tendencies. Regarding "pure" disease-prone types without adequate self-healing traits, 8 of 395 corporate leaders, or 2 percent, reported having a complex disease-prone combination (e.g., Type C/Type 3 or Type C/Type 6), and another 8 of the 395, or 2 percent, reported as "pure" Type C. This finding of a 4 percent "pure" disease-prone trait in corporate leaders supports Hart and Quinn's earlier study findings (1993; see Chapter 2). In short, given the percentages of the "purely" self-healing and of the "disease-prone" types in this corporate leader sample, 13 percent and 87 percent respectively, Hypothesis 8.1 appears to be supported, with a slight overrepresentation on the "pure" self-healing types and with a slight underrepresentation on the projected "disease-prone" types.
- Consistent with Hypothesis 8.2, no significant difference was found between the top management's and the second-tier's self-healing Type 4 mean score (both were about 7.7). But, as predicted, significantly higher mean scores were

found on the disease-prone Type 2, Type 3, and Type 6 predispositions for the strained second-tier group. Both the top-management and the second-tier group were quite Type C in nature, with the antiemotional and overrational, cancer-prone Type 5 mean scores being about "6" for both groups.

- Consistent with Hypothesis 8.3, the female corporate leaders' mean scores on type were generally not significantly different from those of their male counterparts. Only one difference was found: the females had a significantly lower mean score on Type 5 (i.e., 5.7), as compared to their male counterparts (i.e., 6.2).

- Consistent with Hypothesis 8.4, the corporate leaders' PSS scores were negatively correlated with their self-healing Type 4 scores ($r = -.40$) but were positively correlated with their disease-prone Type 1 ($r = 0.56$), Type 2 ($r = 0.61$), Type 3 ($r = 0.55$), Type 5 ($r = .16$), and Type 6 ($r = 0.51$) scores.

- Consistent with Hypothesis 8.5, the corporate leaders' self-healing Type 4 mean score was strong and considerably higher than 5 ($M: 7.59$), and their antiemotional and overrational Type 5 mean score met or exceeded 5 ($M: 6.05$). Also, as hypothesized, the corporate leaders' disease-prone Type 3 ($M: 3.17$) and Type 6 ($M: 3.67$) mean scores were greater than 2 but less than 5. Surprisingly, given the earlier reported Type A proneness in middle managers, and contrary to Hypothesis 8.5, the corporate leaders' Type 2 mean score was considerably below 5 ($M: 2.09$).

- Consistent with Hypothesis 8.6, the highly stressed corporate leaders reported "shotgun" influence strategies—placing a considerable amount of their energy on the assertiveness-upward and on the assertiveness-downward strategies and using a variety of other upward and downward influence strategies. Despite this energy-draining trait, the shotguns were still quite self-healing in nature, even considering that their Type 4 mean score of 6.96 was significantly lower than that of their less-stressed counterparts ($M: 7.85$). As hypothesized, both the Type C ($M: 5.17$) and the Type A ($M: 3.39$) traits were relied upon for coping by this highly stressed corporate leader segment, thus reducing their capacity to be more fully self-healing. While the narcissistic and likely substance-abusive Type 3 pattern presented in fair amount in the highly stressed shotgun segment ($M: 4.03$) and was nearly double that of the lowly stressed segment ($M: 2.28$), the mean score for this Type 3 trait was below 5. Finally, shotguns were more likely to be found in the second-tier group rather than in the top-management group. Thus, given these findings, Hypothesis 8.6 appeared to be fully supported.

- Consistent with Hypothesis 8.7, the corporate leaders who were highly paid tended to be self-healing ($M: 7.41$) but—contrary to what many adults in society might think—significantly less so than their less well paid counterparts ($M: 7.73$). As hypothesized, the well-paid types tended to be in the top-management rather than in the second-tier group, were male, and were, on average, 53 years of age. Also, compared to their less well paid counterparts, the highly paid corporate leaders had significantly higher mean scores on the narcissistic and possibly addictive Type 3 ($M: 3.13$) and on the possibly addictive Type 6 ($M: 3.59$) traits, though both of these mean scores placed below 5. Finally, the highly paid corporate leaders reportedly rely on a "friendly upward" and on a "co-alition upward" influence strategy to get their compensation package returns. Given these findings, supporting the notion of a well-compensated "old boys' network," Hypothesis 8.7 appeared to be fully supported.

THE BOTTOM LINE

This chapter opened with a case on several Canadian corporate leaders who had taken part in our national questionnaire study. The picture drawn by the respondents was one of having to be a workaholic in order to be successful on the top rungs of the business ladder. Hammond and Estill delineated two disease-prone predispositions that seem to manifest, in various degrees, in workaholic corporate leaders: the Type A variety—who work long hours, lead a rather task-obsessed life, and admit, on being told, that "a balance" in their lives is missing, and the Type C variety—who work long hours, lead a rather task-obsessed life, and deny that they have an "imbalance" problem.

The questions then arose, In present-day Canadian corporate leaders, how common are the Type A and Type C predispositions, relative to the self-healing Type B kind? What other disease-prone traits manifest in corporate leaders as a result of today's "taxing" corporate environment?

Perhaps the greatest surprise of the phase 2 analysis, given previous reports on middle-level managers, was that the respondents appeared to be, in large measure, a self-healing /Type C combination or a complex self-healing/disease-prone combination rather than a "purely" Type A variety. Finally, consistent with Hart and Quinn's 1993 assertions, only 13 percent of today's "taxed" Canadian corporate leaders appear to be "purely" self-healing, with the majority—87 percent—reporting some degree of disease-proneness. As Hart and Quinn found, only 4 percent were "purely" disease-prone.

REFERENCES

Bainton, C. R., & Peterson, D. R. (1963). Deaths from coronary heart disease in persons fifty years of age and younger: A community-wide study. *New England Journal of Medicine, 268,* 569–574.

Borgeois, L. J., & Eisenhardt, K. (1988). Strategic decision processes in high velocity environments: Four cases in the microcomputer industry. *Management Science, 14,* 816–835.

Cahoon, A. R., & Rowney, J. A. (1984). Managerial burnout: A comparison by sex and level of responsibility. *Journal of Health and Human Resources Administration, 7,* 249–264.

Cooper, C. L., & Davidson, M. J. (1982). The high cost of stress on women managers. *Organizational Dynamics, 10,* 44–53.

Cooper, C. L., & Melhuish, A. (1980). Occupational stress and managers. *Journal of Occupational Medicine, 22,* 588–592.

Davidson, M. J., & Cooper, C. L. (1980). The extra pressures on women executives. *Personnel Management, 12,* 45–51.

Grossarth-Maticek, R., & Eysenck, H. J. (1990). Personality, stress and disease: Description and validation of a new inventory. *Psychological Reports, 66,* 355–373.

Hambrick, D. C., & Fukutomi, G. D. S. (1991). The seasons of a CEO's tenure. *Academy of Management Review, 16,* 719–742.

Harris, M. (1997). Letters: Is your career killing you? *Canadian Business, 70,* 15.

Hart, S. L., & Quinn, R. E. (1993). Roles executives play: CEOs, behavioral complexity, and firm performance. *Human Relations, 46,* 543–574.

Jacques, E. (1986). The development of intellectual capability: A discussion of stratified systems theory. *Journal of Applied Behavioral Science, 22,* 361–383.

Jick, T. D., & Mitz, L. F. (1985). Sex differences in work stress. *Academy of Management Review, 10,* 408–420.

Kegan, R. (1982). *The evolving self.* Cambridge, MA: Harvard University Press.

Kipnis, D., & Schmidt, S. M. (1988). Upward-influence styles: Relationship with performance evaluations, salary, and stress. *Administrative Science Quarterly, 33,* 528–542.

Leiter, M. P. (1991). Coping patterns as predictors of burnout: The function of control and escapist coping patterns. *Journal of Organizational Behavior, 12,* 123–144.

Meier, S. T. (1983). Toward a theory of burnout. *Human Relations, 36,* 899–910.

Morrison, A. M., & Von Glinow, M. A. (1990). Women and minorities in management. *American Psychologist, 45,* 200–208.

Nelson, D. L., & Quick, J. C. (1985). Professional women: Are distress and disease inevitable? *Academy of Management Review, 10,* 206–218.

Partridge, J. (1998). Options spell pay dirt. *The Globe and Mail,* pp. B1, B6–B7.

Pell, S., & D'Alonzo, C. A. (1958). Myocardial infarction in a one year industrial study. *Journal of the American Medical Association, 166,* 332–337.

Piotrowski, C., & Armstrong, T. R. (1989). The CEO: An analysis of the CNN Telecast "Pinnacle." *Psychological Reports, 65,* 435–438.

Powell, G. N. (1990). One more time: Do female and male managers differ? *Academy of Management Executive, 199,* 68–75.

Robinson, P., & Inkson, K. (1994). Stress effects on the health of chief executives of business organizations. *Stress Medicine, 10,* 27–34.

Stamler, J., Kjelsberg, M., & Hall, Y. (1960). Epidemiologic studies of cardiovascular-renal diseases: I. Analysis of mortality by age-race-sex-occupation. *Journal of Chronic Disability, 12,* 440–455.

Tillson, T. (1997). Is your career killing you? *Canadian Business, 70,* 78–84.

CHAPTER 9

Corporate Leaders: A Revealing Disclosure of Their Long-Term Moods and Mood Disorders

No one could stir up a crowd like Gerald Pencer, the head of soft-drink upstart Cott Corp., who passed away earlier this year. In 1993, Mr. Pencer surprised shareholders by strolling through the crowd, Oprah-style, interviewing representatives from companies that bottled his product. Mr. Pencer's most memorable hour came last June, two weeks after surgery for a malignant brain tumour. He jogged into the meeting, dressed in a white robe and bright-red boxing gloves, while the theme from *Rocky* played and spotlights swirled around the darkened room. The baseball cap on his shaved head said it all: The Magic is Back. After an emotional speech, he asked shareholders to stand, hold hands and sing Dionne Warwick's 1985 hit, *That's What Friends Are For.*

—J. Heinzl et al. (1998)

A CASE IN POINT

The following piece appeared in *The Globe and Mail* on December 6, 1997 (Yakabuski), describing Canada's recent concern about the health of one of our most successful and controversial businesspeople, Pierre Peladeau:

The television satellite trucks parked outside Montreal's Hotel-Dieu hospital since Tuesday are the symbol of a province on tenterhooks. Everyone, it seems, wants to know. One network even interrupted a Canadiens [hockey] game, a normally sacrosanct event in Quebec, to broadcast a Wednesday night press briefing on the fragile state of Pierre Peladeau.

The scene outside the downtown hospital, for which Mr. Peladeau helped collect more than $9 million in 1997 as president of its fundraising drive, is eerily reminiscent of another vigil that consumed the province three years ago when Lucien Bouchard lay near death only a few blocks away at Hopital Saint-Luc.

The then-Bloc Quebecois leader's miraculous recovery from the flesh-eating bacteria that claimed his left leg irrevocably ensured his mythical status in his native province.

What lies ahead for the Peladeau myth? For now, even doctors cannot say whether the curmudgeonly 72-year-old Quebecor Inc. founder and controlling shareholder will emerge unscathed from the coma he has been in, attached to an artificial respirator, since suffering a massive heart attack this week.

But what is certain is that the irreverent media mogul is not alone in his struggle. He has most Quebeckers resolutely on his side. "The emotional attachment Quebeckers have shown for Mr. Peladeau is something exceptionally rare for a multimillionaire businessman," observes Christian Dufour, a political science professor at Montreal's Ecole Nationale d'Administration Publique. "But Mr. Peladeau is part of the fabric of Quebec. He has remained very close to the people, very authentic, despite his enormous success."

Indeed, Mr. Peladeau has proven remarkably attuned to popular culture in Quebec for someone whose own tastes are unmistakenly high-brow, ranging from Balzac to Beethoven. His flagship *Le Journal de Montreal*, a tabloid founded during a protracted 1964 strike at *La Presse*, thrives by offering readers a raunchy mixture of crime, celebrity chatter, and carnal indiscretions.

The Peladeau paradoxes do not end there. Behind the street-talking iconoclast is a well-read intellectual with a master's degree in philosophy. *Le Journal* is the polar opposite of *Le Devoir*, the fledgling snobby broadsheet that Mr. Peladeau bailed out in the mid-1980s. The annual "pow-wow" at his sprawling Ste-Adele estate looks a bit like a pool party at the Playboy mansion, with its beautiful women and pop music stars. But Mr. Peladeau's true passions are classical music and the Orchestre Metropolitain du Grand Montreal, which has depended on him as its biggest benefactor for years.

Even so, the Peladeau myth at home is founded first and foremost on the triumph of the little guy in the face of adversity. In a province where home-grown business legends are a still rare phenomenon, the Quebecor chief has earned adulation by surmounting alcoholism, Manic-Depression and ostracism from the business establishment.

In the rest of Canada, Mr. Peladeau is largely known for his incendiary comments about Jews, women, and the feasibility of Quebec separation. But on both sides of the two solitudes, there is no disputing his business acumen.

Since rescuing a dying weekly newspaper with $1,500 borrowed from his mother in 1950, Mr. Peladeau has built Montreal-based Quebecor into Canada's second-biggest media empire with annual sales of $6.3 billion and 34,000 employees.

Le Journal de Montreal is one of the world's largest circulation French-language newspapers and Canada's third-biggest daily. His commercial printing operations, held through 81%-owned Quebecor Printing Inc., are the world's second biggest, span three continents, and count such publications as *Fortune* magazine and France's glossy *Le Figaro* as clients. And Donohue Inc., two-thirds owned by Quebecor, is one of the country's biggest newsprint producers.

"If you were to make a list of the 10 top businessmen Canada has produced, his name would have to be on it," says Andre Gourd, a former Quebecor executive who left the company in August, 1997, for consultants Arthur Andersen Mallette Maheu. Mr. Peladeau is also known as an unrelenting boss, chewing up and spitting out executives on a moment's notice. Mr. Gourd knows that first hand. In 1991, Mr. Peladeau fired him as president of wholly owned Quebecor Communications to install his son Pierre Karl, now 37, in the job. Mr. Gourd harbours no hard feelings. He reconciled with Mr. Peladeau and rejoined Quebecor in 1995 for a two-year stint as vice-president of government relations.

Mr. Gourd puts his former boss on an equal footing with such Canadian business legends as Paul Desmarais, Conrad Black, Jim Pattison, Ken Thomson and Laurent Beaudoin. But if Mr. Peladeau has earned a place among such illustrious company, he has done so not by embracing the stuffy convention of the business establishment, but by defying it.

While Mr. Desmarais and Mr. Beaudoin have adopted the traditional federalist colours of Quebec business leaders, Mr. Peladeau alone has flirted with the separatists, even voting "yes" in the 1980 referendum on sovereignty-association. He refused to endorse either side in the 1995 vote on sovereignty, but has repeatedly repudiated the independence disaster scenarios evoked by his business peers.

"Bullshit," Mr. Peladeau retorted when Mr. Beaudoin complained about the deleterious impact of political uncertainty on Quebec's economy at a major summit organized in March, 1996, by Mr. Bouchard. The tell-it-like-it-is forthrightness is Mr. Peladeau's stock in trade. Mr. Gourd recalls a 1981 meeting in Paris between his former boss and the publisher of the renowned *Larousse* dictionary, where the aspiring media mogul suddenly asked the aristocratic Frenchman how much he wanted for his company. Needless to say, the unsolicited offer from the irreverent Quebecker—then known only for the racy, crime, and entertainment tabloids he owned back home—was politely refused. But the rejection did not deter Mr. Peladeau from relying on the same determination and self-assuredness to get his way most of the time.

For that power of concentration, Mr. Peladeau has often credited his late mother, Elmire, a woman he worshipped intensely. Mr. Peladeau inherited his entrepreneurial flair, at least in part, from his father. Henri Peladeau made enough of a small fortune to install his wife and seven children in an Outremont address. Unfortunately, by the time he died in 1935, shortly after the young Pierre's 10th birthday, he had lost it all on a pulp and paper scheme gone wrong.

The family kept the house in Outremont, but apparently none of the lifestyle that one normally associates with the affluent enclave that hugs the northern slope of Mount Royal. Mr. Peladeau's own descriptions of his adolescence are ones of relative poverty as his mother struggled to raise him and his six siblings on her own.

Even so, Mr. Peladeau did briefly attend the elite College Jean de Brebeuf boys school—until he was expelled for frequenting the nearby tavern one too many times. He quit drinking in 1974.

The media mogul got his start with the purchase in 1950 of *Le Journal de Rosemont*. And from the start he demonstrated a knack for striking populist chords: The grey weekly was transformed overnight with Mr. Peladeau's first publicity stunt, a Miss Rosemont beauty contest.

Still, where Mr. Peladeau has been remarkably successful in producing newspapers that francophone readers seem to lap up, his populist recipe has largely floundered when tried on English-speaking audiences. Quebecor lost tons of money and some of its credibility on an unsuccessful Philadelphia paper he closed in 1981 and on the *Montreal Daily News*, a tabloid that hardly got off the ground before it was shut down in 1989. Quebecor's only remaining English-language tabloid, *The Winnipeg Sun*, appears, at best, to be holding its own.

Mr. Peladeau wanted to try again in the English-language market by tabling an offer last year for Sun Publishing Corp., and its Toronto, Ottawa, Calgary, and Edmonton tabloids and *The Financial Post*. The reaction from some English-Canadian commentators was as swift as it was virulent.

Mr. Peladeau was tarred as a racist, a sexist, an ex-alcoholic and, above all, a "separatist" in the pages of the very papers he wanted to buy. Columnist Allan Fotheringham, among others, agreed with *The Post* editor Diane Francis that "the idea of Peladeau for a boss would be too much to stomach." The incident was emblematic of the gulf between English- and French-Canadians in the way they view Mr. Peladeau. But it was not the first time this dichotomy in linguistic opinion had shown up. In 1989, Mr. Peladeau was roundly condemned outside his home province for declaring: "The big problem with women in business is this: They try to seduce too much." In Quebec—where political correctness has proven no match for the province's Latin temperament—the comment only seemed to augment the Peladeau myth.

A couple of years later, there was more outrage in English-Canada when news of Mr. Peladeau's latest faux pas crossed the linguistic barrier. He was hauled over the coals for telling *L-Actualite* magazine that Jews "take up too much space." Again, in French Quebec, the declaration was largely forgiven as an unfortunate indiscretion reported out of context.

For the most part, the attacks outside Quebec slid off Mr. Peladeau's back. But he conceded at Quebecor's annual meeting in 1997 that he "needed nerves of steel" to endure the "smear campaign" that he hinted partly cost him the Sun group deal.

Thwarted in his bid for a coast-to-coast empire, Mr. Peladeau turned his attention to a new endeavour: television. In April, 1997, Quebecor purchased Quatre-Saisons, Quebec's money-losing third network, and Mr. Peladeau vowed to work his populist magic to draw viewers. For the man at the head of a $6.3 billion colossus, Quarte-Saisons is clearly small potatoes—"a toy to play with"—in the eyes of one observer.

But Mr. Peladeau seemed to have taken to the task of turning Quatre-Saisons around with particular zeal. On Tuesday, shortly before his heart attack, he could be seen characteristically wagging his finger at the network's advertising sales staff in a motivational video taped that morning. Only time will tell whether Mr. Peladeau will ever return to Quebecor's 13th-floor head office to see the fruits of his pep talk. But much of Quebec is praying that he will.

Endnote: Pierre Peladaeu died on December 24, 1997.

INTRODUCTION

In Chapter 5, starting with the case of narcissistic, very successful, and manic-depressive G, we talked about several traits that psychosocial experts believe are likely found in corporate leaders, in varying degrees: narcissism, mood disorders, and antisocial traits, including substance abuse. Chapter 9 continues on this theme, focusing on the likely prevalence and assessment of these three predispositions in the Canadian corporate leader sample.

How many present-day corporate leaders would self-report as having the hypomanic "creative potential" of other eminents in the arts and in politics? How many corporate leaders, like Peladeau, would admit to battling "the bottle" and manic-depression and continue to stay "on top" of the corporate ladder? Such questions motivated us to search for a third time into our database to try to find some answers to these mood and related issues.

THE PROCEDURE FOLLOWED IN THE CORPORATE LEADER STUDY

The Inventories Selected or Developed for Assessing Narcissism, Mood Disorders, and Antisocial Traits

Assessing Narcissism, Denial, and Antisocial Traits. We sought an inventory that could assess narcissism and antisocial traits, such as suppressed rage and substance abuse, along with personality type. Thus, in addition to the reasons cited in Chapter 8 for selecting Grossarth-Maticek and Eysenck's (1990) 70-item inventory to assess type, it was our inventory of choice for assessing narcissism and antisocial traits.

The Type 3 scale of the 70-item inventory assesses narcissism (e.g., "I believe in the saying: 'What's in it for me?' " and "I am convinced that I am very important, and that I should be in the centre of everything that happens"), antisocial traits like suppressed anger/rage (e.g., "I am often anxious in situations which are completely harmless" and "When I come up against a problem, however small, I tend to exaggerate it"), narcissistic, antiemotional traits (e.g., "I only consider people emotionally important to me who are absolutely and totally on my side" and "When an emotionally important person hurts me very slightly, I immediately distance myself from that person"), and narcissistic double standards (e.g., "I demand very high moral behaviours from others, such as absolute fidelity, but I do not practise these myself").

The Type 5 scale further isolates the overrational and noise-denying tendency (e.g., "I cannot allow my behaviour to be guided by emotion" and "In all aspects of my life, I find it important to look at things in a rational, not emotional way").

Finally, the Type 6 scale of the 70-item inventory isolates the narcissistic, possibly criminal, and possibly substance-abusive tendencies (e.g., "When I expect an emotional response from a person, I cannot tolerate any delay and require instant satisfaction," "Most people only serve to satisfy my needs; for example, they are sexual objects, or provide me with money," and "Certain things like money, alcohol or drugs, satisfy me more than emotionally important people").

Assessing Mood Disorders. Finding a self-report inventory to assess mood disorder behaviors was a major hurdle, since none exists. As noted in Chapter 5, the diagnostic tool often used for assessing mood disorders in clinical circles is an interview guide, called the SADS, developed by mental health experts Endicott and Spitzer (1978). Because of the perceived need by clinicians to more easily assess working adults' mood disorder behaviors, we developed, with the assistance of Dr. Jean Endicott, the Manic and Depressive Behavior Self-Report Inventory (MDBSI), consisting of 31 behavioral items. Because of its self-report nature, the MDBSI was considered to be suitable for use in circumstances in which there was no current episode of extreme illness, such that the client was rendered incapable of concentrating on, or responding to, the items.

Unlike the SADS, the MDBSI was not designed to include such specific symptomatology as schizoaffective disorders, panic or phobic disorders, Briquet's disorder, or obsessive-compulsiveness. Also, unlike the SADS, the MDBSI was not intended to measure change in the respondent's condition.

The wording of the MDBSI was designed to mimic that of the SADS. An attempt was also made by us to include an almost equal number of bipolar I (or manic tendency) and bipolar II (or depressive tendency) items. The seven-point scale used for the items was developed according to criteria for the six mood disorder classes reported in the DSM-IV (American Psychiatric Association 1994).

In short, the primary objective of the MDBSI was to yield a "likely" description of the corporate leaders' (or clients') mood disorder behavior conditions, based on their bipolar I (BPI) and bipolar II (BPII) scale scores. The BPI range was from 0 through 112, with higher scores representing a stronger manic tendency. The BPII range was from 0 through 105, with higher scores representing a stronger depression tendency.

Using the respondents' BPI and BPII scores, we placed the scores in the appropriate mood disorder class(es). Because respondents' sets of scores could, in some cases, place in more than one of the six classifications, all of the relevant classifications were listed. Given that the cutoff scores used by us to classify the respondents are undergoing validation testing in a psychiatric population, they will not be described further.

The six mood disorder classifications listed in the DSM-IV, with distinctive frequency periods shown in italics and with course particulars given in parentheses, are described as follows (American Psychiatric Association 1994):

1. *Negligible Bipolar I, Bipolar II, or Likely Bipolar I and II Tendency*: Defined as negligible behavioral tendencies relating to Bipolar I and Bipolar II and being of insufficient number, severity, pervasiveness, or duration to meet full criteria for a Manic or a Depressive Episode.

2. *Bipolar I, Hypomanic Tendency*: Defined as a distinct period of abnormally and persistently elevated, expansive, or irritable mood and behavior that lasts *at least 4 days*. This period of abnormal mood and behavior must be accompanied by at least three additional symptoms from a list that includes inflated self-esteem or grandiosity (nondelusional), decreased need for sleep, pressure of speech, flight of ideas, distractibility, increased involvement in goal-directed activities or psychomotor agitation, and excessive involvement in pleasurable activities that have a high potential for painful consequences. This list of additional symptoms is identical to that defining a Manic Episode, except that delusions or hallucinations cannot be present. (A Hypomanic Episode typically begins suddenly, with a rapid escalation of symptoms within a day or two. Episodes may last for several weeks to months and are usually more abrupt in onset and briefer than Major Depressive Episodes. In many cases, the Hypomanic Episode may be preceded or followed by a Major Depressive Episode. Studies suggest that 5%–15% of individuals with hypomania will ultimately develop a Manic Episode.) (pp. 335–338)

3. *Bipolar I, Manic Tendency*: Defined by a distinct period of an abnormally and persistently elevated, expansive, or irritable mood and behavior. This period of abnormal mood and behavior must last *at least 1 week* and must be accompanied by at least three additional symptoms from a list that includes inflated self-esteem or grandiosity, decreased need for sleep, pressure of speech, flight of ideas, distractibility, increased involvement in goal-directed activities or psychomotor agitation, and excessive involvement in pleasurable activities with a high potential for painful consequences. If the mood is irritable, at least four of the above symptoms must be present. (The mean age at onset for a first Manic Episode is the early 20s, but some cases start in adolescence and others start after age 50. Manic Episodes begin suddenly, with rapid escalation of symptoms over a few days. Frequently, Manic Episodes occur following psychosocial stressors. The episodes usually last from a few weeks to several months and are briefer and end more abruptly than Major Depressive Episodes. In many instances—50%–60%, a Major Depressive Episode immediately precedes or immediately follows a Manic Episode.) (pp. 328–332)

4. *Bipolar I, Mixed Episode Tendency*: Characterized by a period of time lasting *at least 1 week* in which the mood and behavior criteria are met both for a Manic Episode *and* for a Major Depressive Episode *nearly every day*. The individual experiences rapidly alternating moods (sadness, irritability, euphoria) accompanied by symptoms of a Manic Episode and a Major Depressive Episode. The symptom presentation frequently includes agitation, insomnia, appetite dysregulation, psychotic features, and suicidal thinking. The disturbance must be sufficiently severe to cause marked impairment in social or occupational functioning or to require hospitalization, or it is characterized by the presence of psychotic features. (Mixed Episodes appear to be more common in younger individuals and in individuals over age 60 with Bipolar Disorder, and may be more common in males than in females. Mixed Episodes can evolve from a Manic Episode or from a Major Depressive Episode or may arise de novo. Mixed Episodes may last weeks to several months and may remit to a period with few or no symptoms or evolve into a Major Depressive Episode. It is far

less common for a Mixed Episode to evolve into a Manic Episode.) (pp. 333–335)

5. *Bipolar II, Major Depression Tendency:* Defined as a period of *at least 2 weeks* during which there is either depressed mood or the loss of interest or pleasure in nearly all activities. The individual must also experience at least four additional symptoms drawn from a list that includes changes in appetite or weight, sleep, and psychomotor activity; decreased energy; feelings of worthlessness or guilt; difficulty thinking, concentrating, or making decisions; or recurrent thoughts of death or suicidal ideation, plans, or attempts. To count toward a Major Depressive Episode, a symptom must either be newly present or must have worsened compared with the person's pre-episode status. *The symptoms must persist for most of the day, nearly every day, for at least 2 consecutive weeks.* The episode must be accompanied by clinically significant distress or impairment in social, occupational, or other important areas of functioning. For some individuals with milder episodes, functioning may appear to be normal, but requires markedly increased effort. (Culture can influence the experience and communication of symptoms of depression. Symptoms of a Major Depressive Episode usually develop over days to weeks. The duration of a Major Depressive Episode is variable, with untreated episodes lasting 6 months or longer. In the majority of cases, there is a complete remission of symptoms, and functioning returns to the premorbid level. Studies indicate that Depressive Episodes occur twice as frequently in women as in men.) (pp. 320–327)

6. *Cyclothymic Disorder:* Defined as a chronic, fluctuating mood disturbance involving numerous periods of hypomanic symptoms and numerous periods of depressive symptoms. The Hypomanic symptoms are of insufficient number, severity, pervasiveness, or duration to meet full criteria for a Manic Episode, and the depressive symptoms are of insufficient number, severity, pervasiveness, or duration to meet full criteria for a Major Depressive Episode. *During the 2-year period, any symptom-free intervals last no longer than 2 months.* The description is made only if the 2-year period of cyclothymic symptoms is free of Major Depressive, Manic, or Mixed Episodes. After the initial two years of the disorder, Manic or Mixed Episodes may be superimposed on the Cyclothymic Disorder, in which case both Cyclothymic Disorder and Bipolar I Disorder are registered as a diagnosis. Similarly, after the initial two years of Cyclothymic Disorder, Major Depressive Episodes may be superimposed on the Cyclothymic Disorder, in which case both Cyclothymic Disorder and Bipolar II Disorder are registered as a diagnosis. (Cyclothymic Disorder often begins early in life and is sometimes considered to reflect a temperamental predisposition to other Mood Disorders, especially Bipolar Disorders. There is a 15%–50% risk that the person will subsequently develop Bipolar I or II Disorder. In community samples, Cyclothymic Disorder is apparently equally common in men and in women. In clinical settings, women with the disorder may be more likely to present for treatment than men. While studies have reported a lifetime prevalence of Cyclothymic Disorder of from 0.4% to 1% in community samples, the prevalence in mood disorders clinics may range from 3%–5%.) (pp. 363–366)

The Reliability of the BPI and BPII Scales

The obtained Cronbach alpha coefficient for BPI (16 items, $n=384$) was an impressive 0.96. The obtained coefficient for BPII (15 items, $n=388$) was an impressive 0.93.

HYPOTHESES GENERATED REGARDING MOOD DISORDERS

The Hypomania Issue

The Presence of Hypomania in Corporate Leaders. Considering that creative types seem especially prone to the Bipolar I, hypomanic tendency (Jamison et al. 1980; Jamison 1991, 1992), including writers, artists, scientists, and political leaders, it would seem reasonable to expect that the same hypomanic trend would hold true for corporate leaders, whose creative talents—like Peladeau's—would be heavily drawn upon to deal with the multiplicity of challenges facing corporations today.

- *Hypothesis 9.1*: It was hypothesized that the mean BPI score and the mean BPII score for the present-day Canadian corporate leaders would place in the bipolar I, hypomanic tendency.

Hypomania and the Job Position Issue. Consistent with the arguments made in Chapters 7 and 8, the strained second-tier corporate leader segment would likely present with significantly higher mean scores on BPI and BPII than their less strained top-management counterparts but still be in the bipolar I, hypomanic tendency class.

- *Hypothesis 9.2*: It was hypothesized that, compared to their top-management counterparts, the strained second-tier corporate leader group would present with significantly higher mean BPI and BPII scores in the bipolar I, hypomanic tendency.

Hypomania and the Gender Issue. Consistent with arguments made in Chapters 7 and 8, it would seem reasonable to conclude that there should not be any significant difference in the BPI and the BPII mean scores for the female and male corporate leaders.

- *Hypothesis 9.3*: It was hypothesized that there would be no significant difference in the BPI and the BPII mean scores for the female and the male corporate leaders.

Projected Distributions of Corporate Leaders' Scores in the Six Mood Disorder Classes

Conjecturing the percentages of corporate leaders placing in the mood disorder classes was a difficult chore, given that a major void exists in this regard in the psychosocial and organizational literature. However, consistent with Dr. Ozersky's (Tillson 1996) comment (in Chapter 5) that manic-depression "self-selects" to "any profession that requires stupendous effort, energy, confidence and willingness to take risks" (p. 26), we suspected that a number of mood-disordered types would surface in this corporate leader population. At a minimum, therefore, we thought it reasonable to conclude that the majority of Canadian corporate leaders would present with BPI and BPI scores indicating a "creative" hypomanic tendency. This projection was strengthened by Jamison's (1991, 1992) consistent research finding of hypomania in eminents in the arts, sciences, and politics. Also consistent with Jamison's (1991, 1992) research findings regarding the presence of bipolar pockets in eminents, we thought it reasonable to conclude that there would be a sizable pocket of high risk-taking entrepreneurial bipolars like G and Peladeau in the corporate leader population.

- *Hypothesis 9.4*: It was hypothesized that the corporate leader group would have the majority (i.e., over 50 percent) reporting that they experienced bipolar I, hypomanic tendencies and a smaller, but significant, segment of the respondents (i.e., greater than 10 percent but less than 30 percent) reporting that they experienced the more pronounced bipolar I, mixed episode tendencies.

The Relationship of the BPI and BPII Scores with Each Other and with PSS Scores in Corporate Leaders

Considering that elevated scores on mania and depression tend to co-vary in clients, and considering that the mood swings associated with severe bouts of mood disorders result in suicide ideation or attempts in about 15 percent of the severely stressed sufferers (Guze & Robins 1970; Black, Winokur, & Nasrallah 1988), it seemed reasonable to conclude that in corporate leaders, respondents' BPI and BPII scores would not only tend to be significantly and positively correlated with each other but also tend to be significantly and positively correlated with their PSS scores.

- *Hypothesis 9.5*: It was hypothesized that the corporate leaders' BPI and BPII scores would be significantly and positively correlated.
- *Hypothesis 9.6*: It was hypothesized that in the corporate leader group, the respondents' PSS scores would be significantly and positively correlated with their BPI and BPII scores.

Influence Strategy Usage and Mood Disorder Scores

Considering Kipnis and Schmidt's 1988 study findings showing a significant negative relationship between the usage of reasoning influence strategies by corporate leaders and the stress levels reported by them, it seemed reasonable to conclude that a similar negative linear relationship should exist between leaders' usage of reasoning influence strategies and the mood disorder scores reported by them. Moreover, along this same theme, it seemed reasonable to conclude that a positive linear relationship should exist between corporate leaders' usage of the remaining POIS influence strategies and their mood disorder scores.

- *Hypothesis 9.7*: It was hypothesized that the corporate leaders' reasoning upward scores and their reasoning downward scores would be significantly and negatively correlated with their BPI and BPII scores. It was also hypothesized that the corporate leaders' remaining POIS scores would be significantly and positively correlated with their BPI and BPII scores.

Type and Mood Disorder Scores

Considering that the mental health literature has reported that adults suffering from high degrees of mania and depression can be narcissistic, hyperactive, depressive, substance-abusive, antisocial, and self- and other-destructive during various phases of their illness (American Psychiatric Association 1994; Black, Winokur, & Nasrallah 1988; Winokur, Clayton, & Reich 1969), it seemed reasonable to conclude that in the corporate leader population, a similar pattern could exist. Thus, we conjectured that elevated BPI and BPII scores in the corporate leaders—indicating a bipolar I, mixed episode tendency—would be significantly and positively correlated with their (1) "anger-in" and "anger-denying" Type C/Type 1 and Type C/Type 5 scores; (2) "anger-out" Type A/Type 2 scores; and narcissistic and possibly substance-abusive Type 3 and Type 6 scores. Finally, consistent with the literature on self-healers, we found it reasonable to conclude that the corporate leaders' BPI and BPII scores would be significantly and negatively correlated with their Type B/Type 4 scores.

- *Hypothesis 9.8*: It was hypothesized that in the corporate leader sample, elevated BPI and BPII scores—indicating a bipolar I, mixed tendency—would be significantly and positively correlated with their Type 1, Type 5, Type 2, Type 3, and Type 6 scores. It was also hypothesized that the corporate leaders' BPI and BPI scores would be significantly and negatively correlated with their Type 4 score.

The Stress Yardstick and Mood Disorder Scores

Considering the stress-coping "success" yardstick described earlier, what could we project about the mood disorder classes likely to be reported by the highly stressed, workaholic "shotgun" segment of Canadian corporate leaders? Considering the different stress-coping styles of Hammond and of Estill in Chapter 8, we further asked, Which type-mood variety would likely be self-reported more frequently by these "shotguns"—the Type C/bipolar I variety or the Type A/bipolar I variety?

Considering Linton, Kuechenmeister, and Kuechenmeister's 1986 study findings on psychiatric patients, which showed that "the introverted" and "the feeling Types" of adults are particularly at risk for mental ill health, and Black, Winokur, and Nasrallah's 1988 study findings, which showed that adults with a more "hyperactive" bipolar I mood disorder are less apt to commit suicide than are adults with a "depressive" bipolar II mood disorder, we concluded that the highly stressed "shotguns" would more likely be classified as Type C/ Type 1 bipolar I (mixed episode) than as Type A/Type 2 bipolar I (mixed episode).

- *Hypothesis 9.9*: It was hypothesized that the highly stressed "shotgun" Canadian corporate leaders would more likely report as a Type C/Type 1 bipolar I (mixed episode) than as Type A/Type 2 bipolar I (mixed episode).

The Compensation Yardstick and Mood Disorder Scores

Because there does not appear to be any convincing evidence in the psychosocial or in the organizational literature that mood disorders are in any way significantly related to the compensation scheme, we concluded that the previous findings regarding the compensation "success" yardstick would remain relatively unchanged with the introduction of the mood disorder scores.

- *Hypothesis 9.10*: It was hypothesized that the entry of the corporate leaders' BPI and BPII scores into the compensation yardstick analysis would produce little significant change.

STUDY FINDINGS

The results of the 400 corporate leaders who completed the 14-page questionnaire on stress, influence strategies, personality, mood, and compensation brought a few surprises when the BPI and the BPII scores were added to the previous data analysis. Our findings regarding this third and final grouping can be summarized as follows:

- Consistent with Hypothesis 9.1, the mean BPI score and the mean BPII score for the present-day Canadian corporate leaders placed in the bipolar I, hypomanic tendency class. Thus, like their eminent counterparts in the arts, in the sciences, and in politics, present-day corporate leaders would seem to have large quantities of "creative" potential.

- Consistent with Hypothesis 9.2, compared to their top-management counterparts, the strained second-tier corporate leader group presented with significantly higher mean BPI and BPII scores but still remained in the bipolar I, hypomanic tendency class.

- Consistent with Hypothesis 9.3, there was no significant difference found in the BPI and in the BPII mean scores for the female and the male corporate leaders. Thus, the myth that women cannot make good corporate leaders because they are "too moody" or "too emotional" just does not wash.

- Consistent with Hypothesis 9.4, in the corporate leader group the majority— 60 percent—reported that they experienced either negligible mood tendencies or bipolar I, hypomanic tendencies. A significant segment of the respondents— 32 percent—reported that they experienced the more pronounced bipolar I, mixed episode tendencies, and another 7 percent experienced bipolar I, manic tendencies or overlapping bipolar I mixed and manic tendencies. Only 1 percent reported experiencing the bipolar II, depressed tendency. Such study findings indicate not only that Peladeau is joined by many other corporate leader colleagues in the bipolar struggle but that Dr. Ozersky's comment about manic-depressives "self-selecting" to such a high-demanding and creativity-requiring career as corporate leadership seems to be supported.

- Consistent with Hypothesis 9.5, the corporate leaders' BPI and BPII scores tended to be significantly and positively correlated ($r = .76$, $p < .01$).

- Consistent with Hypothesis 9.6, the corporate leaders' PSS score was significantly and positively correlated with their BPI score ($r = .61$, $p < .01$) and with their BPII score ($r = .76$, $p < .01$).

- Consistent with Hypothesis 9.7, the corporate leaders' reasoning downward score was significantly and negatively correlated with their BPI score ($r = -.44$, $p < .01$) and with their BPII score ($r = -.21$, $p < .01$). Contrary to predictions, their reasoning upward score was significantly and positively correlated with their BPI score ($r = .34$, $p < .01$) and with their BPII score ($r = .27$, $p < .01$). Also consistent with Hypothesis 9.7, most of the remaining upward and downward influence strategy scores of corporate leaders were significantly and positively correlated with their BPI and BPII scores. Across the board, these findings suggest that when corporate leaders have to influence upwardly, the experience is generally perceived by them to be mood-disordering, regardless of the strategy used.

- Consistent with Hypothesis 9.8, in the corporate leader group, elevated BPI and BPII scores—indicating a bipolar I, mixed tendency—were significantly (p

< .01 level) and positively correlated with leaders' scores on Type 1 ($r = .31$, $r = .50$), Type 2 ($r = .60$, $r = .61$), Type 3 ($r = .76$, $r = .58$), Type 5 ($r = .15$, $r = .11$), and Type 6 ($r = .66$, $r = .61$). Also consistent with Hypothesis 9.8, the corporate leaders' BPI and BPII scores were significantly and negatively correlated with their Type 4 score ($r = -.31$, $p < .01$ and $r = -.39$, $p < .01$, respectively).

• Consistent with Hypothesis 9.9 and contrary to previous reports assessing only Type A predispositions in corporate leaders, the highly stressed "shotgun" corporate leaders classed more as Type C/Type 1 bipolar I, mixed episode tendency than as Type A/Type 2 bipolar I, mixed episode tendency.

• Consistent with Hypothesis 9.10, with the entry of the corporate leaders' BPI and BPII scores into the previously analyzed compensation "success" equation, the profile remained unchanged. The highly compensated corporate leaders tend to be particularly well versed in "making deals" upwardly and downwardly, they have a slightly higher narcissistic Type 3 and hard-driving/competitive Type 2 predisposition than their less well compensated counterparts, and they tend to rely more heavily on the "friendly upward," the "coalition upward," and the "higher authority" influence styles. They tend to be males, in the top-management group, and in their 50s.

THE BOTTOM LINE

This chapter opened with a case on one of Canada's most successful, yet controversial, business leaders, Pierre Peladeau. As we opened Chapter 9, we pondered how many present-day Canadian corporate leaders would self-report as being "creatively" hypomanic and how many would self-report as being more mood-disordered like Peladeau.

Recall that in Chapter 8, we found that about 13 percent of the corporate leaders self-reported themselves as being "purely self-healing," given their personality and behavior type scores only. When the corporate leaders' BPI and BPII scores are also taken into consideration, the number of "pure self-healers" reduces to 9 percent when scores exceeding the hypomanic tendency are considered. So, does the thrill of being "in" or "near" the top of corporations have a high personal price tag attached to it? It looks like it.

REFERENCES

American Psychiatric Association. (1994). *Diagnostic and Statistical Manual of Mental Disorders. Fourth edition. DSM-IV.* Washington, DC: American Psychiatric Association.

Black, D. W., Winokur, G., & Nasrallah, A. (1988). Effect of psychosis on suicide risk in 1593 patients with unipolar and bipolar affective disorders. *American Journal of Psychiatry*, 145, 849–852.

Endicott, J., & Spitzer, R. L. (1978). A diagnostic interview: The Schedule for

Affective Disorders and Schizophrenia. *Archives of General Psychiatry*, 35, 837–844.

Grossarth-Maticek, R., & Eysenck, H. J. (1990). Personality, stress and disease: Description and validation of a new inventory. *Psychological Reports*, 66, 355–373.

Guze, S. B., & Robins, E. (1970). Suicide and primary affective disorders. *British Journal of Psychiatry*, 117, 437–438.

Heinzl, J., Church, E., Partridge, J., Lush, P., & McFarland, J. (1998). Those wild and crazy annual meetings. *The Globe and Mail*, May 1, p. B23.

Jamison, K. R. (1991). Manic-depressive illness, creativity and leadership. In F. K. Goodwin & K. R. Jamison (Eds.), *Manic-depressive illness*. Oxford: Oxford University Press, Chapter 16.

Jamison, K. R. (1992). Mood disorders and patterns of creativity in British writers and artists. In R. S. Albert (Ed.), *Genius and eminence*. Oxford: Pergamon Press, pp. 351–356.

Jamison, K. R., Gerner, R. H., Hammer, C., & Padesky, C. (1980). Clouds and silver linings: Positive experiences associated with primary affective disorders. *American Journal of Psychiatry*, 137, 198–202.

Kipnis, D., & Schmidt, S. M. (1988). Upward-influence styles: Relationship with performance evaluations, salary, and stress. *Administrative Science Quarterly*, 33, 528–542.

Linton, P. H., Kuechenmeister, C. A., & Kuechenmeister, S. B. (1986). Personality type and psychiatric symptom formation. *Research Communications in Psychology, Psychiatry, and Behavior*, 11, 37–49.

Tillson, T. (1996). The CEO's disease. *Canadian Business*, 69, 26–28, 33–34.

Winokur, G., Clayton, P. J., & Reich, T. (1969). *Manic depressive illness*. St. Louis: C. V. Mosby.

Yakabuski, K. (1997). The paradoxical Monsieur Peladeau. *The Globe and Mail*, December 6, pp. B1, B4.

CHAPTER 10

Corporate Leaders: How They Would Likely Place on the Trustworthy–Transitional–Toxic Leader Scale

> The strength of the criticism lies only in the weakness of the thing criticized.
>
> —a thought from Longfellow

A CASE IN POINT (JANG 1998)

Gulf Canada Resource Ltd.'s new president and CEO is not afraid of a few bumps. During a ski run in Colorado just days before he took over the company's top job in February, 1998, Richard (Dick) Auchinleck raced over some moguls so quickly, his left ski broke.

"I was skiing pretty hard and the ski just exploded. It was really quite something. I skied the rest of the way down on one leg."

While Mr. Auchinleck may be a daredevil on the slopes, his corporate style is aggressive but not as bold as that of his predecessor, J. P. Bryan. Mr. Auchinleck wants to reduce Gulf's $2.78-billion debt. To do so, he is unloading non-core holdings, both big and small, in a divestment program aimed at chopping that figure $1.85 billion by early next year.

He announced plans on March 20, 1998, to sell offshore oil properties in the British North Sea for $590-million to Oklahoma City-based Kerr-McGee Corp. And Mr. Auchinleck is taking commercial flights for his business trips, in contrast to colorful Texan Mr. Bryan, who travelled in Gulf's private Challenger jet.

The company found a buyer for the plane last Friday, and Mr. Auchinleck, 46, celebrated the $12.5-million (U.S.) sale by indulging in a plate of chicken wings—a snack to help fuel his six-foot-four, 240-pound frame.

"We made a bit of money on selling the Challenger," he said in an interview this week from Denver, where the company's executive offices were relocated from Calgary by Mr. Bryan a year ago. Although Mr. Bryan left Gulf, the company will keep its executive offices in Denver for several years because it can't afford to waste time and money moving back to Calgary, Mr. Auchinleck says. However, he is careful to avoid criticizing the jet-setting ways of Mr. Bryan, a financier who went on a shopping spree during his three-year stint as Gulf's CEO.

The acquisitions revived the company, turning it from a money loser into a profitable oil and gas producer. Gulf posted a $37-million (Cdn) profit in 1996, and earned $204-million last year, after piling up losses totalling $645-million from 1990 to 1995. However, Mr. Bryan paid for a good portion of his shopping by borrowing, adding about $1.6 billion to Gulf's already substantial debt load before he resigned on Feb. 9. Still, the comparisons made between Mr. Bryan's flamboyant style and the new CEO's disciplined approach don't intimidate Mr. Auchinleck.

Gulf's off-the-wall annual report last year described Mr. Bryan as "eclectic" and a "Renaissance man" who revelled in being a "creative contrarian," while concluding that Mr. Auchinleck, a senior vice-president at the time, was a "mild-mannered" guy who worked like a "mechanic." It also pointed out that Mr. Auchinleck's "known weaknesses include single-malt whiskey, Cuban cigars and vintage sports cars."

The Vancouver-born Mr. Auchinleck, who graduated with a science degree in chemical engineering from the University of British Columbia in 1976, is determined to slash Gulf's debt by selling off assets. He admits his new business strategy may seem dull after Mr. Bryan's penchant for publicly criticizing everything from Quebec separatists to British oil executives to Calgary's business elite.

Mr. Bryan is quick to defend Mr. Auchinleck from those who say the new CEO—a 22-year veteran at Gulf who worked his way up the ranks—is a boring guy. "I think Dick is pretty colourful and funny. He's got a different style than me. He's an engineer and I'm a financial guy and it's a totally different focus," says Mr. Bryan, who resigned after losing a battle with Gulf's board over what to do about the company's debt.

While Mr. Bryan wanted to preserve Gulf's assets and put off attacking the debt until next year, the board pushed for a faster approach. Mr. Bryan says he still thinks the company could have delayed or toned down its debt-reduction strategy, but "the last thing I want to do is leave the impression that there's friction between Dick and me. I tell you, from the bottom of my heart, I applaud what he's doing."

Robert Hinckley, an analyst with New York-based Merrill Lynch & Co. Inc., says Mr. Bryan was the right executive to expand Gulf and Mr. Auchinleck is the right successor to nurture it. "J. P. got them growing again. If you can fault J. P., he relied too much on the leverage of the company. What Gulf needs now is to operate what they've got in the best way they can. Dick is an aggressive operating guy, which is what the company needs now."

Mr. Auchinleck says Gulf has a lot of work to do, budgeting about $875-million for capital spending this year, compared with $664-million in 1997. Gulf will become a company with fewer assets, although it is maintaining its widespread focus with holdings in places such as Western Canada, Indonesia, Australia, and the Netherlands sector of the North Sea. However, the company plans to sell non-core items such as natural gas processing and gathering assets in Western Canada for $200-million and some Nevada real estate for $30-million.

"People are beating on us and saying J. P. loaded us with debt. But we're taking a minor course correction," Mr. Auchinleck says. "The toughest thing is reassuring people that there's nothing fundamentally wrong with Gulf. The legacy that J. P. left us is a strong company that's very well-diversified." Mr. Auchinleck is confident that Gulf will stay on course. He hopes to blaze his own trail, too, realizing there will undoubtedly be more bumps ahead.

INTRODUCTION

Now that we have heard from the corporate leaders themselves—both from our questionnaire study and from Gulf's outsider and insider CEOs, Bryan and Auchinleck (who were reluctant to criticize each other's style), I am going to try to answer the question: How would today's corporate leaders likely place on the trustworthy-transitional-toxic leader scale?

TODAY'S CORPORATE LEADERS: TRUSTWORTHY, TRANSITIONAL, OR TOXIC?

A Review of Whicker's Definitions. Referring to Chapter 3 and Marcia Whicker's (1996) definitions for trustworthy, transitional, and toxic leaders, one can see that embedded in her definitions for these three classes is the stress-coping-type "success" yardstick. For example, Whicker suggested that the trustworthy leaders are the self- and other-healing, prototypically high n-Pow and n-ActI leaders who not only value their own self-esteem and that of others but who put the goals of their organization and the well-being of their followers ahead of their own personal gains. The transitional leaders, while not as self-healing and other-healing as trustworthy leaders, are neither uplifting in their long-term impact on others nor purposely malicious toward them. Somewhat lower on the n-ActI than their trustworthy counterparts, the transitional leaders are more narcissistic, disease-prone, and self-absorbed than the "purer" trustworthy types. Finally, the toxic leaders, representing the higher disease-prone end of the leadership continuum, tend to be quite narcissistic, malcontent, and self- and/or other-destructive. Not only do toxic leaders often succeed by tearing others down, but, like G, they glory in their own turf protection and have a tendency to "control" followers rather than uplift them.

Further, Whicker placed, as real-life cases in point, John Kennedy and Lee Iacocca in the trustworthy leader category, Michael Milken and Ross Perot in the transitional leader category, and Richard Nixon and Ross Johnson in the toxic leader category.

A Review of Hart and Quinn's Estimates. Though Whicker did not attempt to estimate percentages for each of these three leader classes in the present-day corporate leader population, in 1993 Hart and Quinn did make such an attempt using a U.S. study sample. This research pair projected that, at most, only 10 percent of those at the top—CEOs and presidents—could be classified as "true" self-healers or trustworthy leaders. Because they are cognitively, emotionally, and behaviorally "highly complex" or "moderately complex," said Hart and Quinn, trustworthy leaders are extremely capable of dealing with the multidimensional and "paradoxical" corporate leader role. The remaining 90 percent, affirmed Hart and Quinn, are either "lower on complexity" or "unbalanced," thus making them transitional and toxic leaders. However, Hart and Quinn did not define the point separating the transitional leaders, who are "complex enough" and "balanced enough," and the toxic leaders, who are either "not complex enough" or "not balanced enough." We were told by Hart and Quinn, however, that only about 4 percent are leader "disasters," presenting in the "low complexity" group.

Present Study Findings. Using the more comprehensive stress-coping-type-mood yardstick from our Canadian corporate leader study, I think that clarification on this dividing point can now be made. First, we'll assume that to qualify as a "pure self-healer" or trustworthy leader, the corporate leader has to self-report as having (1) a score of 5 or higher on the Type 4 scale *and* (2) a score lower than 5 on the disease-prone Type 1, Type 2, Type 3, Type 5, and Type 6 scales *and* (3) BPI and BPII scores placing in the "negligible BPI or BPII" or in the creatively "hypomanic tendency" class. Given these three criteria, only 9 percent of the present-day Canadian corporate leader sample would be classified as trustworthy leaders. This finding is consistent with Hart and Quinn's estimate of about 10 percent in the U.S. sample.

If we were to further assume that to qualify as a "somewhat balanced" transitional leader, the corporate leader has to self-report as having (1) adequate self-healing Type 4 tendencies (i.e., a score of 5 or higher on the Type 4 scale) *and* (2) a score of 5 or higher on one or more of the psychoneurotic Type 1, Type 2, or Type 5 scales *and* (3) a score below 5 on the narcissistic and antisocial Type 3 and Type 6 scales *and* (4) BPI and BPII scale scores in the "negligible" or creatively "hypomanic tendency" classes, then 41 percent of the present-day Canadian corporate leader sample would be classfied as the "somewhat balanced" transitional leaders.

Finally, if we were to further assume that to qualify as an "unbalanced" toxic leader, someone who is either self- and/or other-destructive, the corporate leader has to self-report as having (1) a score of 5 or higher on the narcissistic Type 3 and/or on the Type 6 antisocial scale *and/or* (2) the BPI and/or BPII score beyond the "creative" hypomanic tendency level, then 50 percent of the Canadian corporate leader sample would be classified as "unbalanced" toxic leaders, in varying degrees. Again, we must allow for some margin of error, given the tentative nature of the cutoff scores used for classifying the mood disorders.

If asked whether the toxic leaders in the Canadian corporate leader sample are more self- or other-destructive, I would have to posit that most are, indeed, self-destructive. While these "toxic" corporate leaders tended to have elevated BPI and/or BPII scores and/or elevated scores on the narcissistic Type 3 and/or the antisocial Type 6 scales, they also tended to have one or more scores of 5 or higher on the psychoneurotic Type 1/Type C, Type 2/Type A, or Type 5/Type C scales. In short, their stress-coping-type-mood yardstick scores loudly and clearly said, "I am experiencing much psychological noise. I have much discomfort. My system is at war with itself."

Yet, paradoxically, as noted in Chapter 9, like G and Peladeau, these organizational "shotguns" also tended to have offsetting "self-healing" capacities and ego strength; their scores on Type 4 met or exceeded 5. This kind of "toxicity" is not the classic psychopathic personality that Dr. Hare was describing and that the media have recently posited are roaming corporate hallways. One can only guess that the toxic corporate leaders' n-ActI, in particular, tries to effect some positive "nonfailure" outcomes from a painful and noise-filled "inner experience." In many ways, these toxic leaders are martyrs or magicians, determined to make something positive out of the negative. I think that G's allusions to "having a family" work atmosphere, "not wanting his company to grow bigger as long as people were troubled and problems were unresolved," and "wanting a fit between himself and the staff and the organization" all spoke to this self-healing n-ActI potential. Plus, as one of his organizational members said, G wanted to do something positive for society. I think that expert Robert Albert (1992) was "right on the button" when he said: "What is important to understand is that creative individuals [like these "toxic" corporate leaders] have the capacity to not deny this pain, but to use it. Very much products of the early years, in which they had little or no say, it is fascinating to see how these confused moments, unexpected losses, loneliness and harsh circumstances can become the framework and tools of their art" (p. 326).

Not too long ago, I was called by a writer who was doing a magazine piece on executive rage (Andrew 1998). When she asked me if I thought that the suppressed rage in corporate leaders would result in other-destruction, I responded that instead of physically crushing people, corporate leaders are more apt to, like G and Peladeau, verbally insult coworkers or consultants or fire people in a fit of pique. They may not be predictable or pleasant to be around, but they would rarely be "deadly" to others. I think that the chances are far greater that these noise-filled toxic leaders would self-destruct in a period of depression or through cardiovascular disease (precipitated by suppressed anger and chronic mania).

Finally, on the compensation "success" yardstick, I would have to conclude that most highly compensated corporate leaders (like J. P. Bryan, vis-à-vis the Canadian scene) would tend to place in either the transitional or the toxic categories. Referring once more to the findings in Chapter 9, the highly compensated corporate leaders did report as keen bargainers who, though friendly, were narcissistic and hard-driving/competitive. Unlike their "purer" trustworthy counterparts, the highly compensated types tended to have adequate, but lower, self-healing/Type 4 potential.

THE BOTTOM LINE

This chapter opened with a case featuring two of Gulf Canada's recent CEOs, "insider" Dick Auchinleck, who just took over the helm, and "outsider" J. P. Bryan, who just left the helm. Besides this difference in CEO-board "game" labeling, Auchinleck came across in the case as quite a moderated "game" player, whereas Bryan came across as a much more hard-nosed, flamboyant, and "creative contrarian." So much for Auchinleck's and Bryan's major differences.

Now for their similarities. Both CEOs appeared to be high n-Pow- and n-ActI-driven types, wanting to pull Gulf Canada through troubled financial times and making Gulf's survival a "priority item" for them personally. Both CEOs had very different styles of influencing others, but their similar "end" justified their different means of getting there. As J. P. put it, "He's an engineer and I'm a financial guy and it's a totally different focus." Thus, both CEOs were "martyrs" or "magicians" in their own right, accepting some self-absorbed "pain" and personal costs rather than corporate failure. Both magicians show that "successful" leaders do come in many personality and mood types, shapes, and sizes.

Part II and Chapter 10, in particular, reinforced the notion that there is more than one way to make it to the top of organizations. Some ways have more personal and organizational costs than other ways. The trustworthy way of leading organizations optimizes the self-healing potential in corporate leaders and in others, but this way seems to be practiced by only 9 percent of the Canadian corporate leader sample and by only 10 percent of the U.S. corporate leader sample of Hart and Quinn. The "less balanced," transitional way of leading organizations appears to have some personal and other costs, and this way seems to be practiced by 41 percent of the Canadian corporate leader sample. The "unbalanced," toxic way of leading organizations appears to have high personal costs for the corporate leaders, in particular—and, at times, for the corporation—yet this way seems to be practiced by 50 percent of the Canadian corporate leader sample.

From this picture comes a relatively happy ending. "Successful" corporate leaders seem to be able to—often against the odds—make a "negative" reality a "positive" reality. The n-ActI seems to be a key "eminence" ingredient that not only makes followers want to walk the path of charismatic, trustworthy leaders but allows psychologically noise-filled toxic leaders to, somewhat magically, effect "success" from their pain. As controversial Gerald Pencer, former head of Cott Corporation, put it, "The Magic Is Back."

REFERENCES

Albert, R. S. (1992). Personal dynamics and creative problems in exceptional achievement. In R. S. Albert (Ed.), *Genius and eminence*. Oxford: Pergamon Press, pp. 325–328.

Andrew, R. (1998). Don't act your rage. *Canadian Inflight Magazine*, 12, 14–19.

Hart, S. L., & Quinn, R. E. (1993). Roles executives play: CEOs, behavioral complexity, and firm performance. *Human Relations*, 46, 543–574.

Jang, B. (1998). Gulf CEO engineers debt strategy. *The Globe and Mail*, March 20, p. B23.

Whicker, M. L. (1996). *Toxic leaders: When organizations go bad*. Westport, CT: Quorum Books.

Annotated Bibliography

For those interested in reading further on the topics discussed, an annotated bibliography of book references follows.

Adler, N. J. (1997). *International dimensions of organizational behavior*. Cincinnati: South-Western College Publishing. This book is essential for understanding the complexities of global management. Important topics covered include the impact of culture on organizations, managing cultural diversity, managing global managers, and managing global careers.

Albert, R. S. (1992). *Genius and eminence*. Oxford: Pergamon Press. This book describes many important topics linked to genius and eminence—including a developmental theory of eminence, the importance of motivation and creative behavior, the "mad" genius controversy, signs and outcomes of genius, family and parental influences on creative behavior, and personality dispositions related to creative behavior and exceptional achievement.

Cooper, C. L. (1983). *Stress research*. Chicester: Wiley. An excellent collection of chapters written by leading stress experts from around the world, this important book includes Selye's "The Stress Concept: Past, Present, Future" and Chesney and Rosenman's "Specificity in Stress Models: Examples Drawn from Type A Behavior."

Friedman, H. S. (1991). *The self-healing personality: Why some people achieve health while others succumb to illness*. New York: Holt. A rather new addition to the personality literature family, this book gives an excellent description of the self-healing personality.

Friedman, M., & Rosenman, R. H. (1974). *Type A behavior and your heart*. New York: Fawcett Crest. Written by the developers of Type A theory, this easy-to-read book describes the causes and effects of Type A behavior patterning.

Goleman, D. (1995). *Emotional intelligence: Why it can matter more than IQ.* New York: Bantam Books. A very easy book to get through, the author covers a number of interesting topics related to emotional intelligence, including the "emotional" brain, the nature of emotional intelligence, emotional intelligence applied, windows of opportunity, and emotional literacy.

Hare, R. D. (1993). *Without conscience: The disturbing world of the psychopaths among us.* New York: Pocket Books. Very easy to read and extremely interesting, this book lists key psychopathic symptoms, develops the psychopath's life theme of "I'm OK; you're not," and gives the topic badly needed scientific rigor—without the boring overtones. The author's obvious intention was to translate the technical material into a form suitable for a broad audience—including corporate leaders, their subordinates, and their spouses.

Jahoda, M. (1958). *Current concepts of positive mental health.* New York: Basic Books. This book gives a good description of positive mental health, a label that has since become known in the psychological literature as positive affect predominance, or PA.

Lazarus, R. S. (1966). *Psychological stress and the coping process.* New York: McGraw-Hill. A book familiar to experts in the stress field, this book details the importance of individuals' unique appraisals of stressors.

Maslach, C. (1982). *Burnout, the cost of caring.* Englewood Cliffs, NJ: Prentice-Hall. This book, written by the developer of the Maslach Burnout Inventory, describes the causes and effects of burnout.

Maslow, A. H. (1973). *The farther reaches of human nature.* London: Penguin. Familiar to most in the organizational behavior field, this book builds on the notion of Maslow's hierarchy of needs and details the important role of self-actualization in human development.

Price, V. A. (1982). *Type A behavior: A model for research and practice.* New York: Academic Press. A comprehensive text on the Type A personality, this excellent book details the psychological, behavioral, and physiological changes accompanying the Type A predisposition and suggests intervention strategies for reducing the destructiveness of this pattern.

Schell, B. H. (1997). *A self-diagnostic approach to understanding organizational and personal stressors: The C-O-P-E model for stress reduction.* Westport, CT: Quorum Books. Besides providing readers with stress-coping feedback, this book gives readers interesting, real-life cases, theories, and remedies for dealing with organizational and personal stress. The C-O-P-E model, developed by the author, serves as the theoretical framework for this book.

Simonton, D. K. (1984). *Genius, creativity, and leadership.* Cambridge, MA: Harvard University Press. An exceptional book that is also an easy read, this reference is a scientific study of historical genius. Its important topics include personality and creative character, productivity and influence, age and achievement, aesthetics and charisma, violence and historical genius, and the laws of historiometry.

Simonton, D. K. (1994). *Greatness: Who makes history and why.* New York: Guilford Press. This exceptionally well written book has coverage on a number of important topics relating to who makes history and why—including the drive to succeed, the famous in their youth, a life-span perspective of

greatness, and the importance of personality and psychopathology in determining greatness.

The diagnostic and statistical manual of mental disorders. (1994). 4th ed. Washington,
DC: American Psychiatric Association. Technical in nature, this book is an
excellent reference text for individuals wanting to become more informed
about the mental disorder terminology used by mental health experts.

Whicker, M. L. (1996). *Toxic leaders: When organizations go bad*. Westport, CT: Quorum Books. A very well written and case-loaded book, it describes the
theory and the personalities behind present-day trustworthy, transitional,
and toxic leaders.

Winokur, G., Clayton, P. J., & Reich, T. (1969). *Manic depressive illness*. St. Louis:
C. V. Mosby. Quite scientific in its approach, it is a "classic" detailing
manic depressive illness. Topics include epidemiologic and diagnostic
considerations of manic depression, a clinical picture of the disorder,
symptoms and course of the disorder, genetic studies and the disorder,
and the question of etiology—biologic, psychologic, and social approaches
to understanding manic depression.

Index

About the Author

BERNADETTE H. SCHELL is a professor in the School of Commerce and Administration, Laurentian University, Ontario, Canada. She is president of her own human resource management consulting firm, is an active stress-management consultant, and has served as a consulting editor for journals in her field. Among her many articles and other publications is *A Self-Diagnostic Approach to Understanding Organizational and Personal Stressors: The C-O-P-E Model for Stress Reduction* (Quorum, 1997).